HOW TO MAKE
SOMETHING
FROM NOTHING

HOW TO MAKE
SOMETHING
FROM NOTHING

Life's ultimate dilemma and how it influences your decisions, your success and everything you do

John Moon

T

Troubador Publishing Ltd
Unit E2 Airfield Business Park
Harrison Road, Market Harborough
Leicestershire LE16 7UL
Tel: 0116 279 2299
Email: books@troubador.co.uk
Web: www.troubador.co.uk

ISBN 978-1-83628-078-1

British Library Cataloguing in Publication Data.
A catalogue record for this book is available from the British Library.

Printed and bound by CPI Group (UK) Ltd, Croydon, CR0 4YY
Typeset in 11pt Minion Pro by Troubador Publishing Ltd, Leicester, UK

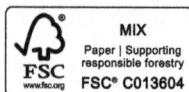

MIX
Paper | Supporting
responsible forestry
FSC
www.fsc.org   FSC® C013604

CONTENTS

INTRODUCTION

Everyone faces daily, hourly and minute-by-minute challenges when making decisions about anything and everything. Do you buy the cake you know is not good for you? Speak to that person you want to interact with or walk on by? Clean the bathroom or watch the TV? Work an extra hour or go home early and put your feet up?

I'm not going to tell you which is right or wrong, but I can show you how important it is to be conscious of your choices and how the millions of decisions you make over the course of your life will determine where you end up. The fundamental thinking driving those decisions is Life's Ultimate Dilemma.

You've probably never heard of me. I have no particularly exciting qualifications and I'm certainly not a guru or motivational mastermind. Others have achieved far more than me in many of the fields I have dabbled in. And I'm quite opinionated about the things I believe in. So why should you read a book written by a random, seemingly ordinary guy that purports to give you an insight into some powerful aspects of life?

The simple answer is because I have been thinking about this kind of stuff since I was young and firmly believe everyone can learn from my story. I've extracted and condensed into this book the significant elements of my life that could help you make a difference to your own or someone else's. Regardless of your current situation and state of mind, if you gain even one insight, it could be transformational. Although the purpose of this book is primarily to inspire those who could use a helping hand to improve their lot, the words I've spent years putting on paper are designed to awaken something in all of us. And I'm hopeful you'll enjoy reading it.

There are thousands of self-help books. I've read many of the best known and learnt a huge amount from them. But I've yet to find one that really relates to someone with a background where buying even one book would have been unthinkable. The grim reality is no-one is batting for you if you have next to nothing. Owning a book is probably the last thing on the mind of someone with only crumbs in their pocket, but being an optimist, I hope this one gets into your hands and inspires you, especially if you have a frustrated desire to improve, but feel it's an impossible task due to either the situation you find yourself in or a lack of guidance on how to do the right things. If this happens to be the first book you've bought or read, then I've achieved one of my goals.

In short, I want to inspire anyone who has the desire to do something with their life. I've used my own story to show you how one ordinary person has been able to achieve success. And if I can do it, then so can you.

True, I wasn't born in a country where families try to survive on less than $1 a day. In comparison to those in that terrible situation, I feel a bit of a fraud. All I have are my own life experiences. Starting in lower working-class England, against the odds, I have put myself into the country's wealthiest 1% of households (according to the Office of National Statistics), mainly due to my successes in the property market.

Throughout the pages of this book, I will recount the experiences that got me there and the insights I learnt along the way. My aim is to help you, or someone you know, to do the same, inspire you to do better, and amuse you too. If you adopt the skills and ideas I share, I'm confident you will enjoy a richer life. If change occurs for just one of you, then it will have been worthwhile.

I know many individuals with tremendous skills in their own fields, but they live almost hand to mouth. It pains me to see the waste of talent, especially when a few small changes could transform their situation.

This book is for you, my friends.

Part One

NOTHING

CHAPTER 1

I'M NOT GOING TO LIVE LIKE THIS

It was a typical British winter's day in the 1960s. Grey, is how I saw it, influenced as much by my mood as the sky. I was about eleven, I guess, and as was often the case when I wasn't at school, I was outside in the back garden of our council house in North Somerset, in my old ripped green coat.

Our house was very basic. With no central heating, it had a coal fire that was supposed to heat the whole place, but ice would form on the inside of the windows in winter. Nonetheless, my mum was fastidious about keeping it clean. The council estate on which we lived consisted of similar houses and families to ours. No-one had the remotest hope of ever being homeowners and, although life was undoubtedly tougher in many other places on earth, *existing* was a more accurate description than *living*.

The coal for the open fire was delivered every so often by a guy we didn't speak to, nor he to us. He arrived and left in a rush of black dust, emptying the heavy sacks into a bunker my dad and I had built in our back garden from breeze blocks. We must have scrounged those from somewhere, as I can't imagine we could have bought them. That day, my job was to chop wood to make kindling to light the fire. When I see cute little bags of kindling for sale outside petrol stations nowadays, it brings a wry smile to my face. Ours was somewhat more essential.

I don't ever recall being asked to chop sticks for our fire, I just knew it was something I ought to do. My dad worked hard enough as it was, riding the 9 miles to Bath to be at work by 7:30 in the morning and not getting home until 6pm as his little moped struggled with the ferociously steep Dunkerton hills. Because of my mum's inability to cope with most aspects of life (more about that later), my dad had very little rest. He would often have to cook our tea after he got home from work (we never called it dinner – that was at lunchtime) as my mum 'had not had time'. Her obsession with cleanliness filled her day, and then often involved my dad being drawn into cleaning something that was apparently 'filthy'. But he would do anything for her and took it all in his stride.

My younger sister Jackie and I had only a small appreciation of the demands made upon our dad at the time, though as we grew older, they became more and more apparent. However, unable to pursue my true passion (more on that later too), I might as well help him out by chopping this week's pile of sticks for the fire. I can't remember where the wood came from, but I think he used to bring a few offcuts home in his pockets from his job as a sprayer at a cabinet makers.

There was a place where we could obtain all kinds of things to help us along with our lives. Nowadays, the place would be called a field and our resource fly tipping, but then, any open space on the edge of a poor estate was a dump. If you had something you didn't need, you took it there, threw it over or into the hedge and forgot all about it. Conversely, if you wanted something, especially if you were a practically minded eleven-year-old boy, the nearest dump was the place to go find it. Wood was a valuable resource, so anytime there was a new load dumped, it was quickly gone.

It was an efficient recycling system as the pile of discarded stuff never grew out of hand. On the contrary. More often than not, we were disappointed more stuff had not been dumped, as we couldn't find what we were looking for. All these decades later, I still have a secret urge to look through the fly tipping in some of the lanes around my home... but I resist, despite my early programming.

Anyway, there I was with our valuable pile of wood which, like most things in my life, I had learnt to chop just by watching my dad. He explained how to hit it with the chopper (we never called it an axe) down the length of the grain. If you got it right, it would split beautifully into easily lit sticks. If you got it wrong, there could be quite a mess, but I would never ask my mum for a plaster as that might involve a rant at me for being stupid. I learnt quickly or I would have become digitally challenged.

Chopping wood wasn't the typical pastime of choice for a boy my age, but there were worse things about my life. At least it was something reasonably satisfying, as I could look at the pile of sticks and feel I had created something. And it would make my dad proud of me.

So, my first major decision concerning my life didn't come about solely because of the wood chopping. The contributing factors had built up over time. Later, I will go into this in more detail, but for now, let's just assume that this revelation came to me in a flash:

"I'm not going to live my life like this."

I guess I've not been the first to say that. It's not even a particularly revelatory thing to say, but when I first started planning this book, I wanted to work out the moment my progress out of what I saw as the gutter of my life began. Being someone who has always looked forward and put as much of the past behind me as possible, I have found it quite a struggle to dig out some of the more significant thoughts and memories. But this is one of the moments which stands out. That's good enough for me.

So, what happened?

Just as I cared about helping my dad by chopping wood for him, I've had a lifelong passion to improve things for others. I've always believed, however scarce the resources you have around you, it is possible to maximise them, often to great effect. Yet sometimes, people resist my advice. The reasons for this are many and complex.

You may think it's harsh to say people choose to be where they are in life. And I understand that. People can be presented with horrendous circumstances, far, far beyond what most of us have encountered or will ever encounter, especially in the Western World. Yet there are countless stories of individuals who have literally dragged themselves out of the gutter and gone on to have a fulfilling life.

Our success or failure is almost always about the myriad decisions we make every day. Just like the modern-day fly tip being the rich hunting ground of my youth, looking at what you have around you in a slightly different way can make a huge difference to your mental state, and therefore what you are able to achieve.

Chopping wood was my opportunity to see things differently and learn from it. We all have abilities and resources which can be used to our advantage, but we don't always use them effectively or perhaps even recognise them. Indeed, the one thing we are really good at is often the skill we take for granted as it is so inbuilt, it doesn't seem special to us. That doesn't mean we have to spend our lives chasing and evolving one particular skill, but being aware there are things we can do to change our lives is very important.

At junior school, our form mistress (that's what we called them back then) asked my class to write down what we wanted to do when we grew up. About nine at the time, I didn't have much hesitation in writing down my career choice, which seemed perfectly reasonable to me. I have always had the ability to make people laugh, so as all the other boys and girls wrote things like 'nurse' or 'carpenter', mine just happened to be 'comedian'. At least it sounded better to me than my dad's job, riding a moped for an hour and a half every day to and from a stinking factory, spraying toxic paint on to pieces of furniture we could never have afforded in our wildest dreams.

I never became a comedian (though some might disagree), but I did change my life in ways which I could never have imagined. In my school days, I enjoyed making people laugh because it gave me satisfaction to see them happy. And it stopped me getting beaten up. As physically small compared with those around me, I needed to develop this skill at a very young age, even before I learnt how to chop wood...

When I think back now to those days of my childhood, it is hard to understand how I kept my vow to create a better life for myself. But in the next few chapters, I will tell you how I made it happen. And you can do the same, even when life hasn't stacked the cards in your favour.

CHAPTER 2

SMALL PEOPLE

It's important to give you some background and context so you can understand what made me into a somewhat grumpy eleven-year-old. This requires me to tell you about my parents' childhoods, as it was their background and circumstances which influenced them and their behaviour. This subsequently became an intrinsic part of my growing up. I'm sure it is the same for most people.

From as young an age as I can remember, it was made very clear to me we were different. Sadly, not in a particularly positive way. As far as my parents were concerned, we knew our place: the bottom rung of the ladder. It was never going to change. The best way to survive was to keep our heads down, do as we were told, never challenge anyone or anything, and be grateful for what we had.

Not a tall story
As well as coming from an extremely poor family, my dad and his eight siblings also faced what is still a somewhat unacknowledged prejudice, even in our more enlightened times. They were rather short. If you were a short female, you were probably treated in much the same way as any other woman. But for a man, it must have been difficult, particularly if you were a manual worker.

I can still remember my grandfather (known to his many grandchildren as 'Granfer'). His father and mother were unknown, even to my dad. They were regarded as so shameful, my dad and his siblings were not allowed to visit them or know exactly where they lived, even though it was in the same small village. All he knew was they resided in some kind of slum, the inference being they were either alcoholics or thieves, or possibly both. Very poor families didn't always register the birth of their children in those days as they couldn't afford to pay the registration fee. My great grandfather may well have been an undiscovered basketball player but nevertheless worked in the local colliery, where most of the employment was. There's no advantage in being tall, working in low mine shafts.

Granfer Moon was pretty short at around the 5 foot mark which, combined with my Gran's 4 foot 9 inches, managed to produce nine kids who, if placed end to end, would be equal to about six normal humans. My dad was 4 foot 11 and a half, which I know is accurate as it is stated in his Army papers. It was obvious my dad's family members were ashamed of their background, which is why they rarely spoke of it. Apparently, it was forbidden to even mention the names of Granfer Moon's relatives, though one did go on to become Chairman of the local Parish Council. A lofty achievement in Moon circles.

Research shows smaller men earn less than taller ones.[1] When you are starting from the poverty line, as my great grandparents were, things aren't looking too bright for you. I don't know how tall my gran's father was, but I do know the family lived in the area of Avon Street in Bath described as 'the place of slums and whores' at the turn of the 20th century. My gran told me the meagre living her father Bill Morgan generated

---

1   M Rozsa, 'Shorter height, lower salary: Height discrimination is real, and can be economically devastating' (Salon, 19 January 2023), www.salon.com, accessed 8 April 2024

came from street fighting. If trouble broke out in that area of Bath, people would advise you to "Call for Bill Morgan, he'll sort it." So even if he was short, he was tough.

If Bill won some money and there was any left after he had bought a few pints of wallop (beer), my gran and her sister would queue up at the back of a bread shop very early the next morning to buy the stale bread from the day before, so they had something to eat. Decent nourishment was not on offer to aid her growth.

By comparison, my mum's family was on another level. Height wise, that is. In line with the aforementioned study, their heady average of 5 foot and a bit brought them into the realms of extreme poverty as opposed to destitution. My mum was also one of nine, but being the youngest, she had the benefit of the older children bringing money from age fourteen, when most of them left school and were sent out to work. Though as her eldest sister was married at age sixteen, the extra wages coming in to the household were somewhat temporary, which may explain why they seemed to have little effect.

One Christmas, Mum told me, she saw a stocking under the tree with something round in it. She was eagerly expecting an orange, which would have been a real treat. But it turned out to be a turnip. My mum blamed her disappointing Christmas gift on her dad, reckoning he had drunk away the orange money, and she carried this grudge with her all her life, regularly telling us he was a no-good alcoholic.

So let's keep perspective. My mum's family was still extremely poor by any standards we use today. There is a tale of a visit by the man who oversaw the dishing out of the equivalent of today's Universal Credit under the ancient Poor Law. Seeing a piece of coconut matting on the cold stone floor of the house, he questioned how such a luxury was affordable. The weekly shilling (now 5p) was stopped.

At this point, I can't help but recall the 'Four Yorkshiremen'[2] sketch from the 1979 *Secret Policeman's Ball*, where John Cleese, Michael Palin, Rowan Atkinson and Terry Jones vie with each other to describe how their upbringing was worse than everyone else's. "Of course, we 'ad it tough" was the unforgettable phrase. Let's just say, my family had what we had and there seemed little way out of it. But there was a way, because I found it. And if I can, then so can others.

Which leads me on to an important point my dad made to me when I was at an early age. In one respect, it helped me tremendously and probably still does to a certain extent. But it also explains his lack of ability to improve his lot and why he always told us to be grateful for what we had and to expect no more.

Reality is perspective

My mum and dad often spoke to my sister Jackie and me about the hardships they endured when they were young. Anyone who lived through the Second World War had faced challenges which must have made the post-war period a relative doddle. My dad told me the best way to survive was to remember something his dad (Granfer Moon) had told him to live by. I'm going to repeat it as close to word for word as I can remember, including my dad's broad North Somerset accent:

"Our father zed you'cn pud up with anything. It don't matter what 'appens to you or whad anybudy duz da ya. Just keep quiet (pronounced 'kwi-ut') and ged on wi' it."

What Granfer meant is it is your own response to external forces which determines how you feel about them. Dad never explained it using those words, but it became obvious to me. In other words, if someone says something to you, it is you who

---

2   https://www.youtube.com/watch?v=qlIXn0r0AY8

decides what meaning that has for you. You can choose to be mortally offended or mildly amused. You might even choose, as Granfer suggested, to ignore the words altogether.

When I was a child, we regularly used to use the phrase "sticks and stones can break my bones, but words can never hurt me" whenever someone said something nasty to us, which seemed to be quite often. I don't hear it anymore – perhaps it should be revived.

So, the first lesson from this book if you are serious about improving your lot is to realise your reaction to any situation determines what you believe that situation to be. In other words, **reality is perception**. If you decide someone has said something offensive or hurtful to you, then you will be offended and hurt. If you decide they don't understand or mean anything hurtful by what they are saying, you could choose to ignore their words completely.

One of the simplest yet most damaging mistakes people make in life is to assume everyone must feel the same way as they do about everything. The reality is actually the opposite. It's much more likely everyone feels and reacts in a slightly or vastly different way to the same inputs, depending on their perception of those inputs.

If we are talking about auditory inputs, ie the things we hear, Granfer and my dad would have found these verbal challenges relatively easy to deal with. "They are only words," they would have said. "So what?" When you are struggling to feed your family and keep them warm, what someone says to you takes on a low level of importance. In our modern age, where obesity kills more people than starvation, some people seem obsessed about minutiae. While I wholeheartedly agree words can be extremely powerful and the effective use of them is one of the keys to success, it's helpful to believe only our own words used on others can have this power.

Tell yourself you have a virtual suit of armour. All the nasty, threatening and abusive words used by those you come into contact with bounce off it. I'm a firm believer in this kind of visualisation and I will come back to it later on. Used in the right way, it will be one of your essential weapons in the quest to rise.

When it comes to physical challenges, some find these easier to ignore than the mental ones, arguing there are actually only mental challenges. In other words, it's how your mind reacts to the big boy thumping you in the stomach because you are smaller than everyone else which determines how much pain you feel. I would suggest it's a little easier to deal with that situation as a mental challenge when you are closer to the size of a normal Homo Sapiens. But perhaps that is just a hangover from my limitation when I was a kid. By the way, in my late teens, I grew to become almost average size – something of a miracle by my reckoning and that of my family.

Anyway, Granfer Moon and Dad learnt it is possible to develop a state of mind where you are somehow numb or immune to all the bad things life throws at you, both mentally and physically. This was a common trait in poor communities, and still is today. "Stiff upper lip" tended to be used more by the upper classes, but as it means hiding all your true emotions, it was certainly relevant to my contemporaries in my childhood. Emotions were luxuries we couldn't afford. It was dealing with the hardships of life which my dad was skilled at, so we will concentrate on that aspect for now.

I grew to understand the stiff upper lip method of coping from a young age, not because of what my dad told me, but from the way he lived his life and his actions. We certainly had some ups and downs, but we just got on with it, as many others did in those days. There was never any thought of blaming anyone else, and seeking help was anathema. That wasn't how the

Moons lived. We looked after ourselves, we weren't beholden to anyone and we never complained.

That was one of the reasons I would never ask my mum for a plaster if I cut my finger chopping wood. It was my fault, I did it, I had to sort it out. Pain could be ignored by getting on with something else to distract me. This concentrating on something else technique is much more effective than you might think.

My learning and experiences over the years have taught me, almost without exception, the way you deal with what seem like inconsequential, mundane and repetitive parts of life is fundamental to programming your mind, and hence your ability to deal with everything. Food is an example. In the 1960s, there were far fewer culinary options. British food was seen by the French as somewhat of a joke, not helped by war-time rationing, which was still very much in the minds of those like my parents. They had become totally accustomed to small meals with little variety, served with a whack around the head from their parents if they complained. Both my parents had to wolf down their meals to stop their older brothers and sisters stealing from their plates as none of them were given enough. One of the reasons my mum was so obsessed with making sure Jackie and I had good food was due to her own childhood experiences. She didn't want us to have to go through the same as her.

One of the ways my dad helped us with the fussiness many kids suffer when it comes to food (especially vegetables) was to get us to eat the bits we didn't like first. "Get those out of the way and the rest will be much more pleasant," he would say. That's another piece of simple advice I took on board from my dad and have applied to many things since. If I had a plate of meat, potatoes and cabbage, I would eat my cabbage first as I didn't like it much. I would end with the meat, so I finished the meal happy (strange and ironic, as I now hardly ever eat meat).

By contrast, my sister Jackie was too stubborn to do that. She only ate the things she liked and pushed the rest around her plate. There would be a daily battle trying to get her to eat everything and I can't remember a time when she actually did.

Mental toughness

The order in which we eat the foods on our dinner plate may sound like an inconsequential matter, but it's one of the fundamental parts of creating the mindset we need to succeed. Throughout our lives, particularly as children, we are conditioning our minds in a certain way. Those with plenty perhaps don't think too much about what they are eating or why they are eating it. They may have lots of ideas and reasons why they have decided not to like or eat certain things, quite apart from health issues. When presented with what we perceive to be less than palatable food, or anything else which we are either scared or turned off by, we invent reasons to justify our decision not to engage.

These thoughts and justifications related to our habits can have a significant long-term effect on us, because every day, we are reinforcing our beliefs and behaviours, usually without realising what we are doing. A lot of being successful is about doing things which others won't do and having the willpower to keep doing them. If your business really needs you to work late every night to get something completed, you have to have the mental stamina to do that.

Like most if not all skills, mental toughness improves with practice and deteriorates without it. If you have been programming your mind all your life to eat things you don't particularly enjoy, is it not logical you will have built a general capacity to resist temptation, such as going home early like everyone else, rather than working late? If you have spent your life eating the meat and leaving the veg, you will likely have less willpower to do what is required when presented with a challenging or, as you see it, an unpleasant task.

It's a complex issue and one of many things in which I have no qualifications to justify what I believe. All I have is a lifetime of amateur study, observation and interest in this kind of thing, so I hope my thoughts will be of some use.

Buddhists place much importance upon the whole matter of eating. I won't repeat it here, but the basis is they believe in being grateful for everything on their plate, not being fussy about what they do and don't eat, and making sure they eat every single scrap they are given. I was sixty-five years old when I discovered this – the Buddhists, one of the most wonderful groups of human beings on the planet, are advocates of something I have always felt and believed in.

Whether or not you pay the price and do the hard things first depends on your decision-making ability. It's part of **Life's Ultimate Dilemma (LUD)**. If you continually go for the easy option, there could be long-term detrimental consequences. Generally, whatever you want in life, there is a price to pay. You either pay it up front and enjoy an easier time later, or vice versa.

That type of thinking was passed down from my grandfather to my dad, who then conveyed the same mindset to my sister and me. Every generation seems to take pride in telling the next one how tough it was in the olden days. Probably because in many families, that is the case. Almost every measure shows the world improving year on year, as documented brilliantly in the book *Factfulness: Ten Reasons We're Wrong About the World* by the late Hans Rosling.[3] It's not surprising parents tell their children how lucky they are, compared with how they had it, because it's usually true. The children never want to hear such

---

3   H Rosling *Factfulness: Ten Reasons Why We're Wrong About The World*
     (Sceptre, 2018)

things and still feel hard done by. And then say the same things to their kids...

Because such progress tends to be incremental, it's difficult for anyone to accept their lot. On the contrary, there are many who constantly live in a state of longing for the illusory 'good old days' when things might have been tough, but everyone was happier.

If you spend some time in your life, especially the formative days, in a state of lack, it tends to create in you a superior ability to deal with many of the challenges life throws at you compared to someone who has lived in a state of surplus. Clearly, if you have insufficient food to help you grow and stay strong and healthy, life's physical challenges may be greater. But if we assume the physical challenges of our age are paling in significance compared with the mental ones, someone who has formed the mental strength to deal with daily hunger will be well prepared to deal with other mental challenges.

Refugees are good examples. They often overcome unbelievable challenges in having to leave their homeland behind. Yet once they are established in a safe country, they can have success well beyond that of the indigenous population. Clearly, there are exceptions either way, but based on my experiences, this is what I have observed.

There is a price to pay for everything. There is a quid pro quo. Although it is possible to develop mental toughness without too much in the way of detriment, for my parents to be able to do so required them to hide their feelings. Emotions were luxuries they could not afford.

I'm absolutely sure my dad loved my mum to bits, but I don't ever remember them holding hands, kissing in front of us or saying "I love you" to anyone, including my sister and me. That's not to say we didn't feel love or have fun, because we did. But there was never any outward expression of love in a verbal sense. I never heard my late mum utter those words, even though I have no doubt she did love us in her own way. I could see my dad's love for us in his eyes and everything he did for us, but it wouldn't have been the done thing to express this to us. It was only on his deathbed my dad finally dropped his guard and told us all how much he loved us.

Instead of verbalising his love for us, my dad used his great sense of humour to find something amusing in every situation, however dire. We never boasted or made too much of anything we achieved, because we were told "pride always comes before a fall". It was better to be quiet and modest and keep our small successes to ourselves, and hope and pray nothing would come along to take them away.

Another phrase which was wheeled out frequently was "You don't know how lucky you are". This related to my parents' version of the 'Four Yorkshiremen' sketch, or if that didn't sound tough enough, my mum knew lots about the poor children of Africa who would be more than happy to eat the scraps Jackie left on her plate and be thankful for them.

So clearly, Granfer's advice rubbed off on my dad, rather too well. Due to his diminutive stature and his willingness to accept whatever he was given, my dad was walked over for most if not all of his life. Anyone who could took advantage of him and treated him like the less-than-complete man they saw him as, aided and abetted by my dad's good nature and his inherent character trait to help anyone whenever he could. Whatever his personal situation, he would give up his time and energy for the benefit of relatives, friends and anyone else who asked, often when he could least afford to.

It was a lovely, admirable trait in many ways, but when he gave help at his own expense and was taken for granted by the recipients, it was a fool's game. This is all too evident when I think of the times we ourselves needed help. My dad would never want to impose himself on anyone and would much prefer to suffer in silence, as he had been taught.

Sometimes, though, we had no choice but to seek the help of others…

CHAPTER 3

SOMETIMES, YOU JUST NEED HELP

I was about seven years old. We had recently moved from our small flat in Bristol to a damp cottage in Midsomer Norton. This was when I first became aware my mum wasn't a person I could always rely on to be there for me. I didn't understand at the time, but I now realise she was suffering from depression.

Her screaming, crying and ranting started quite soon after our move. She blamed it on the cottage reminding her of her 'awful childhood'. Seeming obsessed with her own mother's death, which occurred when I was around two years old, she would cry and cry about it for hours. She told us her father was an uncaring alcoholic who spent any money the family had on drink rather than the food they needed. This may or may not have been an exaggeration. Although it is true to say Granfer Bill was a regular fixture at his local, he seems to have been more of a character than a rogue, as shown by the fact a road in the area was named after him some years after his death.

This particular Sunday morning, my sister and I became aware of our mum being in a far worse state than usual. She was upstairs, crying and screaming, Dad keeping her as calm as he could while bringing us into the bedroom to look after us at the same time. Jackie was only about three years old, as strong then as she is today, so I don't remember her being upset or distressed about the situation.

My mum was in bed with a tray of breakfast my dad had made for her. It hadn't calmed her. She picked up a knife and, in front of Jackie and me, started to cut her wrists. Dad grabbed her arm, but she kept trying to saw away with the knife on her other wrist, screaming she was going to kill herself unless he did something. I'm not sure what she wanted him to do, but whatever it was, it was an impossible ask.

I doubt she really wanted to end her life in front of us. Nevertheless, that was the moment my dad must have realised he couldn't cope with this alone.

As we had only recently moved house, we didn't know anyone except the neighbour. Mum had told us he was an ignorant, filthy grunter of a man, so Jackie and I were a bit scared of him. Some of our aunties and uncles lived in the area, but we had no car, no phone, nothing. There was no public phone box anywhere near us. Even if there had been, how would two small children have got to it?

At times like these, people clutch at the tiniest straw. I said we knew no-one in the area, but that wasn't quite true. When Mum walked me to school, we occasionally saw an old lady who lived in a bungalow further along our street. She was 'posh', which meant she owned her own house rather than living in a rented place like ours. Moreover, it looked very clean and tidy with hydrangeas growing in the small gravelled front garden. Only posh people had hydrangeas.

But what really propelled her into the upper echelons of poshness was she had a telephone. To us, this was the modern-day equivalent of owning a private jet. It was almost beyond our comprehension. Anyone who had one was bordering on being royalty.

Our mum was suspicious of everyone and had made us

believe most people were out to get us or take advantage of us, so it was better not to get involved with anyone. Mrs Hydrangea was probably old enough not to be any threat, so it was OK to talk to her. But not for very long. Just in case.

I assume it was my dad's idea to ask her to help us. Things must have been absolutely desperate because never, in any circumstances, would he normally have asked a favour of *anyone* and therefore been in their debt. That just did not happen. This time, though, he had to break his sacred rule. There was only one way to seek help. He couldn't leave my mum for a second. I would have to go.

I guess it was only early, but like many older folks, Mrs Hydrangea was up and around. I was a little scared knocking on her door and I don't remember exactly what happened immediately thereafter or how I explained what was going on, but she must have got the message and phoned the emergency services.

The next thing I recall is seeing my mum, tied down with leather straps on some kind of stretcher, being put into an ambulance, with a crowd of neighbours gathering around to take in every bit of the excitement. This would be a major problem and a reason we couldn't have stayed in that cottage after this incident. There was one thing more important to my mum than anything else in her life, including us, my dad and God. It dominated most of her thinking and the actions she took.

Reputation is everything

My mum was obsessed with what people might think about her. Although we were very poor and lived from hand to mouth, she would do all she could to put on the appearance everything was perfect. It was her overwhelming raison d'être, so the ignominy of this situation would be unbearable for her.

Obsessive cleaning was part of this. It was essential to her for people to know she had a clean house. It's something I can relate to, up to a point (I will tell you later about my rental property experiences). I realise my mum went too far, cleaning at the expense of many other things, but at least we had some kind of pride in the house we lived in, which is a simple yet vital example of how we can all make the most of what we have. One thing anyone can do is keep their surroundings clean. You may not be able to afford cleaning products, but water and a cloth and some hard work will usually do the trick.

My mum's obsession with what people thought of her manifested itself in rather more complex ways than just cleaning. She had devised a set of rules which could not be broken, whatever the circumstances. This is something everyone does, to a greater or lesser degree, but for my mum, it was mainly about show.

The swan analogy is a good one here. We see a beautiful bird, gliding serenely along on the surface of the pond. What we don't see are the little legs, flapping like mad underneath. My mum had to present her family to the world as though we were as posh as Mrs Hydrangea. I have no idea whether she fooled anyone except herself, but the thought others might talk about us filled her with horror. Being forcibly restrained and removed from her house broke that illusion of poshness a little, even though she had probably been sedated and knew little of it.

As we had no means of transport ourselves and because our dad understandably wanted to stay with our mum, Jackie and I were allowed to travel in the ambulance as well. I remember feeling excited by this and cheekily asking the driver if he would make his siren go. Obligingly, he did, which to me offset all the trauma so far that day.

From that point on, our little family was never quite the same. My mum was admitted to the Mental Asylum in Wells where she received treatment. I remember some talk of her being given electric shocks to her brain, though I'm not sure if that happened; just the thought of it is enough to traumatise me. Either way, she was there for some weeks, while Jackie and I went to live with her sister in Chippenham. We didn't see my dad while living there, but at least Jackie and I were together. She was a great sister and very much a tomboy, so we got on well.

On the move, again

Eventually, my mum was released and the local authority decided the damp cottage was not suitable for us. So, in 1966, we were allocated a council house in a place called Westfield, about 2 miles away. I suffered badly from Tonsillitis and went into hospital to have my tonsils removed. While I was having that done, the move to Westfield took place, so I returned to a different home and, hopefully, a new start for my mum.

Our new house was certainly an improvement on the cottage. It had a decent-sized garden front and rear, and a bedroom for both Jackie and me. We continued to attend the same school as before – St John's in Midsomer Norton, which meant a thirty-minute walk every day. We were the only pupils from Westfield as my mum insisted we must go to a Church of England school. Part of the walk was along the pit path, a scary, lonely track where bullies and other weirdos could get you, but those whom my mum looked up to (the posh people) would surely think more of us if we went to a Christian school where we would be protected from the evils of the world more effectively than those who ran their lives without the help of a deity.

After being accompanied to school for a couple of days by Mum, Jackie and I were left to make the journey on our own. After I left junior school at eleven, my sister had to make that 2 mile journey entirely on her own. She was eight years old. And like all our family, she was tiny compared with everyone else. But she was strong and determined and I don't remember her ever complaining (I wonder where she got that from).

None of our neighbours could work out why we attended that school when there was a perfectly good one on the edge of our estate, but my mum knew best. Perhaps she did – things turned out OK for us in the end, though it took a long time for me to realise this.

CHAPTER 4

WHAT HAPPENED NEXT

Although having one coal fire in the living room to heat the whole of our house wasn't great, my mum was the major source of my discontent as an eleven year old. You may have heard the phrase, 'wherever you go, you take yourself with you'. This was exactly the case after our flit from Midsomer Norton.

My mother might have escaped the reminders from the cottage she felt triggered her issues, but part of her treatment was the prescription of Valium, which she quickly became addicted to. As I grew older at Westfield, I became more and more aware of what I saw as her illogical behaviour and how she was affecting all our lives. A particularly distressing episode was one which must have been incredibly upsetting for my dad, given everything he had done for her and how much he cared for her.

Money, or rather lack of it, had always been at the heart of our family. My dad never earnt a great deal, even at the end of his working life, but he always endeavoured to be frugal and would have saved whatever pennies or halfpennies he could. But he was always frustrated by my mum. Driven by face saving and the importance of putting on a show, if there was any spare cash, she quickly utilised it. Although to be fair, she spent it as much on us as she did on herself.

Sadly, there were often occasions when she utilised the cash rather too swiftly, so the week's food budget, which had looked reasonably healthy on day one, disappeared on things we simply couldn't afford. Partly so we looked good in front of the neighbours, she would pay the local butcher to deliver meat on a Monday. His shop was only a few minutes' walk away, but she was far too busy cleaning to have the time to go there. There was never any question of setting a budget or asking what it cost; the delivery simply arrived and my mum paid without question. Then we ate like millionaires, for one or two nights at least.

Even at my young age, I could clearly see we simply could not afford what my mum was buying when her purse was full at the beginning of the week and empty by day three. Sure enough, reality quickly hit us.

Leading up to her death in 2023, my mum suffered from Alzheimer's, and during its onset, she would accuse everyone she came into contact with of stealing from her, often things which didn't exist. This was rather clever of them, but also very upsetting, especially for her granddaughter whom she accused of stealing a non-existent ornament. Because she had this condition, though, people were understanding and accepted her ridiculous allegations accordingly.

What only Jackie and I knew was this paranoia had been going on for most of our lives. It was all very real at Westfield, the Alzheimer's just made it happen more frequently. Rather than admit her ineptitude at balancing her budget (we will explore that important skill later in the book), my mum decided to blame someone else. In this instance, it happened to be my dad.

There was no money for food as the end of the week approached, and as far as Mum was concerned, there could only be one reason for this: my dad had been stealing from her purse. In theory, that could have been true. In reality, I would have an easier time believing Martians were living under our stairs. My dad lived a selfless life. He had no time or money to pursue any hobbies, no close friends or social life. He didn't drink or smoke and devoted every moment when he was not working to taking care of my mum and his children.

I am convinced he would have done anything for us, whatever the cost to him. If my mum made a demand, however illogical or unreasonable or difficult, my dad would do his best to make it happen. It never made sense to me, but he almost worshipped her. From what I gathered from the few conversations we had regarding this, she was the only girl he ever asked for a date and he was blown away when she accepted. From then on, she could do no wrong.

And yet, despite all that, my mum decided to make one of the most distressing allegations it is possible to make against any human being, let alone one who would have laid down his life for her. It didn't matter what my dad said, however much he tried to calm the situation and to deny taking one penny, my mum was adamant he had stolen from her. The only saving grace was, like many of her rants, she quickly forgot the incident ever happened. In fact, she would later deny she ever said anything like it. And as you now know, my dad had the mindset to be able to deal with it and we moved on. Money was found, probably from the pot set aside for coal, and we were able to eat.

It's probably becoming a little clearer now why my wood chopping epiphany occurred. But to reiterate the point, let's go back and set the scene for how we became a family.

Love and marriage

My dad left school at fourteen and immediately got a job with a piano making company, where he learnt the skill of French polishing. This is the dying art of making wood look like the pieces we are all familiar with from TV programmes like the

Antiques Roadshow. In those days, expensive furniture was laboriously polished by hand.

His passion, though, was cars, which led to him teaching himself to repair and spray bodywork. Despite his low wages, his frugality allowed him to buy his own car, one of the first people to do so in his small village. Living at home would certainly have helped, though to add context, it took him about eight years of saving to acquire the funds to buy his second-hand Austin 7.

Not known for the power of its engine, my dad's 7 was particularly bereft of urge, made apparent when it was tackling one of the many steep hills in the area. Or rather, not tackling it. But at least he could get out of the small village, even though that involved reversing up some of the hills as the car was incapable of climbing them forwards, and take a bold trip to a dance in a nearby town. There, he met my mum.

In the 1940s and early 1950s, families like those of my parents did not have telephones. Actually, we didn't have a phone at home until the mid-1970s, and only then because my sister and I defied our parents and had one installed. The solution to making arrangements with someone you had no efficient way of contacting after you had left their presence was quite simple: you devised a plan, and you stuck to it. You kept your word because that was not only the correct thing to do, but also how society, at least the poorer parts of it, functioned.

So, having plucked up the huge amount of courage he required to speak to my mum and seemingly established some kind of connection with her, my dad made an arrangement to see her again in a month's time at the next dance. There was no question of it being any sooner, as he needed another four weeks of work to save up enough money for fuel etc. Thankfully, she honoured that arrangement, or I probably wouldn't be here to write these words.

The ease with which we can communicate with others is another example where surplus can lead us to become less admirable as humans. Taking the ability to communicate for granted, and holding so little value in your word that you treat arrangements as disposable is not a recipe for success, particularly in business. The ability to trust in an arrangement is at the core of a civilised society yet treating arrangements with the same disdain as fast-food wrappers or cigarette butts discarded without any thought is not a rare occurrence. **Reliability** is one of the key components in making something from nothing. The last time I looked, it didn't cost much money or effort to be a reliable person, and it's a valuable asset you can develop to help you move on to greater things.

The Austin 7 soon made way for a slightly more powerful Morris 10. This was an essential component in my dad's courtship of my mum, as their villages were not within walking distance, and were separated by a number of those notorious hills. Then the courtship evolved into marriage, which brought with it the requirement for a home. In the 1950s, everyday items such as furniture, crockery, cutlery and bedding represented a huge investment for the average working-class person. It's easy to take for granted today's affordability of such items, where things like electric kettles are so inexpensive, they are regarded as disposable. Cheap household goods were simply not available back then. People kept things for many years, until they could no longer be repaired.

My mum took this to heart. She and my dad had managed to save a small amount of money to enable them to start a home together, which he would dearly have loved to use as a deposit for their own home, albeit a very modest one. My mum, always with an eye to what others might think, was not prepared to manage with second-hand stuff or hand me downs, and instead blew everything they had saved on new and relatively expensive household items. My dad told me they had boxes and boxes of stuff to go into a house. The wedding day was set, the reception paid for, the arrangements made. Just one vital thing missing: the house to put the stuff in. No money left as a deposit to buy their own place. Not even enough for the first month's rent.

Whoops! Despite my dad's parents living in a three-bed council house with four of his eight siblings still in residence, the newly wed couple started their married life in a 'spare' room. It's lucky everyone in the family was so tiny.

As accommodating as my grandparents would have been and as accepting as my dad always was, my parents were soon desperate for their own place, mainly because my creation coincided with the consummation of their marriage. The solution came from a garage, based in the Clifton area of Bristol. My dad obtained a job in the body shop, spraying cars. He was skilled enough to show he was capable of working on the Rolls Royce of Cary Grant and the Rover of then TV celebrity, Johnny Morris, both Clifton residents. More importantly, the job came with a flat.

Almost as soon as they had moved there, I came along.

The tale of the missing savings stamps

Although the Moon and Tamblyn families were far from wealthy and firmly working class, by the time of my birth in 1957, some of my relatives had managed to drag themselves out of extreme poverty. They were both very close families and, for some reason, they found me to be a rather adorable baby and wanted to give me presents. Wisely, my parents suggested they buy National Savings stamps instead of actual presents. Some of them spent sixpence on me (that's 2.5p in today's money), while the wealthier ones would splash out on a half crown savings stamp, a whole 12.5p.

These stamps could be stuck into a Savings Book and would

be something for me to use when I was older, even gaining interest. It seemed incredible to me someone would give me money (interest) for doing nothing except having the good fortune to possess the money in the first place. It was a great idea and I recall hoping to make the most of that concept in the future. Meanwhile, as the birthdays and Christmases rolled by, my little pot built up quite nicely, reaching an almost unbelievable £12 by the time I was around six. Bearing in mind my dad only brought home £9 per week in wages, I was the wealthiest member of our family…

The flat, on the ground floor of a Victorian house, was a bit weird in that the two bedrooms were on one side of the entrance lobby and our kitchen and living room on the other. So we had to cross through the communal hallway to go to and from the bedrooms. When I say two bedrooms, my room was not much more than a large cupboard. When Jackie was born in 1960, there was nowhere for her to sleep except in her cot in my parents' bedroom. This was not an ideal situation, so as she grew older, my parents' search for decent accommodation became paramount.

Although my dad's ancient Morris 10 soldiered on for the first few years we lived in the flat, its age and our lack of money forced it into the hands of the scrap merchant. I vaguely remember riding in it. Despite me only being about three years old at the time, my passion for cars was already evident. I used to sit on the front passenger seat, held by my mum (different times). While dad drove, I would move the gear stick to the correct gear, with him using the clutch. He told me later in life I always knew which gear to go to and never missed a change. I must have loved it, as it put me on a path where cars and motorsport became an intrinsic part of my life.

I remember being very sad when the Morris went, especially as we were then without transport, but I didn't envisage that state would continue for the next ten years or so. There was no question of my dad having enough money to buy another car, though occasionally he was allowed to borrow one from his employer. We made up for it by spending time together, looking at other cars on the road and those in the garage my dad worked at. I quickly learnt the names of all the cars I saw and could recognise the sounds they made. Sitting in the front bedroom window, listening to the sound of an approaching car, Dad and I would play a game to guess what make it was. It was a lovely game, costing nothing yet giving us great pleasure – which just goes to show that the best things in life often are free. I had a pretty good hit rate, but cars had much more distinctive sounds in those days, so it was a lot easier than it would be now.

By the time Jackie was outgrowing her cot, my mum was desperate to move and had decided she wanted to be close to her family home. At least we could see her relatives then, as we rarely did in Bristol. But how could we move when we had no way of viewing properties in the area we wanted to be? And how would my dad get a job there if he couldn't attend interviews or make telephone enquiries? The biggest challenge, though, was finding a rental house with no deposit while persuading a landlord to take on a family with one wage earner who was only barely surviving and planning on changing jobs.

A particularly upsetting experience was recalled by my parents in detail years later when I fully understood the significance. A newspaper advertisement popped up for a car sprayer in the town of Frome, a job which came with a company house courtesy of the garage owner. My dad somehow made it to Frome and was offered the job and the house, which he accepted. He then resigned from his current employment and made all the arrangements to leave.

I remember us driving to Frome in a car, ready to move house. I have no idea where the car came from, I can only remember being greeted by the shocking news there was no job for my dad after all. And, obviously, no house. We had to return to Bristol, where my dad begged for his old job back and for us to be allowed to stay at the flat. Luckily, both were possible. 'Beg' was the word he used to describe this, another of the very few times in his life when he had no choice other than to seek help.

After that blow, we nevertheless managed to find the little cottage in Midsomer Norton, where Dad subsequently secured employment as a car sprayer. So, how is this part of the story related to my National Savings stamps? Have you guessed yet?

After the cost and frustration of the aborted move to Frome, the situation for my parents was desperate. No money, no help, no hope. Apart from my £12 in savings stamps. Yes, that was used to pay for the removal lorry which took our stuff to Midsomer Norton and to help us get through the first week there, as my dad had no work arranged. When the cottage came up, we just had to go and work the rest out later.

It was some time before I found out my money had been 'borrowed', but I remember being absolutely devastated and feeling I had been cheated. I was about ten years old when I looked in the little savings book and saw there was only a couple of quid there, rather than the relative fortune I thought I had. Mum was initially evasive and tried to tell me I was mistaken about how much I'd had, but eventually she explained they'd had no choice other than to use it, promising she would pay it back to me.

More than fifty years later, I am still waiting…

As an adult, I completely understand why my money had to be used. Who knows where I would be now if my parents hadn't used it? But as a child, I was very upset. I started this book by recalling one of my pivotal life moments and this was undoubtedly another. It created an unshakeable conviction and determination in me that I would have my own money which no-one could take away from me and I would never have to do what my parents did to me. Whether that thought occurred at the moment I found out about the missing money or whether it built up over a period of time, I can't say. But one thing is for sure: it has become an intrinsic part of me.

In our modern age, it's become traditional, some might say essential, for parents if they can, to help their children on to the so-called housing ladder. Some also pay huge sums towards their kids' education or to travel the world, buy them their first car etc.

I often smile at this. From an early age, I (albeit unknowingly) started subsidising my parents, a situation which barely changed throughout the rest of their lives. With Jackie, we even bought them their own home. Jackie paid for them to go on their one and only foreign holiday, and when my mum became the victim of fraudulent postal competition scams, we dipped our hands in our pockets again, so she had enough money to buy food.

I'm telling you this not for sympathy or with any bitterness, but because it's important you understand the context of my life and what drove me. This background will provide that context, and as we get further into the book and deeper into the tips and techniques you can use to help yourself, we will refer back to those important moments.

CHAPTER 5

SUCCESS ISN'T ALWAYS WELCOMED

So, I'm eleven, I've perfected my wood chopping skills and I know I want my life to change somehow. What I don't know is this process has already started.

When I was ten years old, the 11 Plus examinations were in their heyday. This was the system (still in use in some areas) where children were all tested on their skills at maths, writing and problem solving. I was always a good writer, a skill my mum told me I developed because she read to me constantly when I was very young. I have little doubt it helped. As with most things, the earlier one can become familiar with a subject, the easier it is in later life. There is little substitute for endless exposure to something, as evidenced brilliantly by Matthew Syed's book *Bounce* which shows you are likely to become extremely adept or even world class at anything you spend 10,000 hours or more practising.[4]

Maths was not my strong subject, but nevertheless, I passed the 11 Plus test, even though almost none of my relatives had done so. The only one I knew of was my mum's cousin. Bearing in mind I had thirty-two aunties and uncles and over fifty cousins, and only two of us had passed, this was a big surprise. And a huge problem.

---

4   M Syed, Bounce: *The Myth of Talent and the Power of Practice* (Fourth Estate, 2011)

Failing the exam would have meant my next school would be a secondary modern. The idea with these schools was children would be taught the more practical subjects, with a view to them aspiring to jobs such as carpenters, car mechanics, nannies or hairdressers. If you were well connected, you might get an apprenticeship which would lead you into the rarefied world of the union-controlled printing industry, where the wages were far beyond those of any other manual job and often in excess of the professions.

Passing the exam, on the other hand, allowed me entry to the grammar school system. In this case, it was Midsomer Norton Grammar, a formal and old-fashioned establishment at the time. Our family saw it as a place where other people went. It's difficult to convey how alien the grammar school would have appeared to my parents but imagine someone from the Arctic Circle applying for a job as a beach masseur in Barbados and you might get the picture.

It might be hard to imagine parents being disappointed at their child's success. But that was the case with me. Like most things in our family, it was my mum's mood and feelings which determined the policy, so it was she who told me I would not be going to the grammar school.

I can't say I had thought much about the possibility of going there prior to passing the 11 Plus. I had always achieved top marks and gold stars for my essays, which I loved writing, but I didn't like maths too much and it never entered my mind it was possible for me to be a little bit cleverer than some others. But passing started me thinking.

After some discussion, it transpired the main reason for my mum's refusal to let me go to the grammar school was a monetary one. No surprise there, then. At the secondary modern, kids were supposed to wear a uniform, but it was very informal. People wore stuff they could buy in ordinary shops, as long as it was more or less in line with the school colours and not too outrageous.

The grammar school was totally different. We saw the posh kids walking to school (even rich parents didn't drive their kids back then) with their immaculate blazers, caps, and ties, believing they were almost from another race, so far removed were they from our humble life. To make them seem even more special, all the grammar school pupils belonged to one of four houses: Blake, Scott, Pollard and Dunstan. There was fierce competition and rivalry between them and the badge of your house had to be sewn on the breast pocket of your blazer. If your parents had gone to the school, it went without saying you would be a member of their house.

There was only one supplier of the school uniform, a small, old-fashioned draper's shop in Midsomer Norton called Callenders, long since closed. Having a monopoly, Callenders could charge whatever they liked. These days, this would be regarded as unfair and immoral, but life was quite different then. The cynical might say it was a purposeful attempt to keep the working classes in their place, making the barrier to entry so high, only the middle classes could send their progeny to grammar school. My mum's cousin, who had passed the 11 Plus exam in 1930, had no possibility whatsoever of going to the grammar school as even ordinary clothes were unaffordable. Her place was given to a girl who had failed the exam. Her parents had more money.

And while things had improved by 1968, that was irrelevant to me. The uniform was far too expensive for my parents, so I would not be going.

To attend or not to attend

Their decision didn't particularly bother me initially. I had been taught nothing like that should affect me, so I just brushed it off.

Like most ten-or eleven-year-olds, I regarded my friends as the most important thing in my life. But then I began to realise my close friends would be going to the grammar school. Perhaps I had been subconsciously seeking out those with an IQ closer to mine, which is the basis of another vitally important life lesson we will cover in more detail later in the book – **choose positive influences.**

The person who was pivotal in prompting me to change my parents' decision was Andrew, the son of the geography teacher at the grammar school. His life and background were extremely alien to me, but we got on well and became close enough that I was invited to his family's house on a posh estate. It was like a mansion to me. I was super impressed. The estate was clean and tidy, there was no dump at the bottom of the road, and his parents were polite, intelligent and welcoming.

When I told him I would not be joining him at grammar school, he could not believe I would pass up the opportunity. Despite his young age, he explained to me how it would be good for me and how I could do well in life if I went to grammar school. I was impressed with what he told me and he was authentic enough (more on this later) that I trusted he was acting in my best interests. My other main friend had also passed the 11 Plus, so I decided I just had to go to the grammar school.

This is when I used a skill which became a vital part of my successes. Children possess all the sales skills anyone will ever need, but many tend to lose them as they grow older. When I say lose, I probably mean they are engineered out of them by what life throws at them. Really wanting or believing in something is a prerequisite to effective selling, and the thought of being detached from my friends gave me all the incentive I needed to make my mum change her mind.

I must have used my skills effectively. The main sales skill most children use is persistence. A kid seems to have unlimited energy to keep on asking the same thing until they get their way, which is kind of what I did. I just kept on and on and wore my parents down until my mum at least agreed they would look at trying to find a way of getting me the uniform. But there was still the question of affordability.

Perhaps one of my parents' most traumatic experiences was going to Callenders. It's hard to imagine how big a deal it was for them. There could be other parents in the shop who might realise we were poor. I recall them being very nervous, my mum especially embarrassed as she knew we couldn't afford any of the stuff. I'm sure the only reason they agreed to go was to placate me. They had no intention of buying me anything and thought I would change my mind when I understood how expensive it was.

But it was even more of a shock than we had anticipated. The cost of just one item was beyond our most pessimistic thinking. When the whole list of what was required had been written out by hand on a pad, it was a ridiculous amount, more than a week's wages. I didn't believe there was any way we could get around that.

But the lady who served us must have picked up on our signals. Perhaps she had encountered folk like us before or was just a good salesperson, as she showed us how the cost could be 'painlessly' spread over some years through hire purchase. That was my first concept of borrowing money. Although my parents were poor, they were never in debt (except to me, ha ha) and my dad would always say we should only buy what we could afford. But perhaps this would be different. You will read elsewhere my advice on borrowing, but only for something which will either grow in value or give you a return on your investment. Perhaps at this moment, I fell into the latter category.

Thankfully, my parents thought so, or were too embarrassed to say no. As soon as we had been shown the hire purchase option and how the payments could be spread over three years, I knew my mum's face-saving gene would kick in. To show we couldn't afford something would have been far too embarrassing, so meekly, they signed on the dotted line and I was kitted out.

Thankfully, everything was good quality, and as I hardly grew in the first three years at the school (probably subconsciously inhibiting my own growth genes so as not to prompt more debt), by the time I required a new uniform, our debt had been repaid. And conveniently, the school then became a comprehensive and the new uniform was much more affordable.

CHAPTER 6

ONWARDS

As we have already touched on, our peers can play a large part in determining what we do with our lives, particularly when we're children. But as with most things, our attitude and reaction to how our peers behave is every bit as important as how they are themselves. This is another thing we will explore in more depth later on...

While I've been writing this book, it's become more and more apparent to me many things I had forgotten or put to one side as being just part of my life have in reality been hugely important. Everything I have achieved, the place I find myself today, has come as a result of the billions of events, interactions and decisions I have made, perhaps almost from the minute I was born.

Just in case you haven't considered this fully before, let me tell you – you are no different. Your thinking and your decisions have the potential to be massively influenced by those around you and what has happened to you. How you react to those things is the key. We will talk about this in later chapters, but for now, let's continue to chronicle the important happenings in my life which taught me the priceless lessons I have used to my advantage.

My posh friend Andrew effectively got me to go to the

grammar school, so his interaction with me is one of the myriad examples of why I am where I am today and not somewhere else. He was a good friend, but as I grew older, my passion for cars grew too, and that was something Andrew didn't particularly share with me. So we drifted apart, even though we were always on friendly terms.

But there was one boy at my new school who was even more crazy about cars than me. Actually, he was crazier about cars than any human being I have ever met. Dave and I became friends from my second year at the grammar school, as he had attended a different junior school to me. Dave's family were far from wealthy, but unlike mine, his parents owned their own house, a small terraced cottage) and worked in jobs which didn't pay a pittance. They even had a fridge! But even more impressive was their car, a Vauxhall Viva they had purchased new in 1967. Dave's father cherished and cared for it like the prized possession it was.

Because Dave became a very close friend (he still is today, five decades later), I was invited into his family's world and treated like one of them. Having insight into a family that on the one hand was similar to mine (two parents, two kids, working class), but on the other hand different (the parents could afford clothes for their kids, a fridge and a new car) was crucial to my development and improvement. I began to see ordinary people could have a life which was so much less of a struggle than my family's, without doing anything radically different. But as we will realise as we progress through this book together, subtly different decisions, distinctions and reactions to the same circumstances can and do have profound effects on how we evolve and what we achieve.

Having that exposure to Dave and his world was, I now realise, one of the most important inputs of my life. Yes, I had been to the posh house where Andrew lived, but his family's world was so far from mine, there was no thought of them being a positive influence. A teacher, especially one at a grammar school, was only just below God and therefore of no aspirational relevance to me.

But when I met a working-class family that didn't live on a council estate and had a nice lifestyle, perhaps the twelve-year-old boy I was thought it might be possible to do the same. Had I only made friends with those who lived in my street, I would have had few positive influences. I'm not denigrating those people in any way, but following the herd and settling for the same as your peers is an all-too-easy path to follow. We will look more closely at **choosing positive influences** later in the book.

Passion

The first important life lesson I gained from being friends with Dave is if you have a **passion**, it is incredible what you can do with it and how much it can influence other parts of your life. I've already mentioned my passion for cars and, as I grew older, motor sport. There were very few ways I could indulge that passion as almost no motor sport was shown on TV, and when it was, my mum would often not let me watch it. We couldn't afford to buy car magazines except on special occasions and we didn't have a car until I was about thirteen.

Dave had access to both these things. He also had a head start on me as he had already built a few trolleys. Typically made from scrap collected from a dump, usually pram wheels mounted on a wooden frame, and string or a pram handle attached to the front axle to steer it with, a trolley was the next best thing to a motorised vehicle. We pushed it up the nearest steep hill (there were plenty in our area), and then hammered down it as fast as we could.

I hadn't built a trolley before I met Dave, but I had helped my dad with all kinds of projects, especially general DIY stuff at home. This instilled in me an all-important feel for practical things. When I discovered the book *Zen and the Art of Motorcycle Maintenance*[5] some years later, it made the importance of being exposed to making things at a young age all too apparent.

Dave and I built or modified a few trolleys which we had great fun with. I dread to think how close we came to serious injury, speeding down the slopes on some of the rough ground near Dave's home. And if that wasn't risky enough, we had a secondary pastime: sitting on books balanced on roller skates which we would race down the steep public roads. No gloves, no protective clothes, nothing. Often, we went so fast, we would catch up with cars ahead of us. Cars were much slower in those days…

But as fun as they were, neither of these things was a substitute for what Dave and I really wanted – a vehicle with an engine. Despite the seeming impossibility of acquiring one, we wouldn't give up on our dream. We had to find a way, and making a bit of money might help.

Our first entrepreneurial exercise was to rebuild and renovate an old bicycle which Dave managed to buy from one of his neighbours for almost nothing . We had already built a little bike from scrap parts obtained from the dump, so we had some experience, and in any case, nothing seemed to faze us. If we didn't know how, we just worked it out.

The new bike came together well. Dave was always good with paint and, having decided to finish it in the colours of the John Player Special F1 cars, he made a lovely job of the gold pin striping and signwriting on the black enamel. Christened the 'Bramble Bug', the newly restored bike was advertised on a card in the local shop window and almost immediately snapped up by a posh guy who wanted it for his son.

---

5   R M Pirsig, *Zen and the Art of Motorcycle Maintenance: An Inquiry into Values* (Vintage Classics, 1991)

I don't remember how much we got for it, but I do remember he knocked me down from the asking price very easily. I had never negotiated a sale before and, feeling I had given in too easily after the deal was done, I vowed not to make that mistake again. Another vital life lesson – **learn how to negotiate**. Nevertheless, we made a good profit as our expenses were negligible and our labour was free.

What's for sure is we were never bored in those days and couldn't wait to be free of school each day so we could get on with our projects. It set the scene for the rest of our lives where we have both always had more projects than we have time for.

Pretty quickly, the next project came along. A posh boy in our class told us he had a 50cc BSA power unit he didn't want. This was a small, self-contained petrol engine, not dissimilar to that powering a lawn mower, with the fuel tank as part of the unit, mounted on a wooden board. It could be the key to us liberating ourselves from the restrictions of gravity to having our own self-propelled vehicle.

But there was the small question of negotiating the deal.

Armed with my experience of selling the Bramble Bug, we aimed to get the engine for as little as possible. As I learnt later in life, the potential buyer has a massive advantage if they are limited in what they can pay and the seller is motivated to sell. Dave and I, then aged fourteen, negotiated the purchase down to 10 shillings, ie 50p. The deal was done.

Finding a way

Collecting the engine was another challenge. It was inconceivable any of our parents would do anything to enable us to bring it home, although by this time, even mine had a car. So we resorted to cycling the mile or two from our houses and strapping the relatively heavy unit to the rear of Dave's bicycle. I still can't imagine how we managed to attach it and keep it there. We then had a slow and nail-biting journey back to my dad's rented council garage in Westfield, where we eagerly devised plans to create our own motorised vehicle.

As usual, we disregarded our lack of money and resources, and simply decided we would **find a way**. This is another vital lesson in how to succeed. Probably from the dump, we sourced a basic frame consisting of a single metal tube bent into a loop upon which was welded an upright where a seat could be mounted. We used this as the basis of the trolley, as having a seat with a back on it would make it seem like a real vehicle.

We built the rest of the chassis from scrounged wood and used the ubiquitous pram handle for steering. Once the trolley began to take shape, our enthusiasm grew to bursting point, so the weekends just weren't enough for us to get it finished in the time we saw as acceptable. There was only one thing for it. We would have to skive (ie play truant from) some of our school lessons. The choice of which to skive was easy. It had to be a Thursday afternoon, which was double games preceded by biology, neither of which Dave or I enjoyed.

We weren't alone, as there was already a skivers' union of naughty boys who used to gather on the nearby coal tip, usually smoking and often getting caught or into even worse trouble. That was not for Dave and me. Rather than furtively creeping out at the start of double games, which was what the others did, we simply walked through the school gates at lunch time as though we were perfectly entitled to do so. I have no idea how tight security is at schools these days, but at the grammar school then, teachers would take it in turns to patrol the front to make sure none of the pupils escaped. Dave and I became so brazen at leaving on a Thursday, there was no question of us being challenged. We still remember the headmaster actually saying goodbye to us on one occasion.

And this leads nicely on to another valuable life lesson: **act**

as if and you can blag your way in and out of most things. My friends will tell you how successful I have become at doing this.

Having escaped the tortures of biology and double games, we would ride our bikes to my dad's garage, where we would work on building the trolley. Luckily, I had a key to the garage as my parents knew it was where I wanted to spend all my spare time, so it was relatively easy to go straight there and work all afternoon without my mum (who was at home all day) knowing.

On one occasion, though, I forgot my gym kit, in which the key to the garage was hidden. There was no question of us not working on the kart (with an engine by this time, it was no longer a trolley), so we had to get the key from the house. I was banking on my mum not being there as she had been planning to go to the shops that day, but nevertheless, I couldn't risk going to the house directly.

My parents gave me 12.5p a day to cover the cost of the school meal, so I was supposed to be in the dining room there, eating it at the time we skived. Instead, I used to buy a packet of crisps and a Mars bar every day from the local shop, and retain a tiny amount of money for myself, which added to my savings. We needed an excuse for Dave to go to the house. He didn't have school meals and my mum knew that, so the plan was for him to knock on our door, just in case she was there. If she was, he would say I'd forgotten my gym kit. And she was there, ready and willing to hand the kit (and the hidden key) to Dave so we could spend the afternoon in the garage.

What two kids will do to pursue their passion.

The Brooklands Bomb

The kart gradually came together. We were used to building trolleys, but something with an engine was a whole new ball game. The main issue was transmission. It was easy enough to mount the engine on to the kart, but without a gearbox or any other means to get the drive to the wheels, we were presented with a tricky problem.

When we were offered the engine, our youthful optimism far outweighed such issues. In life, it's easy to get consumed with detail before we even start a new project, something I see all too often. We must always **seize opportunity** when we can. A quote from General Patton I've used over and over again in my life is: "*A good plan violently executed now is better than a perfect plan next week.*" None of us knows what awaits us in the next second, minute, hour, day or decade. There is little in life which will hold you back more than procrastination. If you want to achieve something, it's almost always better to get on with it now than to wait. Another analogy I use relates to tying your shoes. If you are in a big hurry, or need to run from danger, it's better to slip both shoes on and get moving, even if the laces are undone. Running with one shoe perfectly fitted and the other one where you left it, is not a great strategy. Something useable or doable is often better than something which is perfect. That's a life lesson, by the way.

Dave and I could have missed our opportunity by over analysing how we would:

1. Get the engine home
2. Convince my mum it was OK to build a powered kart
3. Find a way to connect the engine to the wheels of the kart
4. Overcome our lack of money to obtain parts
5. Find somewhere to drive it when we finished the kart

But instead, we just ploughed on, confident we would find a way. You could say it was madness or youthful naivety. Certainly, I had spent as much as I wanted to on buying the engine, as I was determined I would never be left without any savings after what had happened to me before. So we had no other money to put towards completing the project. We had no parts, few tools, a garage without light or power (every hole had to be drilled using a hammer and a nail, often taking hours), and nothing but our enthusiasm and ingenuity to see us through.

After much puzzlement, we decided the only way to get the kart to move was to use belt drive from the shaft of the engine to one of the rear wheels. But we had no pulley to mount on the shaft or the wheel and no drive belt. Moreover, we calculated the pulley on the back wheel had to be relatively large to make the kart low geared enough to be able to pull away from rest. We didn't even know if such a pulley existed. What we did know was if it did, we would be unable to buy it.

Luckily, the dump came up trumps again. A small pram wheel, devoid of tyre and wired to the spokes of the wheel of the kart, would substitute as a crude pulley. Sorted. But what about the engine pulley and drive belt? We found a few old car fan belts, but they were all too short.

Dave's dad came to the rescue. He worked at a local paper bag and printing company which used huge machines to produce on an industrial scale, and agreed to liberate a suitable pulley and belt from the old stock at the factory. What a relief.

We also came up with the idea of making a clutch of sorts. Without one, the kart's engine would be connected directly to the back wheel, effectively making it impossible to pull away from rest without ripping the engine out of its makeshift wooden mountings. By rigging up the rear axle of the kart to swing backwards and forwards using wire connected to the pram handle, we could tension and release the belt. It worked surprisingly well and allowed us to have the kart's engine running while we were stationary. To pull away, we lifted the handlebars, thereby tightening the belt and giving us drive. Just like a real car, ha ha.

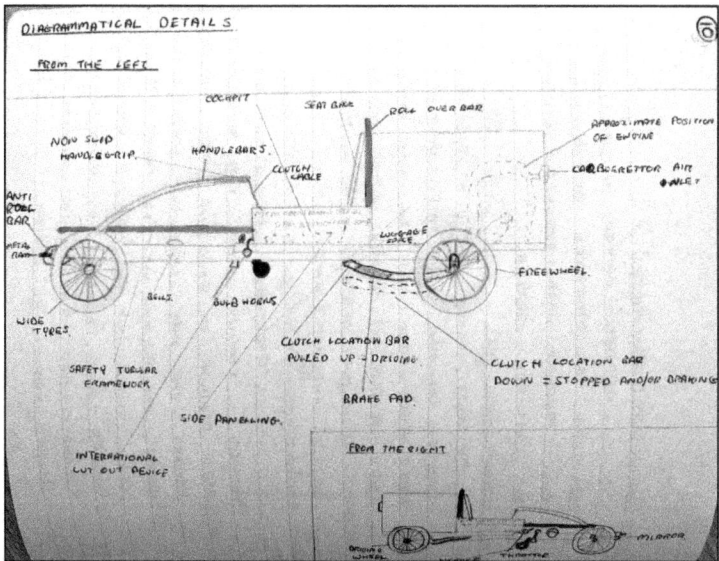

Part of the original plans for the Brooklands Bomb from September 1971. I documented all of our projects in detail in a school exercise book. It's fascinating to re-discover them 50+ years later

You may have noticed I haven't mentioned brakes yet. That was a challenge, once more solved with crude ingenuity. The bar attached to the rear axle of the kart – an integral element of our clutch – came forward to just under the handlebars. Dave's dad found some discarded flexible brake lining material from a machine at his work, which we wrapped around the bar and secured with wire (wasn't everything?). When we pressed down on the handlebar, the material would rub on the ground and slow us down. Slightly.

I've only just discovered such a brake has a name and was used on early cars. It's known as a sprag.

So, the kart came to be, and we christened it the 'Brooklands Bomb'. It gave Dave and me hours of pleasure and frustration as we hammered it around the streets of my parents' council

The finished article, ready to be raced around the streets. The old crash helmet was donated by a neighbour, who cared for our safety more than we did.

estate, frequently repairing it when things went wrong. But it came to an end on a fast left-hand bend, when the tension on the drive belt was too much. The engine ripped out of the chassis, bounced across the road and buried its drive shaft into the tarmac, cracking the carburettor in the process. That was that, as we couldn't afford to buy another carb. And in any case, it was time to move on. If we had spent another summer driving on the public roads in a homemade motorised vehicle, we would probably have been locked up.

And fifteen-year-old kids need a proper car!

CHAPTER 7

MOVING UP

My forthcoming fifteenth birthday was another pivotal moment in my life. In those days, fifteen was the age when you were allowed to leave school. Both my parents and all their many relatives had left the minute they were able, as the mindset was to get out and earn some money. My dad left school at fourteen and my mum at fifteen, so to them, it was obvious and natural for me to leave as soon as I was old enough.

As usual, it was my mum who drove this, telling me that on my fifteenth birthday, 20 January 1972, I would be finding a job, so I had better decide what I wanted to do. In 1971, it had been announced the leaving age would rise to sixteen the following September, so for Mum, it was important I got out before that happened.

Hoping I would be able to better myself in comparison to them, my parents wanted me to take up an apprenticeship. They assumed I would be a car mechanic, such was my love of cars, but I knew this was not something I would want to do, day in, day out. My dad suggested electrician, but the thought of crawling around in lofts didn't fill me with any joy.

Once again, it was my pals at school who were the main influence on my decision and, unsurprisingly, none of them were leaving at fifteen. Some would be staying on to do A levels, which was one step removed from space travel in its infeasibility as far as my family was concerned. But with the same determination I had adopted when I decided I was going to the grammar school, I made up my mind my mum would not have her way.

Luckily, there was a parent-teacher evening scheduled for the limbo period leading up to my birthday. Somewhat meekly, my mum told my English teacher I would be leaving school imminently. English was my best subject and I excelled at it to the point I had wanted to be a journalist until I discovered A levels were an entry requirement. It was going to be tricky enough to be able to take my O levels!

The teacher diplomatically explained making me leave would be a great shame as I had some potential. Again, my mum's overwhelming desire to save face came to my rescue and she humbly accepted the teacher's suggestion I stay on. Well, almost. As soon as we had left the building, she decided I could only stay if I got a part-time job to bring some money into the house. Ironically, my mum didn't particularly want any of the money I earnt, she just thought I should have some in my pocket.

I didn't have a problem with this deal. It seemed fair enough and I would be working full time in just over a year anyway. And it would help me towards my goal of owning a car. But even though I applied for a few jobs, my youthful looks and diminutive stature were a barrier. No shopkeeper wanted someone who looked no more than eleven years old serving behind the counter and there didn't seem much else available.

At the end of our road was a guy with a window cleaning round. In the absence of any other applicants, he took me on to clean ground floor windows. It was a job I quite enjoyed, even in the winter months when the water was freezing, as it allowed me another insight into the lives and homes of rich people. I still remember most of the houses on our round and smile to myself when I see the ones I regarded as mansions. I can't imagine what I would have thought about the lovely house I live in now. The wages were pretty good compared with what other kids were getting in shops etc. In old money, ie pre decimalisation, it was 2s/6d or, as we now know it, 12.5p per hour. A gallon of petrol was about 6 shillings, so I could work an evening or a Saturday morning and have enough to buy a gallon to use in the Brooklands Bomb and, later on, my next project with Dave. As I was not used to having any money of my own, it was also great to be able to buy the occasional car magazine, which I read with relish and learnt a great deal from.

But now I'd caught up with my peers who were used to having money to spend, my eye was soon on a bigger prize. I was only two years away from being old enough to drive legally on the road and therefore buy a car. When you are fifteen, two years seems like an eternity, but nevertheless, I knew if I started planning now, I had a chance of realising that goal.

The most important decision of my life

Goal. A small word, but what a significant one. At the time, I had no idea how significant it would be in my life. Indeed, it was many decades before I realised that.

I was in my tiny bedroom, thinking about the marvel of having an income and feeling something profound. I remember the moment quite clearly. At my age, I obviously had no debts or financial responsibilities, so effectively, I had a clean slate. Surely, with a little sense, I could only move up from there. As long as I saved more than I spent, then my life must get better.

It seemed simple, and to be honest, it still is. Of the kids I knew who either earnt money or were given it by their parents, most spent it almost immediately. Dave was the exception (he hasn't changed), so he was a good role model for me.

Given the way my mum spent any money which came her way, I was already of the opinion I should be more careful if I wanted to achieve something worthwhile. I guess, without realising it, I had developed an intrinsic savings habit, but just to make it even stronger, I did something incredibly important which became key to much of my success. I wrote the following words in capital letters on a little scrap of paper I carefully placed in a metal Riley's Toffee tin, which I still have:

I PROMISE THAT FROM THE 7th MAY 1972 I WILL PUT ALL MY WAGES IN THIS TIN & WILL NOT DRAW FROM THEM UNTIL I HAVE ENOUGH FOR A CAR.
SIGNED
J. moon

Since that day, that piece of paper has been with me, surviving many house moves, clear outs and emotional rollercoasters. Admittedly, it was forgotten in recent years, but then I discovered it again when I was thinking about writing this book. It could have been an inspiration to get me started.

As we go on, we will talk more about the importance of goals and this little piece of paper. There's something profound about writing down things we really want to achieve. There are lots of reasons why this act to manifest what we want in our lives is so powerful, but one of them is when we write down an idea or a goal, and then return to it later, it's as if a third party is advising us. As we will often listen more to others than our internal dialogue, it's effective to talk to ourselves as a stranger.

But for now, let's get back to the next learning project, sometime in the middle of 1972.

Our first car

After the demise of the Brooklands Bomb, Dave and I were desperate for more motorised experiences. Both of us knew how to drive a car, even though we had never had any tuition. We were so passionate about our hobby, we studied in every way possible how cars worked and how to drive them. It's amazing how much you can learn by observation, so on the few occasions when I travelled in a car, I would be engrossed in every detail of the process, visualising how I would do it. As I touched on in Chapter 2 and will return to in more detail later in the book, **Visualisation** is a key to succeeding.

Very occasionally, my family would take a trip to the seaside. Our closest beach was Weston-Super-Mare with a huge expanse of flat sand, often deserted in those days, on which cars were allowed to park. After much badgering, my dad finally agreed to let me drive our worn-out Hillman Husky (bought for £9) up and down the sand. It was my most amazing experience to date.

But Dave and I needed our own car. How would this be possible for two fifteen-year-old kids? Just as our dream of creating the Brooklands Bomb had materialised out of nowhere, so did our first car.

One of my dad's brothers was a panel beater and car sprayer who did lots of work for friends, neighbours etc. One of his clients had an Austin A35 beyond any kind of economic repair due to the dreaded rust bug, which was a big issue in those days. My dad and his brother were well versed in filling in huge holes in bodywork, sometimes with the most unlikely of materials. Unthinkable today. I would help out whenever I could, furthering my learning. I could rub down and prepare bodywork to a reasonable standard by the time I was fourteen – probably better than I can manage now. This A35 was well beyond those skills, though. The sills and floor were so rotten, you could see the driver's feet from the outside. The owner had abandoned it at my uncle's workshop, so he asked if I would like it. Saying yes was the easy bit...

The car was about 5 miles from where Dave and I lived. Even if we could get it home, we couldn't keep it on the road and certainly couldn't drive it on the road, even though we had chanced it with the Brooklands Bomb.

Sometimes, though, you have to be **prepared to break the rules.**

We had the idea of taking the car to an old, flattened coal tip close to Dave's house. It was in a somewhat run-down area and didn't seem to belong to anyone, so just like people would use the field near my parents' house as a dump, they did the same here. The main advantage was the large flat area, out of sight of the public road, which would make a perfect test track for the car.

We just had to get it there. This was where my dad and his brother came to the rescue. They borrowed an old Land Rover and, one dark night, hooked up the A35 and towed our new car to Midsomer Norton. It had no MOT, no lights, no insurance. My uncle drove the Land Rover and my dad piloted the A35 to the coal tip, and then they left it to us to do with as we could. It was quite a risky adventure even in those days, but I'm guessing my dad's desire to help his son far outweighed the laws he was breaking. He was my hero and my uncle was not far behind.

The car's inability to run under its own steam was rectified with some cleaning of the spark plugs and points (cars don't have points these days – it's all done by electronics) and charging of its battery. Sounds simple, but we had to remove the battery, strap it to Dave's bike and take it to his parents' shed as his dad had a battery charger. In fact, we had to do this whenever we wanted to drive the car as the battery was so worn out, it would go flat if left idle for any time. It was also liable to go missing as it was an easily stealable item that would fetch some instant cash at the scrap yard.

Cash to run the car was not something we had in abundance, so again, we hit upon an ingenious idea. We spread the word amongst Dave's neighbourhood kids that we would give rides around the tip in exchange for a few pence. We were both fast drivers, so for the kids who packed into the car, it was a thrilling experience. And not at all dangerous, of course...

I still have the little leather diary (left behind by the car's previous owner) in which I recorded our income and how many miles we had driven each day. Luckily, the coal tip was behind a petrol station, so fetching fuel was quite easy. We usually bought half a gallon at a time and would drive the car until it ran out.

Our biggest challenge was getting the car to start. The battery soon became incapable of turning over the engine even when fully charged. In those days, cars had starting handles to turn the engine over when the battery was flat, but our car was too worn out for that to work. So we had to resort to push/bump starting it. Despite its relatively small size, the A35 was a very heavy car for two young lads to push, and none of our passengers would turn up until we had it going. There was a small slope on to our track and it was necessary to get the car some way up it to give it enough momentum to start before we ran out of room. But it was so hard trying to push it up that slope and I was tiny.

We devised another ingenious plan. By putting the car into reverse gear, we could wind it up the slope inches at a time using the starting handle before the great launch. This in itself was a huge lesson in **LUD**. If we tried to make life easy by failing to wind the car sufficiently far up the slope, it wouldn't have enough momentum to start, so we would have to push it all the way back and try again. On the other hand, we didn't want to expend any more energy than necessary by winding the car further up the hill than it needed to be. I can't tell you how exhausting that was. Our best bet was to wind the car just a little further up the hill than we wanted or had the energy for, to give us a better chance of it running.

Boy, that was nerve wracking. It was at those times Dave and I would say to each other, "Who else would do this?" – a phrase we would utter on numerous occasions in the future when we required commitment way beyond anything the average human is prepared to give. Certainly, no-one we knew had our passion to achieve what we wanted to achieve. Perhaps our grammar school peers had too easy a life. Or were they just more sensible than us?

If you choose a hobby such as ours, it makes a big difference to how you deal with life. If Dave and I had been interested in football, all we would have had to do was acquire a ball. Although boots and kit would have helped, they weren't essential. As long as we had a ball, we could have started some kind of game.

The skills we needed to build and enjoy driving a car were so all encompassing, we had no alternative but to learn about engineering, planning, the art of driving, generating money, administration and, in some cases, avoiding the law. Dave and I developed all those attributes just to drive our little car around an old coal tip. They were amazing things to learn at such a young age and they have helped me all through my life.

We also had to learn how to deal with disappointment.

Dave sitting in the A35 with the slope leading up to the coal tip. John sitting on the roof.

Entering the adult world

It was Christmas of 1972. Dave and I already knew the car was vulnerable to sabotage by ne'er-do-wells, which was partly why we used to remove the battery every time we left it. We had experienced a few small acts of vandalism to it, but it wasn't exactly a concourse example, so we lived with it. But over the holiday period, someone decided to destroy our dream, smashing the windscreen and pushing the car into something solid which bent things enough to make it undriveable.

That's a lot worse than someone stealing your football. But we dealt with it. We had no choice. Using the ethic my dad had instilled in me, I didn't let the loss of our beloved A35 affect me too much, even though inside I was extremely angry about it. As I've learnt as life has progressed, forgetting about something painful is an effective way of dealing with it. In most cases, it's useful to have a poor memory for things which don't serve you. So, I quickly forgot about the A35 and started focusing on getting a real car for when I would turn seventeen in just over a year's time.

There was the small matter of my exams in between. In those days, the first important exams after the 11 Plus were O levels. Despite skiving double games and biology on a Thursday afternoon, I was a reasonably diligent pupil and managed to gain eight of them, including – ironically – biology. My only failure was maths. This too is ironic, given I have since spent most of my adult life in the financial industry. But I was ill on the day of the exam, so I have an excuse.

Shortly after the demise of the A35, I began thinking about getting a full-time job. Turning sixteen in January 1973, I would leave school soon after the exams in the July of that year, but I had no idea what I wanted to do. I loved cars, but I didn't want to get my hands dirty. Even though I wasn't at all scared of doing so and actually spent every spare moment immersed in dirt, oil and grease as a hobby, I didn't fancy doing so to make a living.

The one and only careers interview I had at school was a joke. I felt the whole thing was a complete waste of my time. The so-called adviser didn't ask any questions about me or my abilities or aspirations. He simply looked out of the window at the printing factory opposite and said, "How about getting a job over there?" That seemed to be the limit of his imagination and ability. I'm not even sure he knew what the factory was. It could have been an abattoir or a xylophone testing plant.

Ironically, having already obtained job offers from two banks, a large electronics company and the civil service, I was tempted by an advert for a business apprenticeship with the printing company. It was a big outfit and close to home, so even though I had accepted the job offer from one of the banks (on a salary of £549 pa), I decided to apply and was granted an interview.

It was the toughest yet most interesting of all the interviews I had attended. The questions were intense and I felt pressure I had not experienced in any of the other interviews. But I enjoyed it, especially when my interviewer tried to unsettle me by suggesting I might be intimidated by some of the tall department bosses like him, as I was so small. I replied that we were about the same when we were seated, so it didn't bother me. Sometimes, being a bit cheeky can help break the ice and gain you some **rapport**, which is what happened here. Shortly afterwards, I was offered a business apprenticeship on a salary far higher than that from the bank. I was fascinated by the job, which involved working my way around the clerical departments to gain experience. But I declined it.

After I joined the bank, I dearly regretted turning down the offer. Bank pay was abysmal, juniors were treated as subhuman (it's called bullying these days) and we could be moved to

Moving Up

another branch, anywhere in the country, at a moment's notice. Coincidentally, Dave had decided to take a printing apprenticeship, so there was another good reason for me to join as it would have been nice for us to be working at the same firm.

But my family's fear of the world and inherent worries about offending people or what they called "letting them down" was a big factor. My mum felt there was no way I could possibly go back on my word to the bank. My parents were people of their word. If they said they would do something they did it, regardless of the personal cost to them. This was instilled into me, and I don't think it has done me too much harm. It's part of the **reliability** I speak about later. I really value people who stick to arrangements. My sadness and frustration is those who do are becoming ever more scarce.

The other factor is my parents were astounded I had been accepted by such an organisation as a bank, which they held in awe. They did not have a bank account and would have been scared just to set foot in the doorway of a bank. And yet I had been offered a job I was now going to turn down! Surely, all sorts of awful things would happen to me as a result and I would never succeed if I went back on my word.

It's hard to comprehend how fearful and uninformed people like my parents were in those days, but they were not alone. What is more strange is in a family where lack of money was at the centre of our lives and no day went by without a reminder of this fact, I was told to turn down a better paying job. My bank salary would equate to around £38 take-home pay per month, whereas in line with the printing industry generally at that time, the apprenticeship was offering well over £60pm with a structured set of increments, so I would be earning £2,000 a year within a very short period of time.

But looking back half a century, I feel I made the better choice, even though it took many years before I was able to realise that. I'm sure I would have done well had I taken the apprenticeship, but I have learnt to **regret nothing** I have ever done, even though some of the things seemed like big mistakes at the time. Because I am alive and well and have achieved a great deal on the path I chose, I don't regret any of my decisions, as who knows where alternative choices might have taken me?

Ironically, my job at the bank only came about because of Dave. We were talking about what we would do for a living and he suggested he would be applying to banks as they offered a secure long-term career. I remember saying that a bank was the last place I would want to work, but when I started running out of ideas, I decided to apply to not one, but two banks. My parents could not advise me in any way regarding career options. The world of work for them was confined to the jobs they felt befitted them, so I was on my own and once again sought the opinion of my friends. One of the banks offered me a job in its Midsomer Norton branch, while the other said I would need to travel to Bristol. The electronics apprenticeship was based in Wells and the civil service offering likely to be Bath where there was a huge Ministry of Defence presence. Two long journeys when I only had a bicycle.

I had no more desire to be an electronics engineer over a banker or a civil servant, so I decided to choose the one which would allow me to ride my bike to work. We are often faced with choices where it seems difficult to know which way to go. Many of us are held back by the fear of making the wrong choice, so we endlessly procrastinate while going nowhere. I've learnt it's much better to **do something**, almost anything, rather than nothing.

Once you've dived in, with the right attitude and work ethic, you can make the most of the situation presented to you and something good will come out of it. If you find it difficult to choose, use a random method such as tossing a coin. Just make a choice – it's always better than letting life choose for you – and then move on. Don't keep looking back at what might have been. If you can't help but question a decision you have already made, ask yourself if you have given that decision long enough for the full consequences to become known. When the late Chinese premier Zhou Enlai was asked about how the French Revolution had influenced the world, his reply was rumoured to have been: "Too early to say."[6]

So, I reluctantly turned down the offer of a printing apprenticeship and in July 1973, I rode my bike to the High Street in Midsomer Norton, wearing an awful blue Crimplene suit, purchased with almost the same fear and angst as my grammar school uniform. I felt the pain of that for some time and it tainted my attitude to my job even before I started.

---

6   'Not letting the facts ruin a good story' (South China Morning Post) www.amp.scmp.com, accessed 11 April 2024

CHAPTER 8

THE WORLD OF WORK

Sixteen-year-old school leavers started in what was known as the machine room at the bank. Midsomer Norton was a reasonably sized enterprise – not as prestigious as the city branches in places like Bath and central Bristol, but big enough to have all the departments a bank branch needed in those days. The 'machine' part of the machine room was made up of the numerous contraptions to process the day's work, most of which came in the form of thousands of pieces of paper such as cheques, paying-in slips and other bureaucratic necessities to make sure everything balanced. Much of it came from the tills, sacks of cheques came in by post through a system known as the clearing, and the staff who worked in the branch's other departments (usually just a desk or two) such as the foreign desk or securities also generated paper which had to be processed.

The first rung of the aspirational ladder was to break free from filming (putting every bit of paper into a microfiche reader to keep a record of it), stamping cheque books by hand (using a somewhat dangerous printing machine which thumped every page with a personalised stamp) and filing away cheques, to operating one of two big machines called terminals. These were effectively early computers connected to a server the size of a large cupboard in another branch.

Terminal operators entered data on a typewriter-style keyboard using a number of codes, all of which had to be memorised if we were to be anywhere near proficient. Sadly, I still remember quite a few of them. I had never used a typewriter before, but I was dextrous and had small, agile fingers, so I was quickly able to acquire a high level of speed. The result of each entry was printed on to a large reel of paper which was the only record for the branch of what had gone on and was essential to look back on if there was a discrepancy.

The women ruled the roost in the machine room, the senior machine operator (SMO) role shared between three young ladies, two of whom were formidable and delighted in belittling a new young male recruit. Those who didn't aspire to climb the career ladder tended to find a permanent home in one of the Grade 2 positions and they ruled their patches with unquestioned authority. Each woman would take turns to be the SMO as, like many of the jobs in the branch, the role alternated.

There was one nice SMO, so my life was easier when it was her turn to be in charge. But despite the bullying tactics of the other two, my mental suit of armour helped me fend off even the most ridiculous assaults. Nevertheless, I remember one example in particular.

I was operating the terminal. I was fast and had an excellent memory for most of the codes, even though I was still quite new. But now and then, something complex came up which didn't appear very often. All the codes were printed on a flat piece of plastic just above the keyboard, which was where we rested the day's work we were inputting. Consequently, most of the text had been rubbed off and the codes were unreadable. Which was why we had to memorise them.

On this occasion, there was one I hadn't come across before. We were so busy there was never any time for pleasantries, so I called over to one SMO and asked her for the relevant code.

She shouted it back to me almost automatically, part of it being a semicolon.

I typed it in and immediately received an error message. Tried it again, same thing. Called to the SMO, "Could you repeat that code?" Same reply as before, same code, same error message.

After the third time I'd asked her to repeat the code, the SMO slammed down what she had been working on, came over with a face like thunder and, telling me what a complete idiot I was, pushed me aside so she could enter the code herself. I watched closely and spotted the issue immediately.

"That's a colon, not a semicolon!" She gave me a look which said, "I know I said semicolon, but you should have known it was a colon", then stormed off. An apology was never likely to fall from her lips, but I didn't have any further nastiness from her. Life lesson learnt: **don't assume those in authority or superior positions know everything or are always right**...

Pay versus prospects

What soon became apparent was just what a poorly paid job I had. The two big printing companies in the area banked with us. Unlike today, where everything happens almost automatically, we had to manually enter all the wage payments for every member of staff. And the printers weren't the only firms whose employee wage details I was privy to.

We were sworn to secrecy and I would never reveal any confidential information about any of the clients I have dealt with over almost fifty years in the financial world. But the work I have done has given me a special insight into people's finances, so I have a perspective which has been both extremely interesting and, at times, unbelievably frustrating. Tempting as it has been to say something, I have always resisted, even when I know someone in financial straits has only themselves to blame, and others who claim to be paupers are rather well off.

When you are aware of exactly what people you know are earning, it's not an issue if your income is on a par with theirs. But when it's consistently, substantially and unendingly lower, then it can be infuriating. That was the case with me. It seemed my frustrations from a young age were carrying on into my adult life, as predicted by my parents.

"We are poor, we've always been poor and we always will be poor. Just be thankful for your lot". Those words resounded in my head on many occasions.

On the council estate where my family lived, almost every school leaver would automatically get a job at the nearby shoe factory. The monotony of the work was offset by a good wage boosted by 'piecework', ie getting paid for what you produced, not the hours you spent on it. Dextrous and hardworking young people could earn a small fortune that way.

Although the prospects in the bank were potentially far reaching, especially for a sixteen-year-old school leaver from a council estate, the road to the top was long, and it required a blind and unquestioning faith and commitment. The latter was probably more important than any other aspect. The bank expected us to be wedded to it. It was necessary to put it before absolutely anything else, including family. As soon as there was a question mark over someone's commitment, their career progression came to a halt in a flash.

Initially, it was easy for me to show this commitment as little was asked of me other than to do my job, reliably and efficiently, which I did. In the days of mainly manual recording of transactions, the most important factor, on which we were tested every day, was being able to balance. Whether we were working the terminal or facing the public as a cashier, we had to add up all debits and credits to equal what we were left with, eg the cash in the till for a cashier. This daily test was often quite traumatic.

The speed at which we could balance was a matter of immense pride and competition. I worked hard to find little ways – **to optimise** – to become more efficient at this as I realised it was one of the few ways in which my performance would be judged. I was at a disadvantage compared with a lot of the other youngsters joining the bank as many came with A levels and didn't look as though they were twelve years old, but there was one advantage to being small: I had very nimble fingers. I quickly got used to the keyboard on the terminal and was able to memorise the location of all the keys. After a few weeks, I was as fast as some of the people who had been at the bank for years and vying to be the fastest of them all. I've always been competitive, and even though it was hard to make a comparison between the people operating the pair of terminals, I decided I would get through my pile of work more quickly than my colleague.

The day before the bank closed for Christmas was when I proved myself beyond doubt. It was the busiest day of the year. The work was arriving in massive piles and I 'went like stink'. But even I was surprised when the manager (who almost never entered the machine room) came out of his hallowed office and congratulated me on how much I had processed.

Progress

As a result of my balancing speed and accuracy, progression came my way and, after about a year, I was allowed to train as a cashier. Here, there were two elements of direct competition with the others. The first was being right at the end of the day, ie our tills had to balance to the penny. In fact, being a penny out was almost worse than being £1 out as we had to do the same amount of investigation to show where we had gone wrong. The second was the speed at which we could balance our till.

I picked up the basics pretty quickly and soon realised

how easily people could become overwhelmed with their till management on a busy day. Cash was much more in use then than now. A business might turn up to a banking hall full of people and tip a massive load of cash and coins on the counter for us to deal with. Although there was an accepted way to present notes and coins and most customers adhered to it, there were a few nightmare clients who could upset our routines by failing to sort out theirs properly.

I got into the habit of managing the cash in my till as I went along and not letting things get out of control. Some cashiers would just stuff notes into their tills and hope they would find time to get them into the correct bundles as the day progressed, but when the bank was constantly packed to the door with customers, this could be tricky. I found ways to optimise every second. Eventually, I became the guy who could balance his till faster than anyone else.

Within a couple of years, I was moved to the Shepton Mallet branch where there were some excellent cashiers who prided themselves on their efficiency. But I was faster than them too and was soon promoted to the SMO position, in charge of the new kids who had just joined from school or those whom the bank had decided were going nowhere.

Another move, this time to the Old Bank branch in Bath, saw me presented with a familiar tactic on day one. This was an extremely busy branch with many of the large shops and the local authority as its clients. The amounts of cash and the pressure on the tills were way beyond anything I'd experienced at the country branches I had worked at before. So, to establish what sort of person I was, the supervisor threw me on to the till on a busy Monday to decide how to categorise me.

It was like being hit with a sledgehammer. Constant pressure, no time for niceties with the customers, just a barrage of money pouring through my window. By this time, I had developed an excellent level of mental arithmetic. Although I had failed my maths O level, by habitually practising and honing the skill, I could add up columns of numbers at a great speed. It sounds unlikely, but when you have a long column of handwritten numbers, it's often quicker to add them up in your head than to use a calculator. A lot of the best cashiers rarely used a calculator and I would show I was as good as anyone.

So, on my first day in the big city, I was absolutely determined to be the first to balance. And I was. Such things spread around a branch quickly and the manager, a formidable man who would not normally deign to even speak to anyone at my level, came out of his office and congratulated me for doing a good job. I knew I had made my mark.

Another important lesson: **establish your reputation early on.**

This allowed me to progress to the area behind the cashiers where all sorts of exciting new tasks awaited, often with fearsome characters watching over them. I worked my way through a number of the jobs and gained a couple of promotions to higher grades, which helped my income a little. But like many things with the bank, the prestige of the position was supposed to mean more than the wages you were paid. It's amazing how easy it is to deceive huge numbers of people to accept this for years at a time without them doing anything about it. But luckily, I had a couple of small sidelines which helped my income.

Moonlighting

Being a fairly large branch with over fifty staff, the city bank presented a number of opportunities. My colleagues all had stuff they wanted to buy or needed doing. All I had to do was meet those needs.

Many of the guys at work would talk to me about cars and soon, I was servicing theirs. I would drive back to their homes after the day's work, complete with the required service items of oil, filters etc, and do the job in their garages or on their driveways. They fed me and I would earn a few extra pounds. I had been getting my hands dirty as a hobby for years, so doing it for a little extra cash was easy.

I also set up a sideline selling wine from the Cash & Carry, a trade-only warehouse close to where I lived. My parents had never had a bottle of wine in the house until then, apart from the Sanatogen tonic wine which was a permanent fixture in one of the cupboards for when someone 'felt ill'. But I was now mixing with a different class of folk who were rich enough to afford Blue Nun Liebfraumilch, the drink of choice for those who had achieved something in life. Armed with a trade card I had blagged somehow, I was able to buy cases of wine to bring into the bank and sell by the bottle, making a little profit for me yet giving the buyers a better deal than they could obtain elsewhere. Low-priced supermarkets destroyed that opportunity, but it worked for a while. I was bold enough just to do this, with no permission sought and no questions asked. This is a philosophy I've employed on many occasions since and only rarely has it backfired.

But cars and motor sport were the only things I truly cared about at the time, so we need to catch up with that area of my life. The success lessons I gained from this passion are every bit as important as the ones I learnt while making a living.

CHAPTER 9

THE WORLD OF RACING

After the destruction of the A35, there was a big hole in my world needing to be filled. What I saw as the most important date of my life (being old enough to drive legally) was now getting into range, so I was able to focus on that, as well as the small matter of passing my exams and getting a job. Even with the latter dealt with, though, when you are sixteen-and-a-half, your seventeenth birthday still seems much too far away.

Dave and I needed some kind of fix. This came from what now seems an unlikely source, but it was another pivotal moment in my life and started me on a path which has brought me huge pleasure, a modest amount of prestige, and achievements I could never have imagined in my wildest dreams.

The local rag, the *Somerset Guardian*, came through our door every Friday and it was soon after I had left school that I spotted the headline, "You could be the one we need to start a car grass track racing club in the Norton Radstock area" (sic). It was placed by an enthusiastic member of the Bristol South club, Clive. Dave and I had never heard of grass track racing before, but it sounded interesting and, after a quick discussion, we decided I would contact Clive. My parents still didn't have a phone, so my only option was to write to Clive at the address on the ad to say Dave and I would help in whatever way we could. I probably didn't mention we were only sixteen.

I didn't hear anything for a week or so, then one evening, Clive turned up at my parents' door. He explained grass track racing, soon to be known as Autograss, was a sport where old cars would be stripped and prepared to race around a basic usually oval track laid out in a kindly farmer's field. It transpired there were clubs throughout the country, though mainly in the West Country and Wales. If we could form our own club, then we would be able to race at a meeting every weekend and even organise our own events at which the other clubs would show up.

There were lots of classes for all kinds of car. The unmodified class for cars under 1200cc was as inexpensive as any kind of motor sport could be. Much as Dave and I would love to have been on the proper circuits of Silverstone and Brands Hatch, that was a crazy dream. I couldn't even afford to go to my local track at Castle Combe as a spectator.

I quickly agreed to help and volunteered Dave too as I knew he would be keen.

Getting race ready

Clive was building a car of his own, so Dave and I were soon spending every weekend riding our bikes to his place in Radstock and getting our hands dirty helping with his Mini. I think Clive was surprised at our knowledge of cars and hopefully we were a genuine help. Before long, we were able to go with him to our very first race meeting near Bristol. And that was it. We had the bug.

Our club was a little slow to get off the ground, but as is so often the case, meeting the right people made a huge difference. An eccentric character, Mike Taviner, – who worked with his dad at a local car body shop was one of those people. He knew *everyone*. As soon as he found out about our club, it took off and we began meeting once a month in a pub's back room close to Mike's workplace.

Having attended our first meeting, Dave and I became even more desperate to start racing. Until we found Autograss, our joint obsessive focus had been our seventeenth birthdays. I had been learning to drive for years, not only in the A35, but in my head, where I visualised every aspect of controlling a car over and over again. I had no idea at the time how effective **visualisation** could be, but it seemed a sensible and logical thing to do. My dad was as keen to encourage my obsession with driving as he could be, so we were both confident enough in my abilities to apply for my driving test before my seventeenth birthday in January 1974.

I thought applying in December would get me a test date either on or soon after my birthday, but in the event, I was allocated a date in March. That was probably a good thing. Although my ability to drive and control a car didn't need much practice, being on the road with others did. But my dad was as good a teacher as he was a driver and the test went without a hiccup. At last, the moment the whole of my teenage life had been building up to had arrived.

With the driving test successfully out of the way (Dave passed a couple of months later), we had to find a way to get a race car of our own. When I say 'race car', what I really mean is an old banger, probably an MOT failure which had had everything stripped out of it apart from the bits that made it stop, go and steer. We would need to weld in a home-made roll cage, secure a full harness seat belt and mount a motorcycle-size fuel tank somewhere safe. When I think of the highly regulated race cars I drive these days, I realise the word 'safe' is a very relative term.

All those things were theoretically within our capabilities, and we knew we could make, fashion and scrounge lots of items which a lack of money would prevent us from buying. But the challenge we found difficult to overcome was a home for the car. My dad's council garage may have been OK for the Brooklands Bomb, but his car filled it most of the time, and we couldn't leave such a vehicle in a public place as we had with the A35.

Although this held us back for a while, Mike came to our rescue. Initially, we didn't know him too well, but after the guy who had volunteered as club treasurer stepped down, I took his place. It seemed logical as I was the only one in the club working in a financial institution (printing cheque books and filing seemed to be sufficiently financial). And eventually, I got to know Mike well enough to pluck up the courage to ask him a loaded question.

"Do you know anywhere Dave and I could build and keep a car?" We hoped there might be space in the yard outside his body shop.

Without hesitation, he replied, "Yeah, at my place." And with those words, he launched Dave and me into the heady world of car racing. Four words which made such a difference to a couple of young lads with an unfulfilled passion.

Another important lesson: **never be afraid to ask for help or advice.**

We quickly found a suitable car: a 1961 Austin A40 in remarkably sound mechanical condition and even MOTed, but with some rust in the wings. It found its way to the body shop in a manner as illegal as that which brought the A35 to Midsomer Norton, though this time under its own steam. There was just the small matter of no tax or insurance.

Dave and I then spent every evening and weekend stripping, preparing and painting it. All this was done outside in the yard with no power, as we couldn't possibly bother Mike and his dad whom we were already seriously indebted to. We were so keen (many would say crazy), we would work on the car at night, even in winter. There was no lighting in the part of the yard where we kept it, so we would push it out to the front of the garage where there was a bright streetlamp we could work under. If we needed to drill a hole in the bodywork, we would use various nails, starting with a very small one to break through and getting progressively bigger, sometimes finishing with a round file. Obviously, this took huge amounts of time, but we had plenty of that and we utilised it to the max. I remember being at the yard one Boxing Day, all on my own, working away. Dave didn't succeed in persuading his mother he needed to leave the family festivities for a while. Another lesson in persistence.

But when it came to the question of making and installing a roll cage, we hit a brick wall, which ironically is when a roll cage is somewhat helpful. A steel cage inside the car, it's designed to protect you from everything coming in on top of you. Thankfully, more help was on its way. Another club member volunteered to do the welding for us. We found some old scaffold pipes, laboriously cutting them by hand with a hacksaw. Scrap metal for the mounting plates was sourced from dumps or scrounged from stuff lying around the yard, which had years of accumulated rubbish. Our total expenditure had still not exceeded the £10 we had paid to buy the car.

With the welding complete, we got to the stage where we needed to spend some money. A full harness seat belt (that's one with two straps which come down over your shoulders and one across your hips) was something we had to purchase new, as was a crash helmet and a tap to turn off the fuel if we crashed.

And somehow, we also managed to build ourselves a trailer to transport the car to meetings. Mainly made from scrap and items we scrounged, we spent almost nothing on it apart from some suspension units we had no choice other than to cough up for.

These things cost more than the car's original purchase price, so they were painful yet necessary expenditure.

And then, we were ready to race.

CHAPTER 10

THE FORMING OF KEY HABITS

Remember my important scrap of paper, my note to save all my income until I could buy a car? My wage from the bank was substantially higher when compared with that of my part-time job while I was at school, but £38 per month in my new bank account was not exactly earth shattering, despite my lack of outgoings. I gave my parents £2 per week for my keep. A modest sum despite my mum's insistence about the importance of bringing money into the house, it nevertheless meant they no longer had to worry about any expenditure on me, apart from Christmas and birthday gifts.

Having started work in July 1973, I had saved over £350 by May of 1974. I'd already had a small amount saved from my window cleaning, so I managed to save an average of £30 per month from my wage of £38. After my keep, my personal expenditure prior to buying my first road car was therefore zero per month.

How could that be? If you're used to spending almost everything you earn, the habits I developed will sound strange, perhaps even impossible and incomprehensible, but I'm convinced they laid the foundations for my success. How did I manage to save almost every penny of my humble wage? The answer is ridiculously simple. Once I had given my mum my keep, I didn't spend anything. At all. Nothing. If it cost money, I didn't have it. If I couldn't find it, make it, scrounge it or borrow it, I didn't have it. I would do anything rather than spend a penny of my earnings.

What are you worth?

This was all with the aim of buying a car. And so, a 1967 Vauxhall Viva found itself outside the door. The £250 I paid for it was a substantial amount of money, more than my dad had spent on his car and far above anything my contemporaries had paid out. Most of the kids in my street around my age and older didn't have a car and wouldn't for many years. But there was a big difference between me and them. While Dave and I were working on our hobby, they would be out spending money.

No doubt prompted by my dad's abstemiousness, I learnt something important at an early age. He had been one of the first to own a car in his village, despite his family being every bit as poor as mine. A car had been extremely important to him, so he decided he would have one and do whatever it took to get it. If that was to the detriment of other things, then so be it.

But there was more to it than that. In the UK, no one is born with debt. A child may have little or no money or assets, but legally, they can't borrow money under the age of eighteen. So the worst possible position a seventeen-year-old can be in is to be worth zero.

Worth. That's an interesting word. I don't hear it used much these days in everyday speech and rarely in the way I have used it most of my life. Along with 'personal balance sheet', this word needs to become part of your vocabulary if you are serious about improving your lot. In case it's not as obvious as it sounds, your personal balance sheet is a snapshot of your worth at any given moment. Your net worth (in this context) is the realistic value of everything you own minus anything you owe to anyone else.

Do you know what you are worth? Why not calculate it now. It's easy if it's just you. If there are two of you and you have joint assets and/or debt, then you either do the calculation to include all your joint pluses and minuses or split each asset and liability down to find out your individual shares.

As my life progressed and I got into the world of property, I began keeping a detailed record of my net worth. We will go into this more later, but suffice to say it's something I recommend you do. It's vital to know what direction you are going in and helps you put your finances into proper and realistic perspective.

When I was a little kid, I had a net worth: the money in my National Savings account. It was only modest, but it was something. My parents had to use it to change their lot, which made me determined never to be in that situation myself. I wanted to be worth something. I know people can be valued for all sorts of things other than money and assets, but those intangibles are difficult to measure. Your true net worth, if you calculate it honestly and correctly, is a way of keeping score.

I wanted to have a value that made me feel I wasn't part of an underclass, as my parents believed themselves to be. But keeping score is not just about measuring yourself against others, but also measuring your own performance. If your net worth isn't increasing, then something isn't working. Most people never improve because they don't measure whatever areas they want to improve in. If that area is your finances, then measuring is simple. If your life's desire is to be a great singer, it's a bit trickier because measuring whether you are improving is somewhat subjective and it's easy to fool yourself.

Although I didn't give the act of measuring my net worth a name, it seemed logical to me at a young age that the only way was up. OK, I had some of my early savings taken from me, but that was a one off. From the moment I started my window-cleaning job, I believed there was no reason why my net worth should not grow in value every single year for the rest of my life.

Let's say I had £30 to my name when I was sixteen. I didn't owe anyone anything. I had a bike I rode to my job at the bank, which could have been sold for about £10. I had few clothes, rarely bought any (I still don't), and my other significant possessions were some tools I had received as birthday and Christmas presents. They may have been worth another £10. So, all in all, I had a net worth of about £50. In other words, five weeks' salary when I joined the bank.

But once I had a regular income, I didn't see how it could be possible for me not to increase my net worth every month.

Little decisions which have grown my net worth

Not everyone sees it that way. Working in a bank and in the finance world ever since has given me an insight into the true state of people's finances. For decades, I have been amazed how many leave school and go almost immediately into a negative net worth situation.

This often happens when people buy their first car. Finance is easy to arrange and before they understand what is going on, their personal balance sheet has a car loan on one side, weighing it down. In theory, they have a car on the asset side of the balance sheet, but guess what? It's almost certain that car will be worth a huge amount less than they paid for it, and probably less than they owe the finance company.

If you are a young person and you have nothing much in the bank other than the dregs of last month's salary, you could have a negative net worth at the very start of your working life. This is not the way to make something from nothing. It's actually the way to make sure you never have anything. I can't stress strongly enough how much I urge you not to get into this situation. If that is how you start off your working and financial life, it is going to be so much harder to manage your finances in the future. I will talk about student loan debt later on.

Of course, we all have essential expenditure. My first month's wage from the bank took a big hit as I had to buy a suit. There was no choice as that was what was required by my employer. In those days, clothes were hugely expensive compared with today; £10 for a horrible Crimplene suit may not seem much, but equate it to a week's wage and you can understand how painful it was. I used my white school shirt and black shoes, so at least that was a saving.

After that pain was out of the way, I could really get to work on my net worth. Little by little, it grew. It was painfully slow, but I was happy to do it and I made sure I wasn't missing out on anything I wanted to do. I just found another way to do it without spending money.

For example, I loved to read about cars and motor sport. But magazines cost money. So, I would walk down to the newsagent and browse the magazines on the shelves. When I say browse, I use the term loosely. This usually means with the intention of buying, which I rarely had. Luckily, I was a fast reader, devouring all the latest news about my Grand Prix heroes or the new Ford Escort, so I rarely missed out on something.

In the bank, my colleagues gathered in the staff room at break times to drink tea or coffee and eat their lunches. Like me, most of them brought a packed lunch, though an ever-growing group would go out and buy what I saw as ridiculously expensive sandwiches. One of the first things I was told about staff room etiquette was how the tea and coffee fund worked. We had to pay a certain amount per month from our salary for a warm drink – the bank was never a generous employer.

Already shell shocked by the cost of my suit, I surprised myself somewhat by standing up to the big guy telling me about the arrangement, informing him I would not be partaking.

From that day on, I never drank anything other than water in my workplace, regardless of where it was. As I type these words, there is a glass of tap water (albeit filtered by my own filtration system) in front of me. The strange thing is, I wasn't a water drinker at home. My mum was a tea addict, moving from one cup to another all day long. I would have the odd cup, but in the summer, the larder was full of sugary fruit squashes, and I was oblivious at the time to their unhealthiness. So it was a bit of a shock only drinking water at work as I had rarely drunk it without a good flavouring of sugary squash. But I soon got used to it and began to enjoy it. A commitment I made almost fifty years ago has not only saved me a huge amount of money, but made me a much healthier person too.

There's another commitment I made in that staff room which has stayed with me until today. As everyone spent most of the lunch hour with their head in some kind of publication, I felt I should do the same. Traditionally, a copy of the day's *Financial Times* was left in the banking hall, theoretically for the clients to read. I had never seen an *FT* before I joined the bank, so I decided I would borrow the copy and have a look while I was eating my lunch.

Like the habit of drinking water, reading such a publication at first seemed strange. Our newspaper at home was the *Daily Mirror*, which was very effective in reinforcing my parents' inbuilt socialism and belief everything in the world was bad, so the *FT* was somewhat of a shock. But it gave me a new perspective on life and I slowly began to see the world a little differently. I probably skipped 90% of it when I first opened it as it would just have seemed like a lot of gobbledygook to me, but the *FT* is not as austere as it looks and has always prided itself on objective reporting. Fifty years later, it's still the only newspaper I read and it's often a place of sanity for me. Another small, seemingly insignificant decision, but the amount of knowledge and insights I have gained from reading that newspaper has been incredible. Imagine if I had chosen to read a tabloid instead and where the years of negative programming from that could have taken me.

I will never be beholden

Until I bought my car, there was little I wanted to spend my money on. I had no transport costs as I cycled to work and my spare time was totally consumed with pursuing my hobby with Dave. Prior to us buying and building our own Autograss car, we would be at Clive's garage, helping him with his Mini, or if that was not possible, then Dave and I would be playing with his Scalextric, set up in a spare bedroom at his sister's house a few miles from my home. Again, I got there by bike and often rode home in the dark with no lights. Saving money on batteries seemed to be more important than preserving my life.

So, my personal balance sheet grew in value, little by little. And by the time I needed money to buy my first car for the road, lo and behold, I had enough. Enough to tax and insure it, too, the latter a substantial sum for a seventeen-year-old. I still have the receipt and find it hard to believe it was £68, just under double my month's wages.

But after I'd paid for the car and the associated expenses, my personal balance sheet was still well in the black. If I cashed in my assets, I would have whatever I could get for the car, probably close to what I had paid for it (I sold it eleven months later for £230, losing £20 or 8% of the purchase price) minus my losses due to the cost of the tax and insurance. I don't remember if I did the actual calculation in my mind at that time, but I've always believed it's essential for me to be in credit, and that my balance sheet must be improving.

If you spend less than you earn, even by just a few pence,

then your personal balance sheet has to improve over time. Compounding is the strongest force in the universe (according to Einstein),[7] so saving even tiny amounts over many years will make a big difference eventually. If you buy things which go up in value rather than decline, then even better. That might be a bit of a clue to some of what is coming later...

Even today, I am reluctant to buy a vehicle which I will lose money on. Occasionally, I may indulge, but until just recently and for the ten years previously, my daily drivers were insurance write offs which I bought inexpensively and ran until they gave up the ghost. I sold the last one very recently. I admit I now have a new car and a fleet of classic cars too, but they generally increase in value, so I can have as many of them as I like :-)

I was chatting to a friend I only meet on an annual ski trip. We were talking cars and I used the phrase 'it owes me very little' about my ex-write-off daily driver. He is a wealthy, successful guy and he found it strange I should use those words. He was even more astounded I should keep in my brain the worth of this car, especially when I have a property portfolio which pales the car's value into insignificance. Perhaps he is right, but the habit of **knowing the worth of the possessions I have**, which I developed from a young age, has been an essential part of helping me to improve my situation. I don't have to do it, I don't need to do it, but it keeps me on my toes, and it builds and maintains my brain so it will assist me in other more important ways.

Prior to my parents permanently borrowing my savings when I was a child, I enjoyed the fact I was worth something when my mum showed me the book with how much money I had. But to then find it was virtually all gone made me feel very vulnerable. As I grew older and began to understand how

---

7   A Roth, 'Compound interest: The most powerful force in the universe?' (CBS News, 2011) www.cbsnews.com, accessed 12 April 2024

little my parents had and how vulnerable they were if anything went wrong, I developed a mindset that I would do whatever it took to make sure I always had something behind me and could take care of myself if something went wrong. This feeling has driven me on, year after year, supported by another idea from my parents that you must not ask anyone for help or become beholden to someone because they have done something for you which you cannot repay.

This was constantly drilled into Jackie and me. Perhaps my parents watched too many gangster films...

I've never imagined the state would support me, even when I had almost nothing. Until recently, I never sought or received a penny from the state. My state pension came as somewhat of a surprise as I rarely thought of it and kind of assumed I might not get one. I've always believed I am on my own and would have to manage if something went wrong.

Most of the big decisions I have taken have been weighed against the possibility of things going against me and me having to sort it out. Although this sounds like a sure-fire way to live an overly cautious life, taking no risks whatsoever, I have never seen it that way. I have just weighed up all the risks, not just the obvious short-term ones. In other words, I examine the risk of failing at today's task against the risk of finding myself relying on the state or others in x years' time because I have failed to do what was needed to improve my own life.

This is where my favourite puzzle comes up again – **LUD**. And it's going to come up a lot more as we progress. It may sound harsh, but there are fundamental choices people make at an early age which instantly put them on a path they are highly unlikely to find a way off. Leaving the family home is one of them.

Clearly, it depends on the exact situation, but in my case, being able to live under the wing of my parents was the only way I could do anything about improving my net worth. I didn't particularly enjoy living there, but the challenge of having to deal with my mum was more than offset by the benefits to my savings. Although the bank moved employees regularly without regard to their family connections, I was able to travel easily to all the branches I was allocated to in the first seven years of my career. Others of my age were moved too far to live at home and it destroyed them financially. All their wages were spent on accommodation, and it took them many years to recover from being put in that situation.

There is always a choice. I know in my heart had I been moved to a branch where I would have had to rent accommodation, I would have chosen to decline and leave the bank. I believe the negative effect of renting on my personal balance sheet would have been more significant than my long-term career prospects. But I was lucky. My move away from home coincided with my desire and ability to buy my first house, a transaction so significant, it became the bedrock of my future wealth.

I feel so sorry for those who have been kicked out of their family homes by their parents or have to leave because of abuse. I don't have any magic answers for you, other than to tell you the principles and lessons I have learnt still apply. It may be difficult, but if you are determined enough, you will find a way. Use the negativity of the situation to drive your obsession to improve. There is no stronger fuel – just burn it in a positive way which moves you in the right direction.

In my early years, it was easy to do my net worth calculation, as my main asset was my car. I usually knew what it was worth and, despite the expense of running it, my savings grew, albeit slowly. But I could see I was going in the right direction. I did all my own repairs and servicing, which massively reduced the ownership cost, and I kept the cars in the best condition possible so I could retain their value.

Apart from university fees, car ownership is probably the

most significant factor in the ability of a young person starting out to improve their personal balance sheet. Insurance alone can be cripplingly expensive, which possibly explains why fewer and fewer young people are choosing to buy a car. Unless you are an enthusiast like I was and prepared to learn everything there is to know about how cars work and what you need to do to look after one yourself, it's going to be a challenge to own a vehicle and improve your lot at the same time, especially if you come from a background like mine. But it's not impossible. There is always a way. You just have to be creative, resourceful and determined.

I will help you to see how this is possible. And you won't be beholden to me. Well, maybe a little…

University and student loans

There was not the remotest possibility of me going to university or even staying on at school after the age of sixteen. But if you are in the position where you are planning to go to university, you need to consider the implications of having negative net worth from the moment you start your further education. Parents, grandparents, aunts, uncles – anyone who knows someone about to embark on student life can benefit from this section too.

Just to be totally clear (I like accuracy), the money the government makes available to you to cover your fees isn't strictly speaking a loan. This is a common misunderstanding, not helped by the fact it tends to be known as a student loan. If we're going to be pedantic, what you are actually taking on is a contingent liability.

What this means is if a certain thing happens in the future, you will have to cover the liability. In this case, it's if you earn over a certain sum of money, then you will start repaying your student loan. It's the same as a company including contingent liabilities in its accounts if it is likely the event they are contingent upon will occur.

If you have a student loan, should you include it in your personal balance sheet? It depends how confident you are about hitting the threshold which triggers your loan repayments. If you are absolutely determined you will use your degree in bagpiping to make your fortune, include it. But if you are pessimistic enough to believe you will never earn enough to trigger the repayments, then don't.

However, the latter is similar to saying, "I don't want to earn too much money as I will pay a crazy amount of tax." Surely, the best thing possible is for you to be in a situation where you pay huge amounts of tax and have to repay your student loan at the maximum rate. That means you are earning even huger amounts of money.

So, perhaps you should include your student loan as a liability in your personal balance sheet. It should certainly give you an incentive to find ways to improve your situation.

If you have yet to take on such a liability, you might want to think about other ways to improve your education while earning money. From September 1973, I began attending evening classes at the Bath Technical College to study for my banking exams. These were in two major parts, divided into various sections and including such things as economics, law and accounting. It took me five years to complete the courses and achieve the letters ACIB (Association of Chartered Institute of Bankers) after my name. Although the qualification doesn't exist in the same format today, it was then the equivalent to a degree and regarded by the bank as such. I certainly learnt much from the courses. And while I was studying for the exams, my net worth was growing every year.

Plenty of young and older people pursue and achieve degrees as part of their career while earning decent money. They might miss out on certain aspects of full-time university life, but perhaps that's a good thing.

This is a classic instance of LUD presenting you with a tricky choice. Will you have a great social life while obtaining a degree and enter the workforce with a negative net worth? And possibly only get a job in a coffee shop, regardless of your qualifications. Or will you get a job where you can study in your spare time, build up your personal balance sheet and probably keep your liver in good shape too? I know which one I would go for. You might be in a situation like mine was and not have the university option open to you. Hopefully, you are starting to realise that apparent lack of choice might be the best thing which could ever happen to you.

If the university option is open to you, consider how much of an effect on your personal balance sheet your decision will make, if you haven't already. Like any decision, what you choose will be massively determined by what is most important to you. What has happened to you in your life so far will contribute to how you will feel about this. There is no right or wrong answer, but you need to be careful to understand the likely implications of your decision.

If you decide to take the leap to university and the loan which accompanies it, do so with a particular mindset, rather than because you feel you ought to or everyone else is doing it. Put some thought into your LUD decision. Are you going to live for today or tomorrow? If it's the former, go and enjoy yourself, but be aware there will be a price to pay later in life. Alternatively, make some goals, follow my advice and decide you are going to do something special.

In a post-Covid-19 world with the threat of climate change ever present, who knows what lies in store? Just make your LUD decision based on considering as many aspects of your situation as you can. Or perhaps you know in your gut, like I did, how you want to go forward in life.

But whatever you do, do it with thought and purpose.

CHAPTER 11

HOBBIES WHICH PAY

Not everyone is blessed in having a job they are passionate about. Even if we have passion for what makes us a living, most of us need a distraction or some kind of leisure pursuit. This was certainly my case when I first started out. In fact, I found ways to enjoy a relatively expensive hobby or interest not only at little or no cost to myself, but as a small profit centre too. This is at the heart of my quest to make something from nothing and in keeping with my long-term view of LUD, while still having fun.

If football is what turns you on, then it's pretty easy to get started. Even if you can't afford to buy a ball, there are plenty kicking around. See what I did there? Such things are so throw away these days (I did it again ☺), you can often find one stuck in a hedge because no-one has the energy or enthusiasm to rescue it.

As you grow more interested in your sport, you might want to watch some of the bigger matches rather than just playing at whatever level you are at. This is where it starts to get more expensive, and where my expertise on this subject runs out. If blagging your way into a Premier League game is on your agenda, I'm sure there is a way if you work hard enough at it.

Life is a little more challenging if your god decides to endow you with a passion for cars and motorsport. We've already spoken of the financial demands of owning even a simple car for the road, but when it comes to racing one, just accept this is potentially one of the most expensive hobbies anyone can choose. I've shown how I managed to get a taste of my passion at a young age, but I did have other desires which I needed to satisfy. One of those was to be a journalist, the only job I really wanted while still at school.

My foray into journalism

My involvement with the Autograss club soon had me thinking of opportunities in the direction of the media. As with most clubs, we found getting anyone to do anything a challenge, and the bulk of the work was done by a small but enthusiastic group of volunteers. In club life, there seem to be two broad groups of people: those who are willing to give what it takes to keep the club alive and those who only take from it what they can.

It seemed obvious to me the club would need some publicity if it was to thrive. We had no money for advertising, but perhaps the local newspaper, the one which published the ad which got me involved, might print an article about the club's very first race meeting.

So, when the club grew strong enough to hold its first event in a field near a little place called Ston Easton, the *Somerset Guardian* knew all about it. There was no email in those days, so using the bank's typewriter, I typed up what was effectively a press release and dropped it off at the newspaper's local offices. The *Somerset Guardian* printed it almost word for word. Although I didn't receive a by-line, that was effectively the start of my second career not only as a journalist, but as the proprietor of my own public relations business.

I was about seventeen at the time. I'd had no training or guidance in how to write in newspaper style, but it never occurred to me anyone should need to teach me. I read the *FT* articles and every motorsport magazine I could skim in my lunch breaks, and realised there are different styles of writing depending on my potential audience. It was just a case of writing in the style appropriate to the person I wanted to appeal to.

I have always loved writing. Just as I am putting words to this book today, back then, they flowed out of me without too much effort, as I was passionate about the subject and felt everyone else should know about it. It seemed obvious to me people would only read my stuff if it sounded interesting and hopefully a little different. I needed to convey my message without it being a sales pitch and keep people's interest.

I carried on writing articles for the local rag, usually a short preview of the meeting coming up, the purpose of which was to attract spectators. It was 75p entrance fee to the meeting per car, regardless of the number of people in it. This was almost the only source of revenue for the club, so it was vital every meeting was a financial success, or we would soon be in trouble. Our main outlay was the payment to the farmer for the use of his field for the weekend.

It took at least a day to build the track. Piles of tyres formed the inside of the corners and we used fence posts and wire rope for the outside. We had to print the programme (I soon got the job of writing the words for that too), hire a sound system and a commentator, and then beg and borrow all the other things which made a meeting happen. It was just like running any business, but for me, the novelty of being treasurer eventually wore off as it was too much like work. When I escaped my day job, I didn't really want to be thinking about financial matters. I was much more interested in being involved in the racing and putting words to paper about my wonderful hobby.

Ladies and gentlemen, do you know where you are?

After a couple of years, we were organising what was to be our biggest race meeting to date. For some reason, the regular commentator used by most of the clubs could not make it. This was quite a problem as a commentator was seen as essential, although I still believe today most people take little notice of them even at prestigious race meetings. I was never particularly impressed with the guy we had been using and I remember thinking I could do better. So, when the opportunity arose, I became the sole volunteer and got myself yet another job.

A little like I had done with writing, I had studied and listened to the words of any commentator I came into contact with. Although there was very little motor sport on TV, I tried to learn from the likes of Murray Walker and the excellent Raymond Baxter. Then, I jumped in at the deep end.

One of the keys to success is saying yes to things – **making a decision** – and working out how you are going to fulfil your commitment later. Of the successful people I know well, most if not all have that kind of attitude. Remember General Patton's words.

Something which was clear to me was I needed to know more about everything I would be talking about than anyone listening. I was already familiar with all the cars and drivers from our own club, though not so much with those from the visiting clubs. So, from the very start of my commentating career, I would spend the morning of the meeting looking at as many of the cars as I had time for and speaking to as many drivers as I could. Being young, I had a good memory, so I could soak up all the details about each and every car, and I found it easy to recall the information once live, helped a little by my poorly scrawled notes.

Getting started inevitably presented something of a challenge. I recall launching into my first words over the sound system with some apprehension, but once they had left my mouth, the adrenaline took over and off I went. I always tried to start off by saying something different to the clichés used by other amateur commentators. My particular hate was "Good afternoon, ladies and gentlemen, and welcome to Autograss racing at xxxxxxx". That seemed a cop out and much too obvious and easy. When did anyone ever go to an event and forget or not know where they were?

"I know where I am," I imagined my audience saying, "I don't need you to tell me. Give me something new and entertaining."

Presumably, people liked my style as I was praised by one normally grumpy member at our next committee meeting at the pub. Without being asked, I became the resident voice. Soon, other clubs started asking me to commentate for them and as my own racing began to wane, it was supplanted by this new skill. These clubs would also pay me, which was a useful addition to my income.

At age twenty-two, I was asked to commentate at the biggest meeting of the year, the National Championship Finals, where clubs from all over the country gathered to decide the year's champions. I was pleased to receive a letter of thanks from the organising club after the event, praising me for my professionalism. That gave me confidence to believe I could possibly do a bit more with this skill…

A pivotal meeting, especially for Jackie

While the praise I received for my commentating efforts was an honour, my love affair with Autograss was coming to an end. The A40 had been rebuilt a couple of times and later we upgraded to a Vauxhall Viva, which turned out to be a poor choice as it was too heavy and not powerful enough. Like my friend Dave, I had a real passion to become involved with proper motor racing, ideally circuit racing. I soldiered on in Autograss for a year or so, racing an unreliable Mini, but it was not the same doing it on my own. Dave had already given up on the racing side of Autograss as his income was by then enough to enable him to make the leap to the circuits via a single-seater Formula Ford. I was able to accompany Dave to a few meetings and finally get to see a real motor race. It seems crazy now to think I have had a lifelong passion for motor sport, and yet my only exposure to circuit racing until my late teens was through magazines and the very occasional slot on the BBC.

So, for a while I fulfilled my need for speed by using my voice instead of my driving skill. Then another door opened in the form of my future brother-in-law, Maurice. Maurice's dad ran the area's largest motor dealership and employed a young lad, Richard, straight from school at sixteen. Richard had been helping Dave and me with our A40 since he was around ten years old and, like us, was obsessed with cars and racing. Even at a young age, he had an incredible knowledge of cars, so working at a garage was an obvious vocation for him.

Maurice was a few years younger than Dave and I, but a little older than Richard. He had been working his way through various departments in the motor dealership and had become friends with Richard, helped by their shared passion for cars. When Maurice came along to an Autograss meeting, we became friends due to our mutual acquaintance with Richard. Then the momentous day occurred when Maurice came to my family's house and met my sister Jackie. A few years ago, they celebrated their Silver Wedding anniversary.

In the late 1970s, it was Maurice's rallying activities which gave me access to another part of the sport. I was soon helping him prepare his cars, and then co-driving for him at various local events. Meeting Maurice was another pivotal moment in my life, only made possible by my friendship with Richard. When Richard began hanging around our A40, Dave and I could easily have told him to get lost. After all, being seen with a ten-year-old when you are seventeen is not exactly the coolest thing in the world. Luckily, we didn't.

There's an obvious life lesson here: **never underestimate any encounter or situation.** The decision you make about whether to interact or not with another human being could change your life completely – directly or indirectly. It could be for better or worse, but what is sure is the more connections you make and the more people you interact with, the more you improve your chances of finding success. You just need to have the awareness and presence of mind to make the most of what is presented to you. I'm not talking about manipulating or using people, but simply keeping an open mind and being ready for opportunities.

Radio star

I was determined to become more involved in motor racing one way or another, but competing at Dave's level was completely out of the question. My bank salary was a fraction of the wages the printing industry was paying at that time. But a move to the branch in Swindon brought with it an unexpected opportunity.

It was 1982 and my career had progressed nicely as I was seen as a good prospect for the future, able to adapt to each new and more prestigious section of the bank without too much trouble. At Swindon, I soon became a manager's clerk, a position which entailed doing all the donkey work for the manager and acting as a go-between with the clients. In those days, a manager at a large bank branch held a prestigious position. They had power to make significant lending decisions and usually ruled their branch with a rod of iron. So being manager's assistant was an important job.

At Swindon, we had some high-profile clients, but the one which interested me the most was the new independent radio station for the area, an ambitious enterprise known as Wiltshire Radio, later to become GWR and now swallowed up into the Heart FM group. This was no amateur local radio effort but a £630k operation, which eventually achieved a market capitalisation of £350m. The station offered a broad range of news-style programmes, but despite the huge amount of money invested into setting it up, it looked to limit its expenditure as much as possible by persuading anyone it could think of to contribute for free. The bank was invited to provide a daily financial report just after the news at 6pm, so the staff were asked if anyone would volunteer. Apart from me jumping at the chance, no-one else seemed interested, though once things got underway, the prospect of local fame appealed to more and more participants.

Soon, we had quite a news team at the bank. We wrote our own reports, mainly using information from Teletext, which was the nearest thing to the internet at that time. We then drove to the studio in Wootton Bassett (now Royal Wootton Bassett) to read our words live to our millions (ha ha) of listeners. With my commentating experience, I found the delivery relatively easy and endeavoured to make my reports as interesting as possible with what can be a grey subject.

But my real reason for volunteering was with a more important aim in mind.

After a few days of reading my reports, I had built up a little **rapport** with some of the newsroom staff at the station. Enough to ask the sports reporter, nice and casually, "Who is looking after motorsport for you?"

I could see his response forming in his brain in the couple of seconds he took to reply. Not only did the station not have anyone, he hadn't considered they should. But with someone asking the question, it put him in a bit of a spot. I knew before he replied that I was in.

"Uh, no-one. Why, do you fancy doing it?" It was the response I wanted to hear.

Like most of my achievements, I had no idea at the time how I was going to do this or where I would get my news. But we're back into the realms of General Patton's advice. Within a week, I was broadcasting my live motorsport report and the station agreed I would keep the same five-minute slot every Friday at around 6:30pm.

While Teletext was useful for the financial reports, this was a bit different. Wiltshire Radio was, as its name suggested, a station for people in and around that county. I hadn't been living in Swindon long so I knew no-one there who could help me. But I was lucky the Castle Combe circuit was in my area and fairly active. Its boss had a certain reputation, something I discovered the hard way when I rang him to introduce myself and tell him about my new radio slot, hoping to be fed with titbits of what was going on, which I could then turn into something newsworthy. I was offering him free exposure and publicity, so I was a little surprised to receive a somewhat cold reaction. But I **persevered** and the coldness thawed, to the extent that six years later, I was asked to take over the circuit's PR, a task I performed for the next thirty years.

But I couldn't base my programme entirely on what the Castle Combe circuit was doing, especially as in the winter months, it closed for all racing activity. I knew a number of competitors from my family's area of Midsomer Norton and Radstock, or at least I knew people who knew them, so I thought of a cunning plan. Even though this area is not in Wiltshire, if my mum and dad could manage to tune in to the station, then people and activities from there would be relevant.

This is exactly what happened. I knew I was pushing the boundaries, literally, but you must **work with what you have** – another important life lesson.

Mixing with the big boys

Gradually, I built up my database of people involved in motorsport. Most of it was done by telephone and any other method I could think of, using the rest breaks I had at the bank. I now had to start buying the relevant media to keep me informed. I couldn't do enough research standing in a newsagent, I was thinking big. Well, big for me – a council-house boy who should have been going nowhere.

The two biggest motorsports at the time were Formula 1 and World Championship Rallying. The former is still so, the latter arguably not. I had to find a reason to cover both as I knew it was a way to gain access to the very top of the sport, something which would have seemed impossible when I was writing my reports for the *Somerset Guardian* about battered bangers driving around a field.

Using the same strategy as I had with my hometown, I discovered both the Williams Grand Prix team and the Toleman F1 team had bases which could, at a push, receive the station. Luckily, a map had been produced showing the extent of the coverage, something the station's sales staff used to persuade potential advertisers. The F1 teams were right on the edge of it...

To give me some credibility and let competitors and enthusiasts know I existed, I advised the UK's main motor sport magazine, *Autosport*, of my weekly radio slot. Somewhat to my surprise, the editor printed my words in quite a prominent place in the magazine and soon afterwards, I received a letter from a PR firm heavily involved in motorsport which happened to look after the Williams team. I was given access to a contact at Williams whom I would call to glean anything I could which might be newsworthy and hadn't already been revealed in *Autosport*. This person was quite a name to those in the know.

Even in those days, F1 teams had an air of unapproachability. Social media was not so much as a twinkle in the eye of the internet and the bank didn't own what we would now call a proper computer. But somehow, I managed to make contact with a guy at Toleman, a helpful chap who had worked at a number of Grand Prix teams.

Using these contacts, I made F1 a regular feature of my reports, though I ensured the ordinary grassroots guys in the sport were featured equally. After all, no-one else was giving them publicity, and if you are seeking sponsorship, you need all the help you can get. Over time, I got to know an incredible number of people, mostly at club racing level, but on occasions, some well-known drivers. Those contacts have been very valuable to me as I've progressed in life, both from a personal and social viewpoint, and in my various business capacities.

It's hard to put a price on **the value of connections**, but I would say this is an essential life lesson. You've likely heard the saying, "It's not what you know, but who you know", yet establishing my network of people cost me absolutely nothing, apart from my time and a lot of effort. Time and effort aren't things you should undervalue, especially when you have lifted yourself into the position of having some kind of business enterprise. Many make this mistake, but when you have no money and no business, using your time and effort to create something for the future is one of the most fruitful things you can do. And the more people you get to know, regardless of how you get to know them, the more successful you are likely to be.

The big advantage I had when creating my network of motor sport people was being able to genuinely give them something for nothing. Few people prefer not to have publicity of any kind, so when someone enthusiastic contacted them and offered to talk about what they were doing on radio, why wouldn't they be happy? Sponsorship is important for a lot of current or would-be racing drivers. Yet I learnt very early on that hardly anyone was proactive when it came to promoting what they were doing. This is why, when I established my PR business, I found it easy to get my stories featured in the media. They so rarely received anything from my sport, they were grateful for anything they could get hold of. This is such a simple, basic thing, but so few took advantage of all this free publicity.

Word got around and as my programme became better known, I found sourcing interesting stories easier and easier. I had great relationships with the drivers and teams I was featuring. The station seemed pleased with what I was doing. The only thing missing was some kind of financial recompense.

Yet, being able to attend the British Grand Prix and interview some of my heroes like Ayrton Senna, Keke Rosberg, Nigel Mansell, Gerhard Berger and Derek Warwick was something money could not buy. Being the first person to interview the 1988 Le Mans winner, Andy Wallace, live on air after covering him and the Jaguar team for the previous twenty-four hours was like a dream come true. It cost me nothing and I earnt nothing from it, but sometimes experiences are priceless.

I was well aware radio stations were not in the habit of paying anything unless they really had to, but after a few years of asking, I began to receive a modest sum, which helped with my pride more than my bank balance. But it was one significant connection which propelled me into another area where my knowledge and enthusiasm could be rewarded.

CHAPTER 12

A DEEPER INVOLVEMENT IN MOTORSPORT

In my hometown was a guy called Dave Whittock who was making quite a name for himself as a co-driver to Swedish rally star, Per Eklund. The duo had a contract with Toyota GB and one of Dave's perks was a nice new Toyota Corolla GT road car, which has now become a coveted classic due to its super little engine and entertaining handling.

I got to know Dave quite well through constantly calling him to find out what he was doing next, and then reporting on what had happened on the duo's last rally. Meanwhile, the radio station had started a general motoring feature. The host, whom I had become friendly with through our mutual interest in cars, would be lent new vehicles from the local dealers and feature them in his weekly slot, giving the dealers publicity and him a free car to drive for a few days.

The Corolla GT was quite a rare car even at the time, so I persuaded him it would be great to feature it in the programme. Dave suggested I call the woman who ran the press fleet at Toyota to see if she would lend me one of its cars. Much to my surprise, she agreed with little hesitation. Not only would she lend me a car, but it was also delivered to my house with a full tank of fuel. And I got to keep it for a week, opening my eyes to a whole new world of fun and opportunity. This really was something for nothing except, once again, my time and effort.

This got me thinking. If Toyota was prepared to do this, then perhaps other manufacturers would do so as well. Once I had completed my road testing of the Corolla and put together and broadcast my radio feature, I felt confident to expand this little enterprise. Bear in mind I was still working full time at the bank and was by now married. With a house to look after and our first child on the way, my life was getting quite busy. But I was never afraid to fill every minute of my day with stuff to do. Things aren't much different now, forty years later.

The second manufacturer I contacted was the UK importer for Mitsubishi, based in nearby Cirencester under the name of Colt Cars. The local element made things a little easier and Mitsubishi models soon started coming my way, followed by various Fords, Vauxhalls, Rovers, Renaults, Hondas, Volvos, Protons, Isuzus, Daewoos and, on one occasion, a Dacia. The German manufacturers were more reluctant to lend cars for something which wasn't broadcast nationally, but with almost a dozen others prepared to help me, I soon had a constant stream of new cars coming and going from my driveway, which kept the neighbours somewhat puzzled. The full tanks of fuel made up for the fact I was doing all this without pay. My road car clocked up very little mileage of its own.

I soon decided it would be nice to feature these cars in print as well as just through my radio slots, so I started making contact with editors of small local freebie newspapers who, I guessed, would be happy to print something presented to them at no cost. It didn't make me any money, but I knew I would fall out of favour with the manufacturers if they didn't see evidence of their cars being featured, and the radio broadcasts went out at various unexpected times, so it was tricky to get recordings of what I had prepared. A small freebie journal in my old hometown of Radstock offered to feature my weekly pieces. If I had no car to test, I could promote something at the Castle Combe circuit, because by this time (1988), the owner had warmed to me so considerably, he was employing me to look after the circuit's PR.

The arrangement with the local newspaper worked very well and gradually, I expanded it to other publications on an ad hoc and mainly unpaid basis. As far as the car tests were concerned, my written pieces eventually took over from my radio broadcasts as Wiltshire Radio evolved into a station more interested in music than anything else. By that stage, because I had established enough of a relationship with the car manufacturers, there was never any difficulty in being supplied with what I wanted.

As I was once told by a man at an airport, "If you establish a reputation for getting up early, you can get up at whatever time you like." I still believe **establishing a reputation** to be an all-important life lesson.

So, even without my radio broadcasts, I was able to carry on with my road tests and took some very nice cars on holiday trips. On one memorable occasion, I was lent a new motor home, which I took on my annual pilgrimage to the Le Mans twenty-four hour race with my friends. Filling it with ten of them, I drove into the City of Le Mans on the night before the race, which was probably not something the donor had in mind as a thorough test…

Spreading my wings

This kind of thing (usually without testing the seating capacity of vehicles beyond its limits) went on for fifteen years until I simply became too busy with my other businesses to find time to write my reports. But in that time, I became known to the Society of Motor Manufacturers and Traders, and got invited on its annual press days. It was possible to drive some amazing new cars provided by the manufacturers, usually at a race circuit such as Donington Park, where my skills of car control learnt in Autograss found me lapping quicker than most of the other journalists. This made me more and more determined to start circuit racing myself. Despite many other pressures, I knew it was something I had to do, but more of that later.

Another bonus of my relationships with the car manufacturers was the invitation to press launches for new models. Some of these were relatively modest affairs in nice country houses where typically, we guests dined to a high standard, and were then given a selection of cars to drive on the local roads. But occasionally, they would take place abroad.

At age thirty-one, I had still not flown in a plane, but in 1988, Mitsubishi invited me to Majorca for the launch of the latest Shogun. Even the flight there presented me with an opportunity. I happened to be seated next to a Danish guy, and as we were both travelling alone, we began chatting. When a hostess asked me if I would like anything to drink, courtesy of Mitsubishi, this gave me some credibility. It transpired I was sitting next to the man responsible for the look of the distinctive Bang & Olufsen stereo systems, which were much coveted at the time. He was suddenly very interested in me as he had also designed a car, bearing many similarities to the B&O sound systems in terms of shape.

At the time, I was still working in banking, but when he asked me the question which strangers almost inevitably ask of each other, "What do you do?" it was natural for me to talk about my motoring and motor sport journalism. Even to this day, I find it a little tricky to answer that question as I am involved in many different enterprises. And when someone asks, I have little time to summarise what I do, as most people switch off after the first few words.

With this in mind, I would urge anyone with ambition to think about and rehearse exactly what they are going to say when asked this popular question. You may need to have a number of stock phrases you can use, depending on who you are talking to. It's the first part of any future sales negotiation and helps with **establishing your reputation** as well as potentially catalysing a beneficial future relationship. Remember, **sales are everything**.

My link to cars as a journalist was enough to get my fellow passenger on the plane – let's call him Jans – excited, as he and the industrialists behind the new car were desperate for some publicity to help get the project off the ground. The car's main unique sales proposition (USP) was being made by what would then have been the only Danish car manufacturer. But Jans and his colleagues had nowhere near enough money, so needed publicity to drum up outside investor interest.

Jans asked me if I would be interested in helping them. It was at this stage I told him about my banking job. My knowledge of the financial world would surely be of help too. I didn't mention I was a relatively small cog in the bank… **only tell people what they need to know** is another invaluable life lesson for the ambitious.

Using my lifelong tactic of saying yes, and then working out how to do it afterwards, I was soon in touch with the main people behind the project, and within a short space of time, I was on my second flight, this time to Denmark. As with all of my extra-curricular activities, I had to take holiday from the bank to do this, but it was exciting and I felt it was worth it. I had no experience in raising funds of the magnitude the manufacturers required, but I did know about generating publicity and I guessed the same principles applied, regardless of the scale of the project.

But it transpired it is a little bit easier promoting car racing on grass in a local rag than an optimistic overseas venture very few in the UK had any interest in. Even with my modest experience, I quickly saw this was a somewhat naïve venture. Apart from Jans's design, which had been made into various models, almost nothing had been done. It would have been a task and an ask of huge magnitude for someone with deep pockets, but these people were doing everything on a shoestring. They were really nice and genuine and I wanted to help them, but I could see this was a waste of everyone's time.

There is a popular question in the motorsport world: "How do you make a small fortune out of motorsport?" The answer is, start with a big one. The same applies to car manufacture. I felt I had done my best. It had been interesting and added to my life experience, so I'm glad I was involved in Jans's enterprise, even though nothing came of it.

Formula 1

The place where most people in motorsport want to be involved in some form or another is Formula 1. My connections with the Williams and Benetton teams gave me the confidence to make more of what I was doing, so in 1983 (and for a few more years thereafter), I applied successfully to obtain not just one, but two press passes for the British Grand Prix at Silverstone. I convinced the organisers I needed someone to help me with my recording equipment, which admittedly was quite heavy in those days, so I could take my pal Dave, who I knew would love the experience as much as I would.

Today, gaining access to the F1 paddock is trickier than getting an audience with the Pope, but back then, Silverstone obliged with the necessary passes. By now, I had started to develop the mindset of being pretty confident I could do something if I wanted it badly enough. But even I was surprised to be able to mingle with the likes of Keke Rosberg (the soon-to-be World Champion) and interview him and his rivals while they tried to relax in their modest deckchairs just an hour or two before qualifying.

I was lucky enough to interview many of the top F1 drivers of the day and even made it on to the grid just before the start of the race on one memorable occasion. Undoubtedly, my most treasured memory is of interviewing a young Ayrton Senna, who went on to be arguably the greatest F1 driver of all time and was given a godlike status in his homeland of Brazil, both before and after his death. In 1984, he was in his first season at the Toleman team, which later became Benetton.

Unlike today, when all interviews with the F1 crowd are prescheduled and accompanied by a public relations (PR) minder, I would simply walk up to a driver and ask him if I could have a few words with him. Some drivers, mainly the top stars, would use an excuse not to talk to me, without saying no directly. Usually, they were stalling for time in the hope I would get the message. I thought this might be the case with Ayrton Senna, who had just completed his qualifying session and was still in his overalls in the garage. Politely, he told he had to do something right then, but if I waited a few minutes, he would talk to me.

I've heard that before, was my first thought. If it had been anyone else, I would have moved on. But he seemed sincere, so I hung around in the pit garage. These days, even the most revered journalist would not be allowed to linger in an F1 team's garage, which are sacrosanct places full of top-secret information. And I was just a local radio station reporter with more balls than manners. I watched as Ayrton went to every one of his mechanics, looking them in the eye, squeezing their arms and thanking them for what they had done for him. He also handed each one of them something, and I don't think it was a £1 tip. It was clearly something which showed his appreciation.

Without his team, an F1 driver is nothing. Even if I had

never spoken to Ayrton again, witnessing that act made him special in my eyes. I was seeing a star in the making and I learnt a lot from watching him in those few minutes. That is the way to motivate people around you.

At the end of his tour of the garage, Ayrton stopped and looked around to see if I was still there. As soon as he spotted me, he made his way over and gave me a friendly and warm interview. How much did that treasured memory cost me? Just my time and patience.

Nine years later, I was sheltering from the rain on practice day for the European Grand Prix at Donington Park. Ayrton Senna walked past me on the way to his McLaren garage. Our eyes met, I nodded, he nodded back. Wow.

Until that first trip to the British GP, I had never been to an F1 race and would not have been able to justify the cost of the ticket, despite my passion for the sport. But as I have practised all my life, you can do amazing things for no cost. I arranged a press car to take Dave and me there, complete with full tank of fuel, and we were fed and watered along with the international press. Imposter syndrome? Never heard of it. The only downside was it spoiled me and I've subsequently found it difficult to attend any event purely as a spectator.

As the world of F1 evolved, muscling into a race became effectively impossible and even a local radio station would have to pay for the privilege of attending, making it totally unviable for me. But as one door closed, another opened.

Rallying

There were lots of local amateur rally drivers I was covering, but Dave Whittock's career was zooming. His successes with Per Eklund in the British Championship soon propelled the two of them into the World Championship, the UK's round of which was the RAC Rally, known more recently as Wales Rally GB, but at its most famous, every motorsport fan in the UK knew it as the Lombard. In those days, it was billed as the biggest sporting event in the UK, because of the millions of spectators who would brave our November weather to stand in a forest or in the grounds of a stately home to see spectacular cars being driven on the limit by some of the best drivers in the world, sometimes only inches away.

At the time of writing, the event is absent from the world calendar as it had become much less popular, possibly because of its sanitisation. But long before my radio work, I would join the millions to see my rally heroes in action, helped a little by my employer. The bank owned the sponsor!

While I was at the Midsomer Norton branch of the bank, a guy a few years older than me joined who was as big a car nut as I was. He was also a member of the bank's motoring club, which I had never known existed. So I had someone I could talk cars with who was much more familiar with motor sport than I was and attended lots of events. As a member of the club, he was invited to help marshal the press day for the 1975 RAC Rally and managed to get me an invite too. So at age eighteen, I attended my first event as an insider, opening my eyes to what is possible if you are either too impecunious or too ambitious to be a mere spectator.

We had a great day, getting close to my heroes, including my all-time favourite, Hannu Mikkola, in the Toyota Corolla Levin. Surprisingly, though, my most treasured memento from the event was the reflective tabard we were given to identify us as marshals and as a vague sap to health and safety, which generally did not exist in those days. Somehow, I managed to acquire a couple of these as I was always thinking of my friend Dave and how we might use them together to our advantage.

A year later, they came into their own. For the first time, the RAC Rally would start from Bath, our home city. Scrutineering is where the cars are checked for safety and eligibility prior to the event, and is an opportunity to see them and the drivers up close. With my valued tabards, I decided we would be attending. But not as spectators on the crowded side of the guard rail. No, we would be mingling with the stars. Which is exactly what we did.

Given my dad's shyness and our family's mantra of staying in the shadows and keeping our heads down, I have no idea where I learnt to blag as brazenly as I did. But I've realised if you look as if you are meant to be doing whatever it is you are doing, then no-one will question you. **Act as if** is a life lesson that has served me well many times over the years.

So, Dave and I walked past security and straight into the melee of scrutineering, seeing the cars close up and really feeling part of the atmosphere. I saw the crowds on the other side of the barrier and, a bit like my moment in the garden at the start of this book, I thought, *I don't want to be like those people.* I would always need to find a way to be on the inside. It began with the grass track club I helped to start and continued to F1, the World Rally Championship and beyond.

That weekend, the first stage of the four-day event was at Dodington Park, now the fabulous estate of James Dyson. Guess what? Dave and I used our orange jackets to enter for free and wandered around mainly unchallenged, apart from one occasion when a guy asked me if I was the sector chief. I was nineteen and didn't even know what a sector chief was...

After that, I was hooked, and every November, I would drive to some of the remotest areas of the UK to follow the event. Seven years later, when the rally returned to Bath, I had become known to Toyota through Dave Whittock. For the 1983 event, Whittock and Eklund had been promoted to the fearsome Twin Cam Turbo Celica, a beast of a machine which had no lack of power, but considerably less grip than its four-wheel drive rivals.

One way or another, I engineered for Wiltshire Radio to agree to live reports from me throughout the event from wherever the rally happened to be. Toyota looked after me for the four days, driving me to as many stages as it was practicable to get to and accommodating me when the luxury of sleep was allowed. Part of the appeal of the rally in those days was its endurance aspect, the crews getting very little rest, testing them to the extreme.

The main challenge was finding a public phone box to call in my reports. This was the time before mobile phones, so reporting this way was commonplace for radio journalists. I had done it many times from the public call box at the Castle Combe circuit (no, the owner wouldn't let me use his landline!) and various other places, but travelling to the wilds of Scotland, Wales and Northumbria was a new challenge. On one memorable occasion, I was live on the radio in the middle of a piece when someone came up behind me, shouting about having to use the phone now and trying to grab it out of my hand. Somehow, I kept my composure, put my leg up behind me and pushed this person away from me and out of the box, all the time continuing with my report. Apparently, there was no indication on the radio station anything untoward had happened.

Sadly, Whittock and Eklund retired from the event after an accident. But the following year, they were back in the same car and finished an incredible third against much more sophisticated opposition.

In 1986, the rally was back in Bath. I had been asked to join the organising committee, looking after publicity, which I saw as a privilege, and it further helped to cement my status within the motor sport community. I'm still in touch with a few of the members of that committee, one of whom is now a great friend. Dave Whittock and Per Eklund had obtained sponsorship from the audio firm Clarion for a European campaign in a Metro

6R4 and a one-off outing on the Lombard RAC. Wiltshire Radio had become GWR and was now a twenty-four hour radio station with a wider coverage and more or less a household name for those able to receive it. I seemed to have become a minor celebrity amongst the motor sport world in Wiltshire, Gloucestershire and Somerset, so people wanted to keep me happy and informed.

Dave arranged for a chap from Clarion UK to ferry me and a couple of others around in his Volvo estate for the whole event. This guy happened to have one of the earliest mobile phones, a bit of a misnomer as it was so big and heavy, it lived in a box on the floor of the Volvo. But public call boxes were still the main method of communication.

I managed without the immobile mobile for the entire event, apart from the evening finish in Great Pulteney Street in the centre of Bath, with no phone box in easy range. I was allowed VIP access close to the finish line and placed the huge box – it took two hands to lift it – on the bonnet of the Volvo. The aerial was around 3m long and would have given me a nasty burn if I'd touched it while transmitting. But it worked and I was able to broadcast a live transmission of the finish of Great Britain's round of the World Rally Championship.

Rally Radio

I recently looked back at my diary from the 1983 event and came across a few words which were to prove to be very relevant in the future. I had met up with a couple of influential people in the rallying world, and one mentioned a rumour of some big money being used to finance a radio service for the rally, which would be made available to any radio station, anywhere in the English-speaking world, free of charge.

Fast forward to 1994 and I was called by a rather focused chap – let's call him Tim – who asked me if I would like to be part of the Rally Radio team providing reports to the UK and the world's various English-speaking radio stations. This was exactly the service I had heard and written about in my diary, and it turned out to be a great experience, a pivotal moment for me, working with Tim and two other talented and experienced reporters, both well established in the motor sport world. I really was on the inside. My radio show was great, I had become a regular commentator at the Castle Combe circuit and was doing the occasional piece on TV, but to work for the official voice of the UK's governing body of motor sport was something very special for me.

It was hard work, but an absolute ball. My brain was as agile as it had ever been, and with many years of radio broadcasting experience under my belt, I was happy to improvise and switch quickly from one station to another. Each station wanted a local angle, so there was a constant search for the current standing of the drivers from that area, all done against the clock and mainly read unscripted within a strict allotment of time. That's one of the most taxing things you can imagine, but so satisfying. I was under no illusions anyone would remember the reporter who spouted up on BBC Radio Scotland every so often, but nevertheless, I was doing something few others will ever come close to. As a bonus, there was the opportunity to interview most of the top drivers when they returned to Rally HQ, and put together short pieces to be used by various stations which either had no local drivers competing or were big enough to want input from the leading drivers.

And I was starting to be paid! That was not my motivation, but it made me feel good to earn even a small amount of money for what I still saw as my hobby. That's the ultimate **getting something from nothing** scenario.

Behind the scenes, though, as our annual reports grew in popularity, competition appeared, trying to muscle in on what we were doing. Tim was a slick operator, but our competitors were using sophisticated devices such as satellite phones to call in reports from deep in a forest. We were always based at Rally HQ, using the official results to prepare our reports, and there would be a delay while we waited for the times to be uploaded to the system. So, if we were up against a particular deadline, I would call contacts I had at a stage end and get them to read out the times to me. That way, I could update my own leader board more quickly than waiting for the official one. If you want to be successful, sometimes you need to know when to bypass the system and break the rules.

Sometime in the middle of the 1990s, the Motor Sports Association asked Tim to bid for the upcoming rally, rather than automatically giving it to him as had happened for many years. Two or three other groups were looking to take the deal away from him, so he was required to present a proposal to a board at MSA headquarters. Tim asked myself and one of my fellow presenters to come along. We had a short meeting prior to the presentation because, in typical local radio style, none of us had pre-prepared anything, so we had to work pretty quickly. It was obvious we had no chance of preparing a conventional presentation in the short time we had, so I suggested we did a mock-up of a typical few minutes in action during the event.

This was another example of saying yes, and then **acting as if**. I guess our enthusiasm and ability to act, innovate and improvise impressed the panel, as we won the contract. I carried on covering the event for some years, until the loss of the main sponsor heralded the beginning of its end as one of the most important sporting spectacles on the calendar.

Tim went on to win various awards for his work. I was sent on a number of missions for him, including covering the famous Circuit of Ireland rally from Belfast and, in complete contrast, the Whitbread Book of the Year awards for late-night radio in London. They were amazing times, all of this accomplished alongside making my day-to-day living. Somehow, I managed to keep all the balls in the air.

CHAPTER 13

ON THE CIRCUIT

Alongside my main employment and all my side hustles, I was building up a motorsport PR business. This had taken off when the circuit owner gave me the contract to look after the Castle Combe PR in 1988. I had already been doing small amounts of work for him, writing press releases and words for programmes etc, but this was a lot more formal. I was on a retainer and for the next three decades, most of the well-written words about the circuit in local and national media emanated from me. The poorly written stuff, I take no responsibility for...

My involvement with my local circuit eventually helped me do the one thing I craved more than anything else: compete in proper circuit racing. After my Autograss exploits came to a natural end, I had a one-off outing in a Sandocross race on the beach at Weston-Super-Mare in 1982 in Maurice's rally Escort, with which I easily won my class and set the third fastest time overall. Perhaps the practice there as a kid in my dad's Hillman Husky helped... Until then, I'd only had an inkling I might be able to compete at a decent level, but that event showed me I had enough skill to get on terms with most people.

But I still didn't have any money, and nor would I for another thirteen years. In that time, I got married and had two lovely daughters, my marriage broke up, I started working for myself and by 1995, I was not in any kind of position to start circuit racing. So, I did anyway!

A friend and I had been pestering the Castle Combe circuit owner to introduce a series for road-going saloon cars. Our idea was we could drive our own car to the circuit, race it and drive it home again. Assuming it still had the required number of wheels. Our pleas fell on deaf ears, until the 1995 season when, without any reference back to us, the circuit announced it would run such a series.

This was the only way I would be able to take up my beloved sport, so despite being in the middle of a marriage break up, with little in the way of spare funds and numerous other barriers which should have stopped me, I made a decision I would find a way to start competing. At the final race meeting of the 1994 season, a little black Vauxhall Nova 1.4, competing in a visiting championship, caught my eye, helped by the fact it was a dominant winner of its class. Almost as soon as the car had come to a halt, I had done a deal with the owner to buy it for £1,250, which I managed to find with a bit of a stretch. Then lots of phone calls and persuasion saw me arrange a number of modest sponsorship deals to help things along. None of them generated any actual cash, but free signwriting for the car, reduced fees from my accountant and a few other freebies were all very helpful.

After finishing second on my race debut, I then went on to class wins for most of the season and was class champion and the official Rookie of the Year for the circuit. I was on my way.

Championship success

The obvious next step was to move to a championship which visited circuits all over the country, to increase my experience. I sold the Nova for a profit (it always helps to have a winning machine) and that, along with the prize money I earnt from my wins, meant my first season of proper motorsport had cost me nothing. Yes, I had more or less broken even, something which rarely happens in motorsport. The payment of prize money for such championships has long since become unviable, so best not to get too excited about trying to emulate me in that way.

What to do next? The idea of being able to drive my race car to each circuit appealed to me. The Castle Combe series was born with that idea in mind, but most competitors transported their cars on trailers. While my Nova was still at the garage of the marital home in Chippenham, I drove it to and from every meeting. By the time the 1996 season was in sight, the marital home had been sold and I had moved into my new house in Bath, with the vital ingredient of its own garage.

I had my eye on the Historic Sports Car Club's 70s Road Sports Championship. This awarded extra points for cars driven to the circuit. Development of the cars was also limited, which helped keep the costs down. But the cost of a competitive car was still somewhat more than the funds I had from the sale of my Nova. I had to find a way to move up a gear.

Two things happened almost simultaneously which allowed me to achieve my latest goal. I knew someone who had bought a TVR 3000M (a sports car made in relatively small numbers) as his first race car and didn't get on with it. He wanted to sell it, looking for a car which would be easier to handle than a rear-wheel drive beast with a 3 litre engine, and I could see it would make an ideal car for the 70s Road Sports championship.

I'd heard about a race-prepared Rover 216 GTi road car which was sitting doing nothing in the yard of a British Leyland dealer in Swindon. I did a great deal on the car, which the dealer seemed desperate to get rid of, and at the same time I pre-sold it in part exchange for the TVR, with very little money changing hands. It was perfect. The buyer got a car he could manage and campaigned it with complete reliability for some years. I got a car I could improve which would be ideal for the 70s Road Sports. I then made it into a championship winner, so it was what I would call a win/win deal.

With championship successes behind me, my automatic mindset was to keep on moving up, so almost as a gut reaction, I put the TVR up for sale. It sold easily at a profit, albeit a modest one. But what to do for 1997?

A disastrous season

In 1996, I'd met a mechanic at a race in Sweden I was doing some PR at, and we became good friends. He was keen for me to move onwards and upwards, and suggested the televised Eurocar Championship. TV's *Top Gear* was a little different in those days to the modern version, but it featured each race, which was obviously appealing. All the cars were supposedly similar, making for close, exciting racing.

By now, my independent financial advice business was starting to go well and had built up a bit of surplus cash, so I persuaded myself it should buy a Eurocar as a sponsorship deal to provide publicity. I bought the 1996 championship-winning car to give me a good chance, as I had in 1995 with the Nova. The mistake I made was going against my previous instincts and collecting the car sometime after the end of the 1996 season and not as soon as it had finished its last race. It's an old trick, but it's easy for unscrupulous sellers to replace all the good bits from a competitive car with worn-out or undeveloped ones. I can't say for sure this was what happened to me, but it was immediately obvious my car was way down on power, even though it was supposed to have one of the best engines.

I initially thought I had overestimated my talent and could not compete at this much higher level. But at the first wet race, I was suddenly on the pace, finishing a strong fifth, despite starting from low down on the grid after the dry qualifying session. Having a car which is down on power is much less of a disadvantage when it rains heavily, as driver skill becomes more important. Unfortunately, that race at Brands Hatch was the only wet one of the year.

It was a horrible season in terms of results. I had spent all my budget buying the car and could not afford to rebuild the hopeless engine. My three enthusiastic part-time helpers and the good humour between us meant we had a great social time, but we were trying to compete with big-budget teams and professional outfits. As far as moving my race career on was concerned, it was a disaster.

When you have had some success and think it comes easily, **don't be complacent**. This is a hugely important life lesson. The next leap up is likely to be tougher than anything you have achieved so far. It's OK to aim high, but you can't cross a chasm in two jumps. And two swallows don't make a summer.

An adventure in Europe

Spending the next couple of years trying to recover from my terrible 1997 season, I decided to go back to racing locally, so bought a Vauxhall Calibra Turbo to aim for outright wins in the Saloon Car Championship. Unfortunately, my choice of car was a poor one. It attracted lots of attention and spectators seemed to love it, but I soon discovered why it was the only one of its kind competing, anywhere in the world: it was very fast when it went, but ridiculously unreliable. Every time I drove it, I led my race, but often that honour lasted only a few yards. I achieved one outright win with the car in a wet race from the back of the grid, but the frustrations totally outweighed the results.

Be prepared for huge amounts of work if you buy or develop something unproven. Innovation is a wonderful thing, but it's tough, especially if you are doing it by yourself. A great life lesson is often to **see what everyone else is doing and improve on that**.

While I was contemplating what to do next, a friend told me about FISC, a championship he had discovered in Europe. It catered exclusively for MG Midgets and Austin Healey Sprites, cars which I'd had an interest in some years before when I attempted the restoration of an early example. He told me the series was partly subsidised with free ferry crossings and a beneficent attitude from the organiser who happened to compete in it himself. The biggest appeal was the chance to race at legendary circuits I could only previously have dreamt about, the greatest of those arguably being Spa-Francorchamps, the home of the Belgian Grand Prix.

I needed little more encouragement. Within days of learning of the series, I had managed to find a lovely race prepared Frogeye Sprite and was setting things in motion to compete in the 2002 season. The pound was very strong to the euro then, so I calculated I could do a season in Europe for the same or less cost than competing at my home circuit of Castle Combe. Another good lesson: **sometimes you have to look outside the box to get what you want.**

Five years later, after the greatest fun and adventures at Europe's top Grand Prix circuits, I completed 2007 and my years in the championship with a wonderful weekend at Monza where I put my Frogeye on pole position, winning the race after an epic duel and setting fastest lap. Even going to Monza (the home of the Italian Grand Prix) was something I thought I would never do. Winning there is an achievement I am unlikely to surpass.

One of the guys I met in FISC recently commented, "As with so much in life, do it before you cannot do it." LUD again. FISC doesn't exist anymore, so we were lucky to be part of it. The friends I made from it are more significant than any of the results or fantastic races, and most gratifying is two of the guys I used to compete against became my team mates in endurance racing, which gave us the opportunity to compete in a pair of Spa 24-hour races and two at the Silverstone Grand Prix circuit. And that same car I bought in 2001 is still a winner today.

Part Two

SOMETHING

CHAPTER 14

THINGS START TO CHANGE

As important as racing was (and is) to me, there was (and is) still a life to be led. When we left my day-to-day career, I was progressing up the ladder at the bank. While I was doing well by the standards of many of my contemporaries in the organisation, there was much about my job I found incredibly frustrating. Although I had the distraction of my radio work while at the Swindon branch, coupled with the challenge of acquiring my first house, I felt there must be a better way to progress in life.

Up until the 1980s, it seemed the only way for me to improve my situation financially was to live an extremely frugal life. But by being thoughtful and, hopefully, clever, I was still able to indulge in the things I wanted to do and I certainly didn't have a miserable existence. My hobby or, more accurately, my passion was being fulfilled and even exceeded in some ways.

But there is no denying, the tiny amount of money I was earning left no room whatsoever for luxuries. And if something went wrong, then it was very painful on the pocket. When you live with your parents, the fear of such things is hugely less significant. A person's place of residence is normally their biggest commitment and potential liability. An issue with your property often brings unexpected costs. If you live in a council house, as my parents did, your landlord will take care of most things. This is one of the principal reasons my parents refused to buy their council property as they could see no way of being able to meet the costs of things which might go wrong.

"What if the roof blows off, what would we do then?" my mum often asked. The fact such things can be insured against only made her more scared, as insurance was yet another cost she and my dad didn't have to cover.

For me, my source of unexpected cost was limited to my cars. Cars were far more fragile and potentially unreliable in those days than they are today. Even in the 1980s, making it to the end of your journey without some kind of drama was by no means guaranteed, particularly if you ran a car from the 1960s as my family and many others did. I serviced my cars myself and kept them in excellent condition, so generally I had few surprise expenses.

On the whole, I was insulated from the world of large expense and able to gradually build up my personal balance sheet. I needed a great deal of patience, but nevertheless, I was on track.

The fun of getting a mortgage

In the late 1970s while at the Bath Old Bank branch, I met a woman who was to become my first wife. She came from a totally different kind of family to me, but was also someone who chose to be a saver rather than a spender, so by the time we set up home together, we both had a decent amount of money to use as a deposit for a first house. This was not because we earned even average wages. Bank pay was well below the national average and everyone we knew earned more than us. We were able to save because we never went on holiday, only had a meal out twice a year (on our birthdays) and generally didn't spend on anything except absolute essentials.

My move to the Swindon Commercial Road branch from

Bath Old Bank was the push we needed to get our own place and, despite my take-home pay being £450 per month and hers £200, we managed to get a mortgage from the bank and buy a three-bed bay-windowed post-war semi in a very nice part of town for £25,250. We had a deposit of £7,650, a relatively large amount of money then, saved painstakingly over many years, so our mortgage was £17,600.

I was twenty-three at the time. One of the features of working for the bank was the ability to borrow money at what was then seen as a very low rate, some 2.5%. While at the time of writing, this is a good rate given current conditions, there are still plenty of people paying less than this if they locked into one of the ultra-low rates we grew accustomed to in the period leading up to 2021. But the world in the early 80s had not seen these low rates.

The other advantage was being able to borrow a relatively large amount compared with our salary. In my case, this worked out at 4x. Not hugely different from today, but good for the time.

However, the bank's rate was not necessarily the bargain it may have seemed to many staff. Offering a low-rate mortgage was a way of our employer tying us in. Whenever colleagues spoke about leaving the bank (an almost weekly occurrence as so many were dissatisfied), the ubiquitous question was "But what would I do about the mortgage?"

When you compare the house prices of today with those of forty or more years ago, you might say it was so much easier for a young person to get on the housing ladder then. Yes, it was easier than it is right now, but other factors placed significant obstacles before that young person. Perhaps the most important of those was the necessity to have a relationship with a building society or bank in order to be granted a mortgage. I remember my 'wealthy' uncle (he and his wife had their own terraced house) telling me when I got my first window cleaning job to open an account with a building society, explaining how it was essential to establish a relationship with lenders who, if I saved with them regularly, one day might see fit to give me a mortgage. How kind of them…

There was also something called mortgage rationing, dictated by the 'cartel' of lenders who determined what they made available to the market. As with lots of business in those days, lack of choice meant the customer had to go cap in hand and almost beg to be given what they wanted.

These days, lending is all about criteria. You either fit them or you don't. In those days, the main lending criterion was a man could only borrow a maximum of around 2.25x his salary and perhaps 1x the salary of his other half, if he was lucky. There was plenty of discrimination, as a woman's wage would never be taken into account in the same way as a guy's and sometimes not at all. Certainly, a woman was unlikely to be granted a mortgage in her sole name. The good old days, eh?

As it happened, my relationship with the building society came to nothing, as the bank which employed me was the obvious place to go for a mortgage. Because moving around the country from one branch to another, often far from our homes, was expected of us, the staff mortgage scheme was more or less essential as it would otherwise have been impossible to comply. The other big issue facing a first-time buyer was the peripheral costs of buying a property were relatively far higher than today. The bank recommended a solicitor from its client base who would supposedly look after us, but that didn't include any kind of help with the cost, as the bill for their basic legal work came out at more than my monthly wage. That was a huge amount of money. Although stamp duty was generally at a lower rate then, there was no free concession as there is today for a first-time buyer, so overall, the barriers to home ownership were considerable for a young person. Just as my parents had found, there was also the matter of the high costs of furniture and fittings compared with today. It's hard to believe now, but a kettle was about £15 – double what you can buy one for today, despite forty years of inflation.

As for furniture, we were fortunate as my dad was practical and would bring home damaged stuff from his job, and then repair it for us. We ended up with a very nice dining table set which I was still using in my holiday lets thirty years later.

The property bandwagon

So, by 1982, I was on the property ladder. I was twenty-five, which seems to be far younger than most people become homeowners these days. A significant factor in this is the trend to continue with education far beyond the age when I left school. This is commendable for young people who want to better themselves through education, a philosophy which is difficult to argue against as expanding one's knowledge and life experience can only be a good thing.

In many instances, the reasoning behind the exodus to uni is simple: get a decent qualification and a profession could be yours. But some who emerge from university end up doing more or less the same job they could have done at age sixteen or seventeen, while they've missed out on many years of income. Yes, they've obtained a different outlook on life and had a great time partying, but their personal balance sheet has probably slipped into the negative and can take a long time to recover.

Given property can be one of the most effective ways to build wealth, I make a strong argument for doing everything you can to jump on to that particular bandwagon as soon as possible. To keep this in context, if you leave school at the earliest age you can and spend the rest of your life in a job paying you minimum wage, it's not terribly likely you will be jumping on to anything except a cheap mattress in a rental property. But if you have some kind of entrepreneurial streak or driving ambition, why not get started on achieving your goals as soon as you are able?

As with many things in this complex life of ours, your decision will take into account a balance of two of my favourite factors: LUD and what's most important to you. Do you decide to do all you can to buy a property as soon as you can and give up most everything else to achieve that? Or are you confident you will emerge from uni with such a great qualification, you will leap into a highly paid job and be able to make up for all the non-earning years quickly?

Whatever you believe is likely to be true for you. You know what I did.

Gardening – the savings and the costs

My first house with my wife was in pretty good condition, but with potential to improve it and therefore increase its value. It had a prefabricated garage which was only just big enough to house a small car. My first idea was to remove the back of the garage and build a more permanent extension to it with concrete blocks. Apart from helping my dad lay a concrete path at our family house in Westfield when I was at school, I had no building experience, but having been brought up doing practical things, I reckoned it was just a case of applying common sense. So I did. I found it pretty hard work, especially the block laying which took me for ever, but eventually I had what I wanted. It might not have been the prettiest thing ever built, but it was hidden from the road in the back garden and allowed me the space I needed to work on my cars.

Another area which required a lot of hard work was the rear garden. Like many houses of that era, ours had a generous back garden, around 25–30 metres long and the same width as the property. The previous owners certainly hadn't been gardeners. The ubiquitous small lawned area and flower beds were OK, but the majority of it had been left to nature, so I wanted to maximise what I had.

So began the laborious process of digging every inch by hand to create something I could grow my own vegetables in. While this decision was partly down to cost saving, it was also something which just seemed normal and natural to me. I had helped my dad to do the same at home and we enjoyed the unrivalled taste of fresh produce which had been in the ground only hours before we ate it.

Luckily, my new next-door neighbour was an obsessive grower of plants. A Polish refugee old enough to be my father, he was not the most outgoing or talkative of men, but we became friendly and it seemed he admired and respected me for my work ethic. Quite often, we were the only two in the street working away in our gardens at silly times of the day.

His entire garden was given over to growing plants from seed, mostly in cold frames he had built from scratch and covered in plastic. He had become well known in the area, and in the spring and summer, a regular stream of customers would come to his door to buy both flower and vegetable plants. He was kind enough to give me lots of plants which were not quite presentable enough to sell, but with care could be nurtured into a decent life. Soon I had a wonderful garden full of colour and taste, and all it had cost me was my own labour and the ability to strike up a good **rapport** with my neighbour. The title of this book springs to mind yet again.

Actually, there was another cost. I was only in my mid-twenties, but after weeks of digging, I developed a bad back. I thought it would go away once I had stopped the bulk of the heavy work, but it didn't.

Eventually and reluctantly, I visited my GP, the first time for many years. My pain was severe enough for him to recommend an X-ray to see what was going on, and to my shock, the results were negative. The X-ray showed signs of extreme wear on one of my joints, and what I had thought was an injury from overuse turned out to be arthritis. The doctor suggested it was going to get worse and spread to other joints. His only remedy was painkillers.

This seemed impossible to me. Old people got arthritis. My dad didn't have a bad back. How could I? The surprise of the diagnosis certainly affected me, but perhaps not in the most obvious way. Almost instantly, I made a decision which has saved me from enduring a very different kind of life.

I am a firm believer in **whatever you imagine becomes your reality**. This is an invaluable life lesson. I just decided the doctor was wrong, I didn't have arthritis. It wouldn't slowly cripple me and I would find a way to manage my pain and do everything necessary to have a normal life.

I asked my GP if there were any exercises I could do to help, but his reaction told me this was something he had never considered. It was similar to when I asked the head of sport at the radio station who was covering motorsport. I knew straight away neither had an answer. The doctor demonstrated a somewhat comical swivelling of his hips, but he was so incongruent, it was obvious to me this was something he had made up on the spot. So I left, vowing not to take painkillers and to find a way to manage.

In brief, I didn't do too well for some years. I tried all kinds of exercise, some of which I now know made things worse. Most of them were to no avail and at best just kept me functioning. In the next twenty years, I had times where I couldn't walk due to the pain and lack of mobility, but eventually, I discovered an exercise regime which develops the supporting muscles, a brilliant physiotherapist, and therefore a solution.

So now, part of my daily routine is around 30 minutes of exercise which keeps my back in shape and puts me in a position where I am healthier and fitter than I was in Swindon in the early 1980s. I can ski faster and for longer than many people one-third my age, and I aim to continue to improve and perfect my fitness every day. And all it costs me is a bit of time...

Learning by doing

Four years passed by in that property, while my time at the Swindon branch of the bank saw me progressing at a pace I felt quite happy with. That period could be summed up as 'learning by doing', though in the interests of understanding how I built up my knowledge and experience, I will give you some of the fine detail.

The customary way we learnt a new task or position in our extremely busy branch was to be thrown in at the deep end to see how we managed. This suited me fine as I have always believed that is the best way to learn (though I draw the line at performing open-heart surgery). Strangely, at a lower level, we had a reasonable amount of hand holding while we learnt, especially as a cashier where the possibility of making a fool of ourselves and, more significantly, the bank was all too obvious. But as we progressed into ever more complex jobs, there was simply no time or manpower available to give us much training.

The kind of person who could learn quickly had a massive advantage. If we could be thrown into a job and still produce the goods, then it was likely we would be given more opportunities. This probably isn't exclusive to banks. If you want to get ahead in life, the best training you can do for yourself is to teach your mind how to learn. No doubt the brain and genes you were born with will have an influence on this, but like with many things, **your attitude will make more of a difference than almost anything else** and will therefore determine how you progress.

My first prestigious job was as manager's clerk to the sub-manager of the lending department. In those days, bank managers held real responsibility and the position was much admired and respected. It took most people many years to achieve even a sub-manager's position. My job taught me a lot about business and dealing with clients, and I found it extremely interesting. I must have performed well as I was soon promoted to the clerk supporting the main manager of the branch.

Like many managers of large branches, he exuded an aura of unapproachability and seriousness, and for a boy from a council house with only a few O levels to my name, this was a daunting job. But I took to it well, using the knowledge I had gained from my banking exams (see Chapter 10) and applying it to real-life situations. I recall my finest hour as spotting an error in the published accounts of a Public Limited Company which banked with us. It was a major embarrassment for the company and the bank kept it as quiet as it could, so my achievement was never acknowledged or mentioned, but must have been taken into account. This was evident when I was asked to step into a couple of jobs which were two levels above my pay grade.

Everyone at the bank was graded into one of five levels before becoming part of the management structure where we would have definite authority over those beneath us. Logically, we started as a grade one in the machine room. A cashier was a grade two and someone doing one of the more complex tasks such as managing the branch's foreign exchange business was a grade three. As a manager's clerk, I was a grade four.

Just below the sub-managers were the assistant branch accountants (ABAs) and branch accountants (BAs). The ABAs performed most of the lending tasks a sub-manager or even manager would do, but with let's say the lower end of the customer spectrum. The morning part of their job was poring over reams of paper data, produced daily, showing who was trying to go overdrawn without permission. The ABAs then had to do something about it, usually bouncing cheques (not allowing the cheque to be paid) and/or writing snotty letters to the customer. It was a mammoth task in a big branch, especially as everything was done manually. Four typists were stationed in our level and dealt with the dozens of letters the ABAs dictated every day. The Swindon branch had a staff of around sixty. These days, a branch that size operates with less than a handful of staff.

My opportunity came when someone was on holiday or off sick. They could have been one of the ABAs or someone above them whom they had to deputise for. With eight people at that management level, there was a regular gap to fill, so once I had shown I could do it, I was often slotted in. The daily challenge of assessing and managing those with fewer funds than they assumed or wished they had, taught me how rampant poor money management was. There was no internet, so people had to keep their own records of how much money they had and when it was going out of their accounts. They could come into the branch to get a statement printed out for them or access a small amount of detail from the cash point, but the availability of information was nothing like it is today, making money management even more important. It seemed to be a skill hundreds of our customers did not possess.

These days, your bank account will not allow you to make card payments or perform transfers when you have insufficient funds, but back then, you could (and still can in theory) issue as many cheques as you liked, regardless of whether you had the money to cover them. You could even come into the branch and encash a cheque without the necessary funds in your account. Incredible as it might seem today, the cashiers had no access to a customer's account balance, so every cashier had an A4 sheet of paper with a list of 'bad' customers to watch out for. If someone on the list tried to cash a cheque, the cashier had to go to the machine room and laboriously check the balance of their account to make sure they had the funds. If a cashier missed a bad customer and allowed them to cash a cheque with insufficient funds, the ABAs would find out and give that cashier a rollicking for what they had done.

The ABA job wasn't a particularly pleasant one in many ways, but it was a step up the ladder. So when I was asked to fill in, I jumped at the chance and took to it easily with almost no training. The two ABAs at Swindon were based in the same open-plan office as me and I had been watching and listening to what they got up to from day one. A little familiarisation with their procedures got me to a position where I was ready to start bouncing cheques and admonishing cashiers – the power!

All this was fine from an experience viewpoint, but did nothing for the money in my pocket. Our pay was solely determined by our grade and that had not changed. After the first year at the branch, I spent the rest of my time there mainly performing duties above my grade, but never earnt a penny more for doing so. I thought it would put me in a line for a big promotion when the opportunity arose. Hmmm…

Attitude is everything

After proving myself as an ABA on the lending side, I was given a chance at the same position in the administration department on the ground floor. This was the area behind the cashiers where huge numbers of tasks which no longer exist were performed, mainly by grade threes. Banks looked after clients' stocks and shares, buying and selling them and making recommendations, while also buying and selling foreign currency. The most complex task was managing the bureaucracy of foreign exchange controls for the business clients who exported or imported goods. I had done this and the stock clerk job at Bath Old Bank and enjoyed it, despite – or perhaps because of – the complexity.

The job of the ABA overseeing the administration department was to sign off anything of importance. The clerks would prepare everything, but it was the ABA's responsibility to give it the authorisation to go ahead. This was arguably the area where the potential for loss was the greatest. A cock-up on a large foreign exchange transaction could cost the bank dearly, while a bank draft issued incorrectly could have a devastating effect on either the client, the bank or both.

The other part of the ABA's job was to watch out for fraud amongst the staff. As most tasks were performed manually, everything had to be checked. This could be an onerous task with the potential for long delays while the checks took place. Occasionally, staff would be found to be cheating the system and lining their pockets, which I guess justified the amount of time the ABAs spent checking. Two people at the Swindon branch were caught while I was there, and another shortly after I left. None of them were reported to the police as the bank preferred to keep such things quiet. And the amounts involved were relatively small, just a few hundred pounds in each case.

Although I was inexperienced at the ABA level, I had a great knowledge of the jobs I was overseeing, so I approached the task knowing what the short cuts and errors could be. It was just a case of looking out for them and making sure nothing slipped through. For a grade three working on the foreign desk, for example, the efficiency of the ABA made a huge difference to their day. Some were super-efficient, while others…

It soon became obvious to me the job was overwhelmingly a delicate balance between making sure everything had been done correctly and not pissing off the people beneath me by being too picky. This was a fine line to tread, but just as there were good and bad ABAs, the quality of those I oversaw also varied immensely. I soon worked out who I had to watch very carefully and who could be trusted to get on with the job. It was a time of my life where I really started to understand why some people are successful and others are not.

When you are on the shop floor with other workers, you see how different people operate in different ways and realise small things can make a huge difference. Like a cashier keeping their till tidy, for example. In a position of authority, especially when this involves much checking of what others are doing, the differences in quality are even more evident. There are multiple reasons why this is the case, probably millions of experiences which contribute to these differences, but if there was one overwhelming factor I had to choose, it would be **attitude**. As an ABA, I knew who had a good attitude and who didn't. And guess which ones progressed the faster?

One of my biggest life lessons has been to realise most people only need to be slightly above average to succeed. We don't need to be superstars, but if we have the right attitude and can show we are at least as good as those around us, perhaps slightly better, we will progress.

So, I was on a roll. I already knew I was on a senior management career path as I had been selected for a particular programme which identified those who were going somewhere. Being moved around between branches was a key element of this and, so far, I had complied. But there was one thing on the horizon which I dreaded: being moved far away from the area I had grown up in. Swindon had been a lucky move for me. It was only an hour from all my old haunts and thanks to my local radio work, my motor sport passion was almost completely fulfilled.

And then it happened. I was called into the manager's office and told I was being promoted to a position at the Plymouth branch. I tried to sound pleased, but there was an important factor involved.

My wife was one of twins and extremely close to her sister, who lived in Chippenham, only thirty minutes or so from us, so she was able to see her regularly. And her father was also in range in Bath. The news, therefore, was not well received. Let's just say there was not a chance my wife would move to Plymouth.

This helped me in a strange way. While I was reluctant to move, my sights were still set on a great career with the bank, so I could have lived with my reservations and accepted the position. But my wife's opinion tipped the scales the other way. I had no choice but to decline, knowing this could well halt my career progression and put me back to inching my way up the ladder at a snail's pace.

As I expected, my decision to decline the move did not go down well. There were very few instances of male staff turning down such offers and from then on, the bank's attitude towards me changed. As did something else in my life…

CHAPTER 15

AND CHANGE THEY DID

Although the work I was doing at Swindon didn't change too much after I declined the promotion, something at home certainly did. My wife became pregnant. And almost immediately, the bank decided I would be moved after all, but to the Bath Stuckeys branch. I didn't have a problem with this as it meant I would be much closer to the area I wanted to be and I could have a house move paid for. This was one of the few areas where the bank was generous. With a little ingenuity, we employees could do quite well out of it.

We were never told too much about what we might be doing at our new branch, but it seemed I would be clerk to the main manager there. This was a job I could do easily, but it was a kind of demotion. The branch, while still a prestigious one of reasonable size, was smaller than Swindon and had no clients of the calibre of the PLCs I had been used to.

But for the moment, all my thoughts were towards the new baby and trying to find another house before he or she came along. Luckily, the bank would offer its staff a free bridging loan to assist with such moves. That meant my wife and I could find a new house without having to sell our existing one. We simply had our house valued and, based on that value and the amount of new mortgage we could afford, we had a budget and could start looking. Our house had increased in value, partly through house price inflation and partly down to the improvements I had made, so we expected to get around £35,000. A nice little profit in only three years. My long road towards improving my lot through property had begun.

My preference was to buy a place in Bath. It would be close to my work, family and old friends, and everything I was interested in. I had calculated we could move up to a nice, detached property in a good area, even in Bath which is one of the most expensive places in the South West. But that was not going to happen. My wife was adamant she wanted to be close to her sister in Chippenham. She even wanted to live on the same housing estate, which happened to be mainly ex-local authority.

As a compromise, I agreed we would move to Chippenham, as long as we found a decent house at the top of our price range. There was no way I was going to move downmarket, even though my wife was extremely risk averse and would have felt comfortable with a smaller mortgage and a more modest house. Looking back now, I see this was where our differing aspirations began to cause cracks in our relationship.

Eventually, we found a really nice detached three bed on probably the best estate in Chippenham. It had a huge garden, room to improve and was within walking distance of the railway station. I did a deal with the vendor at what I thought was a good price of £50,500. This was 1985. It meant increasing our mortgage but, while I had received only modest wage increases in my time at Swindon, our frugal lifestyle and close managing of our finances meant we could cope with the new repayments quite easily.

Chippenham was about thirty minutes' drive from Bath and just about the same from Swindon, so eyebrows were raised in the bank when I put forward my house move application.

Normally, when the bank provided assistance with a move, it expected its member of staff to live close to the branch they worked at. But I gave the management the story my wife needed to be near her sister so she could help with the new baby, and my application was accepted.

We were only in the house for a short time before Rachael came along. I was twenty-eight and had little idea about raising a family or what looking after a baby might involve. I wasn't anywhere near ready to deal with it, but as with most things in my life, I wouldn't change a thing about it. The biggest shock was discovering Rachael was a very demanding child, making her presence felt from the minute she arrived, using the medium of crying almost without a break, day and night.

Despite my extreme fatigue from lack of sleep, I still wanted to improve our lot. The house needed plenty of redecoration, which I tackled in earnest and had soon transformed it into a very comfortable place. And although there was a small garage attached, I decided to build another detached garage on some unused land on the side. I was determined to have somewhere big enough to house a car project, perhaps a race car one day.

Settling at Bath Stuckeys

Meanwhile, the new job was rather less fulfilling. I had gone from being an up-and-coming man on the move to someone doing just another job, albeit an important one. I quickly realised I was there simply to do this one job, day in, day out. No variety and no opportunity to fill in at the higher levels.

Additionally, my manager was an old-fashioned, traditional type. He addressed all the male staff by their surnames, sometimes preceded by Mr, but he was usually in such a foul mood, the start of an interaction tended to be "Moon!" booming out of his office. To say the relationship was formal would be an understatement, though managers like him were not unusual in those days. But I was determined to win his respect, so I guessed the only way to make my life easier was to **establish a good reputation** as fast as possible. It was head down and work hard to gain his trust from day one.

That part seemed to work well and I soon found my feet. The work was somewhat tedious and many of the bank's procedures seemed ridiculously old fashioned, but once I had organised myself, I found enough time to devote to my radio work during the spare moments of the day. Although my broadcasts were only weekly, they still needed a reasonable amount of preparation, and the motor sport slot required quite a lot of research and gathering of information, mainly by calling competitors and event organisers. With a young, demanding baby, I had no time to do any of these things at home, so I had to find a way to do them while I was supposed to be doing my day job.

Looking back, I find it intriguing I was able to juggle these two opposing forces, especially with a manager as strict as mine. I remember on a few occasions being on the phone to one of my motor sport contacts with my manager pacing in and out of his office, becoming more and more impatient as I kept him waiting. How did I get away with it? I can only say it was due to establishing my initial reputation. If that kind of thing had happened early in my time there, the situation would have been different. But luckily, I had a few weeks before Rachael was born in which to put everything into my new job and gain the manager's trust. By the time Rachael arrived, my feet were under the table.

A harsh introduction to property investing
One of the bonuses of being transferred to Bath was Adrian, a friend I had made at my first branch in Midsomer Norton. He had been based at Stuckeys for some time, so filled me in

on what to watch out for. Adrian had an interest in cars and I'd introduced him to the world of motor sport, firstly through the local Autograss club and later to other parts of the sport. He knew my oldest friend Dave well, and the three of us formed a close friendship which still exists today. I really value it.

Adrian eventually found himself sitting opposite me in his new role as clerk to the assistant manager. This was great in many ways, especially when Adrian mentioned something which turned out to be highly significant to me.

It transpired some of his clients were property investors in Bath, buying houses and letting them, mainly to students. The term 'buy to let' did not exist then, but essentially, that was the market they were in. And one of the few sources of finance available to them was the bank. Building societies were too conservative to lend on such speculative ventures.

Adrian and I started chatting about this. It seemed these landlords were doing well out of their speculation. The property boom of the 1980s had started, so the idea of owning a second house which was paid for by someone else and might grow in value was appealing.

Adrian and I decided we should do something, ideally involving Dave as well. Dave was still living at home with his parents, so was the ideal candidate to be a front man for our purchase. He could buy it in his name with a residential mortgage, but it would effectively be owned and run by the three of us.

We began a search and found a two-bed flat just off the prestigious Pulteney Street in Bath, one of the best locations in the city. We agreed a deal at somewhere around £27k sometime in 1986. That little flat would be worth more than 10x that now. The deposit was only a few hundred each, so it was a painless way of getting our first investment property.

Dave was earning more than enough to obtain a mortgage

to buy the place and soon it was ours. Was this a somewhat foolish and risky venture? After all, Adrian and I had invested our money in a property which belonged to someone else, who could easily walk away and leave us with nothing. But I had known Dave since we were eleven and I had total trust in him, as I did Adrian. So the answer to the question is, it depends on the circumstances.

Breaking/bending the rules is almost essential if you want to get anywhere in life from a standing start. We had no idea about how to let a property, or anything else about buying to let for that matter, but after a couple of disastrous attempts at renting it to tourists, we found two student sisters to occupy the flat. We had kitted it out with second-hand furniture and, in our usual style, managed to get it up and running without spending anything significant on it.

Almost without us noticing, property prices started to increase strongly, particularly at the end of 1988 and into 1989. By then, I had changed jobs twice (more of that later) and Adrian had moved branches to Gloucester. He was performing a similar role as he had before, but this time some of his clients were speculating short term on the growth of house prices in the boom time of the mid-1980s. The idea was to buy off plan, and then sell at a profit as soon as the property deal went through.

Buying off plan means committing to the purchase of a property which is not yet built and probably only exists as a drawing. It's a popular ploy for developers to encourage buyers to acquire their perfect plot on a new estate, snapping up the best houses in advance. If this is for your own occupation, it's a reasonable thing to do and often essential if you want to get in at the outset. But as a speculative purchase, it has some potentially large risks attached, the biggest of which is a property price crash.

Guess what happened in 1990? After the UK joined the European Exchange Rate Mechanism, one of the biggest crashes in house prices of all time came with it, arguably the one with the most significant impact on homeowners. Lenders foreclosed on distressed borrowers, creating a fear of both the housing market and the cost of mortgage borrowing. The pain was felt by many for years.

As you may now have guessed, our trio got in on the boom. There were huge new housing developments being built around Gloucester, so we decided that was the place to buy, not factoring into account the possibility of oversupply. The thought of prices falling hardly entered our minds. A weekend trip to Gloucester found us a little three-bed terraced house and we put down a deposit to secure it, with completion only a few months away. We would sell it as soon as we had completed and pocket a nice profit.

There was the small matter of financing it. By then, I was in the mortgage business in my new role, acting as a broker, but the investment property market was still new and I just couldn't find a lender to assist. So I did something which I now see as incredibly stupid, but it seemed to be a reasonable risk at the time.

My family home in Chippenham had more than doubled in value since we'd moved in, so I found a lender who would give me as much money as I wanted as long as I didn't borrow more than 75% of the property's value. Such deals were known as 'self-certification'. There were no questions about my income, or much else really, and soon a nice lump of money was on its way to enable us not only to buy the new house outright, but to pay off Dave's mortgage on the Bath flat, as he wanted to buy something for his own occupation.

I had taken on a huge risk, with all the liability for the borrowing solely down to me. We didn't even draw up any kind of agreement between us, but these were guys I knew well and we trusted each other implicitly. I wouldn't recommend doing it that way to anyone else. When you're entering into any kind of financial/business relationship with others, it's really important if not essential to draw up a partnership agreement to cover all the eventualities which might occur. I advise my clients on this all the time.

Nevertheless, our plan would have worked out just fine if the completion date for the house had not been deferred and deferred, time and again. Those delays to completion saw the boom period pass over, and then the market plummeted in 1990. By the time we had completed, prices had fallen 10% or more and we were stuck with the house. Our choices were to either sell at a loss, which none of us wanted to do, or hold on to the property and rent it out in the hope the value might recover. We decided on the latter, utilising a local agent. But the rent would not even cover the mortgage (interest rates went skyrocketing to around 15%) and the tenants trashed the place. We kept it for a few years, but eventually had to throw in the towel, selling it at a small loss having learnt a number of lessons. Luckily, our Bath flat had retained a lot of its value, so once that was also sold (much later on), we had made money overall.

One of the biggest lessons we learnt was when you buy something desirable of which there is limited supply (like the Bath flat), there will almost always be a market for it. When you buy something which is one of many thousands (the Gloucester house), it can be difficult to move on again when the market isn't booming.

It was all good experience. Despite the failure of the Gloucester house project, I was still theoretically keen on trying to make money with property. But a few things got in the way before I was able to have another go…

CHAPTER 16

IF YOU THOUGHT THAT WAS CHANGE

It didn't take me too long to become disillusioned with my job in Bath. I felt I had become just another employee of the bank. The recognition I'd had at Swindon was gone. Stuckeys was too small for there to be any openings where I could gain experience, and I could see myself stagnating.

What should I do? I couldn't influence my situation with the bank. I wouldn't move to another area, I had already worked at the two most prestigious branches in my region, and the regime at my current branch was like something from the 1950s.

I looked at various possibilities, but kept hearing about other staff moving to an up-and-coming bank which had just started emerging from its old-fashioned guise. I guessed it would want people with my kind of experience and I was right. I made an application, had a couple of interviews and a job offer was forthcoming.

The bank would be moving into commercial lending, having only previously serviced personal customers. My experience would be valuable and I was told my career path would be straight and fast. Unfortunately, the bank had very few large branches, so I would need to join an even smaller one than I was used to, to learn its systems. Being offered a position in a small branch in Trowbridge was not the level of progress I was happy with, but I was frustrated where I was, so it seemed I had to make a change, even though it wasn't quite the leap I was hoping for.

It's often better to take something less than perfect and use it as a stepping stone to something else, rather than do nothing and hope the situation you are in will magically change. **Stagnation is the enemy of progress.**

I soon realised my new employer had some way to go to become a credible rival to its big brothers. My manager and sub manager were both decent people, but nowhere near the calibre of staff I had been used to working with. The manager's usual modus operandi when presented with a new business case was to sit on it for a week, mulling it over before declining to help. He was so cautious and unskilled in assessment, it was easier for him to say no than to take a risk. Once again, my job was to support him and sometimes fill in for the sub-manager who had a dual role of managing the admin side of the branch and controlling the lending for most of the personal customers. I found it less than challenging and somewhat frustrating to deal with cases which I thought were straightforward while those above me perceived them as a big challenge.

However, there was one area where this bank was light years ahead of its rivals. This aspect made the move worthwhile and lay the foundations for a new career which lasted me for over thirty years. Lesson learnt: **never judge anything until you truly know the full implications.**

Sales skills

One of the keys to the bank's success was its ability to cross sell products to its existing clients. The main high street banks had an array of other products, such as insurance, pensions and investments, but these were virtually ignored. In contrast, my new employer made promoting these products a core part of what every staff member was required to do, years before the other banks cottoned on to this.

Moreover, each branch had an in-house salesperson who was remunerated almost entirely from the products they sold. The staff were supposed to identify opportunities to refer customers to the salesperson. It was the customer-facing cashiers who had the main opportunity to do this by chatting to people to see if they could provide leads. But more often than not, it simply came down to using a spurious excuse to refer customers to the salesperson, who then set about their pitch.

Unlike most of the staff, who hated the pressure of sales, I found it interesting and was keen to know more. The bank sent me on a few courses where I learnt some very valuable and useful techniques, and I was rather good at engaging with customers, finding out if they had a need and then putting them in front of our salesperson, who would fulfil it. We both benefitted, the salesperson from the extra commission from the clients I sent his way, and me from listening to him and learning a new skill.

But there was still an elephant in the room. It was one I had chosen to ignore when I made the move, which shows how a giant pachyderm can live in your vicinity without you noticing when you are focused on something else. It was inevitable it would show itself eventually, though, and just before my second anniversary at Trowbridge, it did.

Any easy decision

I was to be promoted to an assistant manager's position... at the Yeovil branch. This was a decent size office and it was a leap which would have taken me many years with my previous employer, even if I had complied with its 100% commitment regime. So I was torn. I discussed it with my wife and decided I would accept, travelling to Yeovil during the week and returning home at weekends. It wasn't ideal, especially as our second child,

Sarah, was on the way. But it was doable. I then told my wider family and prepared myself accordingly, only for another offer to arrive totally unexpectedly...

As you may remember, my sister's husband, Maurice, met Jackie through me. Our joint love of motor sport soon saw Maurice integrated into my group of friends, and then my family. But Maurice's background was the polar opposite to ours. His father, despite coming from humble beginnings, had built from scratch one of the most successful businesses in the area, mainly selling new and used cars. He had multiple outlets, and over the years, his dealerships encompassed Ford, BMW, Alfa Romeo and Vauxhall.

By the late 1980s, Maurice's father had semi-retired from the business, leaving Maurice and one of his brothers to run it day to day. One of the most successful parts of it was a finance company which had been set up by Maurice's father to finance the cars the dealerships sold. Like many aspects of the family business, this was an unusually forward thinking and impressive achievement, and would be extremely difficult to replicate these days without a substantial amount of backing.

One of the secrets to its success was the ability of the guy running it. I don't know what his background was, but he ran a very tight ship and had built a strong business with an impressively low default rate (the percentage of clients who didn't make their payments compared with the total amount loaned). But his conservative approach and somewhat blunt nature meant the working relationship with Maurice and his brother wasn't perfect. Plus, he was coming up to retirement age.

Unbeknown to me, the news of my move to Yeovil prompted Maurice and his brother to consider replacing their finance man with me. Within days of receiving the promotion offer from my employer, I had another to consider.

It was an easy decision. Being part of a much smaller outfit, where my input could directly influence what happened, was the main attraction. Working with people I knew and respected was a close second. Maurice's office was still just under an hour's drive from Chippenham, but it was a lot better than the long trek to Yeovil.

To give me some introduction to the business, a handover period was arranged. This turned out to be a perfunctory explanation of the basics – all useful, but it did not prepare me at all for the horrors of car finance, which can trap the unwary. I sensed there was an air of resentment from the departing finance man, which was understandable given how long he had worked for the family. Being replaced by a relative of your bosses can never feel great.

Car finance – a whole new minefield

I had been used to dealing with customers who were generally honest and upright. Banks were much more formal places in those days and there were huge numbers of people (like my parents) who did not have bank accounts. While we had to be careful when underwriting a lending proposition, we had lots of information about the person making the application and it was rare to assist anyone who didn't have a decent track record.

The world of car finance was somewhat different. And looking back on it now, I see my personality type was not at all suitable for the task. Dealing solely with the clients brought to the finance company from the garages' own business was not really a problem. All the lending was done on hire purchase, so the car acted as security. Maurice's brother was very good at valuing vehicles and we never lent more than we could realistically expect to sell the car for. The flow of business was strong and everything was dandy for a year or two.

It was when we started attracting business from outside

the family garage the problems began. I was totally naïve to the pitfalls this might bring and, without going into lots of detail, I was completely conned by some very unscrupulous and shady individuals. My optimistic nature always sees the positive possibilities in whatever situation is presented to me. So when someone gave me the opportunity to write huge amounts of new business, seemingly guaranteed by them, my instinct was to run with it.

What could go wrong?

As it happened, almost everything. The people I was dealing with were nothing short of crooks. It transpired the deals were not at all what they appeared and soon, it was obvious we had a very big problem.

It was then I realised why my predecessor had the kind of character he had. To stay alive in that business, you need a pessimistic and inherently suspicious nature. That was the opposite to me. Not being warned about the potentially catastrophic consequences of getting things wrong didn't help, but I'm not sure a warning would have made too much difference as my 'possibility thinking' might have been too strong to resist.

Somewhat luckily, though it seemed almost irrelevant at the time in the light of the problems on the finance side, I had been using some of the skills I had learnt to cross sell other products to the finance company's clients, typically life insurance, income protection, mortgages, pensions, and car and home insurance. It wasn't anything to write home about, but it was a thread that was gradually growing and was something I enjoyed doing, despite working long hours to fit in the car finance in the day and seeing clients in the evenings. I wanted to be a one-stop shop who could provide anything financial the average person needed.

Although this was positive in one way, working in the evenings kept me away from my young family and I began to realise my marriage was not what it should be. And the more time I spent away from home, the more I felt something needed to change. I began staying with my parents during the week (they lived close to the office), ostensibly so I could see my clients, but it also meant I did not have to return home. I would only go back at the weekends.

The more I did this, the more I wanted something different. I knew I was ambitious, but my wife's contentment came from having zero risk and staying well within her comfort zone. I couldn't achieve the things I wanted with that kind of handbrake, but I was pulled back into the family situation by my two little girls, whom I adored. It was an incredibly hard time and, looking back now, I'm not sure how I managed to get through.

When it was clear the finance company needed serious help, the brothers made the correct decision to reappoint my predecessor to oversee the mess and see what he could do to retrieve the situation. He had so much more experience than me, and I was so shell shocked at the extent of people's dishonesty, there was little I could have realistically done to help.

Despite my ineptitude, the brothers offered me an office to work from at their premises, so I could continue with the financial services business. It was more than generous in the circumstances, but it didn't feel comfortable. Just down the corridor was someone working on sorting out my mess, so I was constantly reminded of the terrible situation I had overseen.

Additionally, another seemingly positive opportunity had come into my life. In reality, it was not all it seemed, but at the time, it appeared exciting and full of potential.

More learning from failure

As you will recall, Dave, Adrian and I owned a flat in Bath which we were renting to two sisters, students at the university. I would occasionally speak to one of them, usually regarding a small issue which needed fixing, but a couple of times, she mentioned a new business she and her sister were setting up. I later realised she was pitching to get me involved. She was either clever in sowing seeds or simply not confident enough to ask me directly, but either way, I eventually took the bait and asked what it was.

She revealed very little other than saying it involved clean air and water, which I found interesting. **Holding back information and not giving too much away can be an effective technique to draw people in.** For a few years, I had increasingly been looking at better eating and health. Such focuses are commonplace now, but in the late 80s, it was rare to meet anyone who cared about whether what they ate, drank or breathed made any difference to their health. If you had mentioned it to anyone from the council estate I grew up on, you would probably have been beaten up…

It's funny how introductions to new ideas come out of the blue, if you are open to them. We are exposed to such things constantly, but most of the time, we ignore them or dismiss them for various reasons. Adrian's parents had split up and his dad's new girlfriend was what we would then have called a health freak. I remember Adrian telling me she had said sugar was bad for us. This was a revelation. My dad had a 10mm layer of sugar on his Weetabix every day. We got through so much of it, my mum was obsessed with not running out. At one point in the dire period of the 1970s when the country was going to the dogs, there was fear of a sugar shortage, so my mum persuaded my dad to convert a wasted section of our kitchen cupboards into a place where she could stack dozens of bags. It looked like a wall of the stuff. Today, half a bag of sugar has been hanging around in one of our cupboards for a decade.

Adrian's sugar comment resonated with me, so I became even more open to ideas on healthy living. I gradually reduced my sugar intake to almost nil and was much more conscious of what I was eating and drinking, discovering a useful bonus of cutting out or reducing various things: I saved a bit of money. Therefore, I was intrigued to find out about clean air and water, and how two young students could make any money out of it. It transpired they couldn't, but more on that later.

The next thing I knew, I was watching a professional video at home in Chippenham while a filter was being connected to my water tap in the kitchen. A little box in the living room was blowing out clean air which had gone through a high-tech purifier. If you've experienced something similar or one of your friends has started telling you about the amazing health products they are now using, then you may have already guessed I was being drawn into the world of network marketing. I knew almost nothing about it prior to my introduction, which was lucky for the girls, as many people get burnt by it and pitching to someone with prior knowledge of it is likely to end in failure. But I had no such preconceptions and was looking for something to move into which might make my fortune.

For a while, the company behind these products was almost a household name. It seemed everyone was either involved in it or hated it with a passion. Most of its products were of average quality and effectiveness, yet sold for extraordinarily high prices. The water filter attachment for your tap was the best and best known, yet I buy an almost identical product right now for less than it sold for in the 1990s.

Whatever anyone might have thought about it, network marketing was very cleverly executed. The clever part was getting ordinary people to use the products themselves and recommend them to their friends and family. There was much sophistication behind that simple concept, and the training and backup available (at a price – which was where the experienced network marketers actually earned much of their money) was superb. I got involved, bought huge amounts of product, moved quickly up the sales league, and then discovered like nearly everyone else involved with that company did eventually, everything fizzles out almost as quickly as it starts.

The company the sisters drew me in to has long been out of business, but the concept of network marketing is still going on in other guises. It can ruin people's lives and cause all kinds of upset between friends and families. Yet the indoctrination and training are extremely clever. I learnt so much about sales which I was completely ignorant of before and I carry some of those lessons with me to this day.

Above all, I grasped the importance of working on oneself. We all have enormous potential if we are prepared to put in the hard work to improve our skills. I was lucky in that I became hooked on learning everything I could about self-improvement, lapping up inspirational books, attending seminars and getting insights into what I needed to be successful. So although network marketing made me no money whatsoever, I don't regret being involved. I also wouldn't advocate anyone to try to make their fortune from it. It's better at helping you lose one. The sisters had to give up their degree studies, and the flat in Bath, and I often wonder how much they regret their involvement.

The theory of network marketing is to build up a vast network of people, just like you, all selling a few products from which everyone benefits. You are given lots of what I now see as disingenuous information to convince you what fantastic value the products are – because there are no expensive shops or retail outlets to finance, you are buying them at less than a normal trade price. In reality, though, many levels in the network, both above and below you, are taking a cut of the profits, so the products would have to be more expensive than elsewhere. But the fact there were no or very few other products like them at the time meant the opportunity to deceive was enormous.

I was one of those who was deceived, but I'm certain I would not have been as successful as I have subsequently been without the fundamental things I learnt in my network marketing days. The overarching life lesson I took away from this difficult time: **be open to learn from every experience, however painful it might be**. It's an essential part of growing and improving. If you don't try new things and fail at some of them, you aren't going anywhere.

CHAPTER 17

THE WORLD OF SELF-IMPROVEMENT

In the mid-1980s I recall seeing an advertisement for a book which would teach me how to become a millionaire. That may still be a goal for many people, though with the inflation we have experienced since then (particularly to house prices), often they are paper millionaires anyway simply through buying a house and living in it.

Back then, I only knew of one millionaire outside of the clients at the bank. The ability to create wealth didn't exist to the degree it does today. I could have a very long argument about why that is and whether it's a good thing or not, but I will summarise my beliefs by saying, "A rising tide floats all boats". Without a liberated capitalist economy of the type we have enjoyed over the last forty years, we would all be much worse off. There would also be less of a gap between rich and poor. But by most metrics and perceptions, people today who call themselves poor have a better standard of living than yesterday's averagely well off, I know which type of society I prefer. Surely, it's better to accept more inequality in exchange for the vast majority being better off? Have a look at how the masses fare in almost every communist regime if you don't agree.

I initially resisted buying the book, but kept seeing the advert for it. Eventually, I succumbed, demonstrating the power of repeated exposure to something. You can wear anyone down if you keep at it long enough. But I can't emphasise too strongly how difficult a decision it was for me to send off my cheque. My wife and I budgeted our income down to the last penny and there was simply no spare money for such things, but something drove me to make the purchase.

Upon the book's arrival, my initial reaction was one of disappointment and the feeling I might have been conned. It was a thin paperback, not the substantial tome I'd expected from the advert making its grandiose claims. Nevertheless, despite its apparent lack of presence, I had spent my precious £10, so I delved into the book to see what I could learn.

Again, I was initially underwhelmed. I recall a trend from the beginning which indicated mindset was one of the most important things to work on if I truly wanted to change my life. This had little resonance with me at the time. I had been brought up to believe we were all victims of our circumstances. Everything we had or did not have was because of where we found ourselves – in my case, at the bottom of the pile. Successful people, the government, God, 'they' and just about anyone else I believed was doing better than me wanted to keep us workers in our place, make sure we didn't succeed and work us to exhaustion for minimum reward. When much of that has been the case for the vast majority of time humans have been on earth, I can understand why it was intrinsic in my parents. But the book was one of my first exposures to an alternative point of view.

The other theme running through the book was the importance of writing down what you want to achieve. You will likely recall from Chapter 7 the little note I wrote when I got my first window cleaning job at age fifteen, my initial foray into goal setting. I had no idea then how powerful this technique is or even whether it would make any difference to me whatsoever, but with an open mind, I thought it sensible to make a promise to myself which might then help me, especially when temptation, distraction or challenges presented themselves.

To discover a book which told me this is one of the key ways to change my life completely was a revelation. I still didn't believe it would make much of a difference, but it would only cost me a bit of time to do it, so why not give it a go? I had to write down ten goals I wanted to achieve. Unlike my note from my teens, I have lost my original list of ten goals, but they were quite ambitious for where I was then (especially for someone who was supposed to think himself lucky he was not in the poor house). At the time, the piece of paper with these goals on lived in the cupboard next to my bed and I read them every night.

My nightly ritual

I also started refining something else I had been doing every night since I was a teenager. No, not that – something in my head.

My mum was full of superstition, and much of her life was governed by what we used to call old wives' tales which were linked to religious or controlling beliefs. From when we were very young, my mum had suggested Jackie and I say our prayers at night before going to sleep. I don't ever recall being forced to do this, or even encouraged particularly strongly, but I had been doing it for as long as I could remember. There was one thing my mum was extremely skilled at, which was showing total congruence with her beliefs, a feature inherent in her family. Most of the Tamblyns have a firm idea about themselves and what they know, and there is nothing you can do to sway them.

When you encounter someone who is 100% convinced of a certain belief with every fibre of their being, and acts and speaks firmly and strongly about that belief, it can be very powerful. It can also be very destructive when the belief doesn't serve you particularly well. Hitler is perhaps the best/worst example, empowering and encouraging people to do unspeakable things because of his unwavering congruency with his crazed beliefs.

As children, we are not only learning machines, absorbing everything coming our way, which is how we all develop our method of being and making sense of the world, we are also susceptible to what could be called brainwashing. We take in inputs from **influencers**, whether they be parents or Russian propaganda departments inventing stories on Facebook, then build our neural networks accordingly. When our neural networks are strong enough, they become unshakeable convictions it's almost impossible to dismantle. When such convictions are formed using neither logic nor reason, it's pointless using logic or reason to dismantle them. The problem with trying to point this out to someone who has this kind of thinking is they tend to believe it's you – along with everyone else – who is brainwashed, so a circular argument is inevitable.

Everyone is good at something and my mum's specialist skill was forming unshakeable convictions which only God Himself would be able to question. She had an entire library of them stored away in her brain, and she passed them on to her children. So this explains why, every night before I went to sleep, I used to say a few prayers.

The Lord's Prayer was one of them. I could rattle through it on autopilot at huge speed in my head, so I never actually listened to what I was saying. I just had to get through it so God wouldn't do something nasty to me. There was, however, another prayer which was rather more positive. I'm happy to report I still say a version of it every night, unless I've had rather too much to drink. It is not what religious people would call a prayer as I rejected all organised religions many years ago. What my 'prayer' consists of are positive statements of gratitude, reinforcements of powerful attitudes and perhaps goals as well.

But the prayer which has been with me most of my life relates to those closest to me whom I love and want to prosper. The words are simple, but they express my gratitude to certain significant people who either are or have been part of my life. They include the usual suspects, along with one or two who could be regarded as insignificant, but have added to my life in a small yet important way.

I regret nothing. Even if I were able to use a time machine to alter one tiny element of my life, I wouldn't. It might change my current situation significantly. I am happy exactly where I have ended up and my nightly 'prayers' express my gratitude accordingly.

Positive influences

I've revised and edited my pre-sleep recitations many times over the years. As I've progressed in life, I have achieved goals which were important early on, so they have been replaced by other mantras and goals. In my time at Chippenham when my elder daughter was old enough to understand such things, I taught her a longish but powerful poem called 'Thinking'. It has helped me improve my confidence and I hope hers too:

If you think you are beaten, you are,
If you think you dare not, you don't,
If you'd like to win but think you can't, it's almost certain you
won't.
If you think you'll lose, you've lost.
For out of this world we find
Success begins with a fellow's will – it's all in the state of mind.
If you think you're outclassed, you are.
You've got to think high to rise,
You've got to be sure of yourself before you can ever win a prize.
Life's battles don't always go to the stronger or faster man,

But sooner or later the man who wins, is the one who thinks he
*   can.*[8]

With mantras, the strange thing is you don't need to understand them completely or for them to be 'true' to have an effect. As long as they serve you positively, they will help you. What you need to do is repeat them regularly, and by that I mean at least daily, ideally when you are relaxed and have time enough to take them in, which is why just before going to sleep is ideal. After weeks or months of so doing, you will hopefully find a change will occur. It may only be very subtle, but something will change.

Your brain can be programmed and re-programmed in a similar way to a computer, believe it or not. It's happening every minute of the day. When you talk to negative people, watch or listen to the news and social media (it's almost all negative in some direct or indirect way) and say unhelpful things to yourself, all you are doing is strengthening your subconscious belief that life is shit. That's not going to help you do anything except limit your potential.

I'm going to talk a lot more about internal dialogue later in the book. Here are more powerful words which helped me so much in the early days of my struggle against my negative programming:

Money needs me more than I need money

This one is designed to change your outlook and attitude to money. If you recite it enough (I say it 3 or 4 times in quick succession and sometimes come back and repeat it again later) it will gradually change any limiting beliefs you may have

---

8   Walter D Wintle c.1905 Unity Tract Society, Unity School of Christianity

about money being attracted into your life. If your over-riding belief about money is its scarcity and how difficult it is to get, everything you do to attract it will be governed by that belief. By believing money is abundant and needs to flow to you of its own accord, you set up the mindset to allow that to happen. Sounds strange, but it works.

This next mantra is one of my favourites. Having enough energy to keep on keeping on, especially when things aren't going well, is one of the vital keys to success. Reciting this may help you. But you might find yourself wide awake very early in the morning, when you don't necessarily want to be...

I am a rhinoceros. I have a damn-the-torpedo spirit. I am full of energy, and I can't wait to get up in the morning to start charging.

I used to have these words pinned up on my wall, together with other inspirational phrases. Even if I only took the words in through my peripheral vision, they helped.

I've never considered myself as being what others might call 'normal' and I take it as a compliment to be told I'm not. But I can only judge the effectiveness of mantras by my own experiences and my decades of observations. I'm happy not to be normal if it stops me being one of the masses who spend their entire lives living modestly without achieving any of the goals they may have had before they started out in the world on their own. He says, sounding like a pompous arsehole...

The world will do an excellent job of keeping you in your place if you let it, especially if you start from a background similar to my own. There are very few resources you can draw upon to dig yourself out of that place. So you have to rely on the most powerful resource you possess. It's sitting inside your skull. You can choose to allow the world to programme it, or you can choose to gradually knock it into shape yourself.

Saying the right words to yourself costs nothing. Even if you are the busiest human on Earth, there are numerous occasions when you can recite positive things to yourself. Expect no miracles. You can go for months or years without consciously noticing any difference. You will need lots of patience. If you don't have patience, acquire some by saying to yourself, "I have infinite patience."

You can help yourself to get almost anything you want by coming up with a phrase which directs you towards that goal, though I cannot stress highly enough that this has to be coupled with action. If you merely sit on your sofa every day saying positive things to yourself, you may feel better, but it's not going to do anything other than that. You have to put in the effort too.

If yours is a big goal, it will need lots of effort. Some things can be achieved quickly, others can take decades and huge amounts of effort, persistence and hard work. You can access those three things without the positive reinforcement I am suggesting, but it will be easier if you add that into the mix. I won't encourage you to be realistic as that mindset is what holds most of us back. It can be great to be unrealistic, but choose your goals very carefully and be absolutely sure they are what you want. It's easy to think you want a certain thing, yet in reality you want something totally different. Putting a lot of hard work into thinking about your goals in depth is crucial. If you start chanting to yourself about goals which you haven't properly thought through, you are wasting your time.

I'm going to give you one final tip. Only say and repeat things in the positive. So, replace "I am not poor" with "I am rich", for example. Your brain cannot compute negatives, eg "Try not to imagine a pink elephant." Say that to yourself and you cannot help imagining a pink elephant. If I tell you to imagine an orange elephant instead, however, it's fairly easy to do. So, if you want to lose weight, state your goal as if you have achieved it already, eg "I am a thin and healthy person". Saying "I will lose weight" is going to achieve nothing.

If you really want to be spooked about the power of this kind of repetition, let me tell you my wife is exactly the kind of person I conjured up in my mind when I was looking for someone to share my life. I thought carefully about the attributes which I believed were important to me, and then kept them in my mind as if such a person were in my life already. Lo and behold, I am now married to that very woman and I couldn't be happier. You could say it's a coincidence, but later in the book I'm going to tell you more about how this kind of thing has served me. It has worked for me so many times, I urge you to treat it as seriously as any other technique I am sharing with you to help improve your lot.

CHAPTER 18

NEW START, NEW BUSINESS, NEW PEOPLE

We're now in the early 1990s. The sisters renting the flat in Bath need to move out as they can't pay the rent. I'm working out of a small office in Midsomer Norton which I know is not right for me. And my marriage is dissolving, slowly but surely.

All of those issues would be solved by me moving into the flat.

Dave, Adrian and I decided I would pay two-thirds the rent the sisters had been paying, which kept things fair with them, and I set up the living room as an office. It was a small flat, but there was room for a decent-size desk which doubled as my dining table and just about everything else. The second bedroom housed my filing cabinets, so my only totally private spaces were my bedroom, bathroom and the tiny kitchen. Clients would come to the 'office', which I would make sure was devoid of as much personal stuff as possible in order for it to appear businesslike. It certainly didn't look like someone's living room.

I did all of this without spending any significant money. My desk (the most important part of the room) was bought second hand, and I managed to acquire/scrounge almost everything else I needed.

Once I had made this move, the gradual trend away from

my family home became more permanent. Initially, I would still visit Chippenham at weekends, but as my work became more and more time consuming, there was almost no leisure time. I woke, went swimming at 7am in the nearby leisure centre, ate breakfast at my desk while reading the *FT*, and then worked through the day with a quick lunchbreak, again taking time to read the newspaper. The evenings were spent either working at my desk, seeing clients or network marketing prospects, or networking at various events I managed to get invited to, mainly by following up every tenuous opportunity I could.

It was not unusual for me to work until 11pm, but it did not seem like a trial. On one occasion, I worked until 4:30 in the morning on the day I was going away on a short holiday with the kids. I was building something for myself and I knew every bit of effort I put in might bring me a reward at some stage. I had left Midsomer Norton with a mere handful of existing clients, so the only way to acquire new ones was to try everything imaginable to talk to prospects. This is where the training I had bought into through network marketing started to pay dividends.

Prospecting

There was a phenomenon some of the network marketing trainers came up with called the Three Foot rule. That meant anyone who came within that distance (about a metre) of you was a prospect, so you should talk to them, build rapport, and then pitch to them. Pre-internet, any kind of relationship, whether it be business, romantic or sexual, had to be started with a personal encounter.

Advertising was one way of kick-starting a connection, but it cost money. I didn't have any to speak of. And advertising was very hit and miss, especially in the areas I was working in. Network marketing was the epitome of personal contact to establish the foundations for a potential sale. So I decided I would meet and talk to as many people as I possibly could using whatever means I could come up with.

This may sound calculating and even perhaps deceitful, but like many things in life, it depends on how the technique is used. Knives can kill people, but they are also the best way I have found of cutting up apples. I could use a banana, but it's more efficient to use a knife, as long as I am careful with it. I haven't tried attacking anyone with a banana, though that might be fun in a *Monty Python* kind of way...

My main advantage when talking to or prospecting new people was my 'possibility cupboard'. This was full of lots of things I could pull out, depending on the circumstances. I had set up my financial business with the intention of providing a one-stop shop for a person's complete financial and insurance needs. So I put myself in a position where I could arrange or advise them on their car insurance, home insurance, mortgage, life insurance, pension and investments. Almost everyone I met had a car and I was interested in cars, so at least I could start a conversation on this topic, and then casually mention I could get them a quote for their motor insurance. If and when I acquired their business, they were then a client I could potentially cross sell other products to.

I actually dislike the phrase 'cross sell', but it's appropriate for that time. For the last 20+ years, I've done everything I can to move away from pure sales and into advice, where I get rewarded for finding a solution to someone's needs and not because I've sold them a product. That doesn't mean I think sales is a dirty word. Far from it. Almost every interaction we have in life is a form of sales. If you want to succeed, getting comfortable with that is vitally important or you won't be going anywhere.

Understandably, we tend to develop **rapport** with those

who are somewhat similar to us. Being in my early- to mid-thirties at that time, I would meet and talk to those in a similar age bracket. Many were homeowners already, so there was an opportunity to introduce them to network marketing. If they were relatively recent homeowners, they probably needed to earn some extra money, as interest rates had skyrocketed up to 15%, so there was also that opportunity to put before them. The possibilities were almost endless and, although my client base was as tiny as my income, I knew if I just kept plugging away, it would grow. It was a bit like my realisation at fifteen years old. As long as I made sure I was adding more to my assets than was being lost, I must improve my lot.

Being human
There was another potential outcome from the simple act of talking to people. I didn't forsake my wife and family because I was looking for love elsewhere. I did something I've rarely known anyone else do, which is leave home without having someone to go to or even in mind. To a person looking from the outside, it must have appeared to be a crazy and inexplicable thing to do. Those who knew my wife and me probably believed I had a different agenda, and someone who was waiting in the wings would soon appear and put everything into context.

That was not the case. I had no-one lined up, in mind or even to fantasise about. I just had a ridiculous drive, forcing me to break away from what many (especially my parents) saw as a perfect situation: a beautiful family, a lovely four-bedroom detached house and a good job. Instead, I locked myself away in a tiny flat, having to scrimp and save every penny to survive and establish/develop three businesses (I also had my motor sport PR).

However, I am human, with human needs, so I was realistic. If my wife was no longer part of my life, eventually I would need a companion, whether that be for the short or long term. Which is a long-winded way of saying that while I was on a quest to talk to as many new prospects as possible, there was also the potential of finding one for whom car insurance was not the main priority...

My means of meeting new people mainly revolved around being invited to or gate-crashing events happening in and around the city of Bath. I was beginning to become known to institutions like building societies, firms of solicitors (one of the people I regularly featured in my motor sport programme was a partner in a family run example) and the Chamber of Commerce, all of which hosted much more in the way of events then than they do now. By scouring the local rags, some of which cost nothing, I could find all sorts of free events where people might gather. It didn't matter too much what the event was, though I had to use some discretion and discernment, as the local Hells Angels chapter might not be the best place to sell water filters. Having said that, one of my most long-standing clients is a Hells Angel. So it's best not to pre-judge too much...

I had also become aware of seminars and training programmes through network marketing. Some of these were specifically run for those in the business, while others were open to all kinds of people. Either way, I could pitch my financial products to the network marketing crowd (though in reality, most were struggling too much financially to be worthwhile clients). And sometimes, my whole cupboard of possibilities could be opened to everyone else.

At one weekend seminar, a young French woman sat next to me. I won't go into detail, but she eventually moved into my flat in Bath and stayed with me for a number of years. Once this had happened, the breakup of my marriage became very real.

I had been happy to keep paying the mortgage on the family house in Chippenham as well as the rent to Dave and Adrian for the flat, as I wanted the kids to have as little disturbance as possible. But now, I couldn't see exactly what would happen. I guessed things would evolve and a solution would present itself. Depending on the circumstances, it's sometimes better to let things develop naturally rather than force them along. As it happened, it was my ex-wife who decided we should sell the family home as she wanted to leave Chippenham.

The year was 1994. Probably the worst of my life by some margin. As well as the pain of the split, my dad developed a brain tumour and died within a few months. The shock to us all was enormous. I had taken it for granted he would always be there and suddenly I did not have the man I admired most in all the world. He was the same age as I am now – gulp.

Just to add to the challenge of the year, my wife's father developed cancer and died a few months after my dad. My children loved both their grandfathers dearly and I couldn't imagine how they would cope with all this, but the resilience of the young is incredible.

The housing market was still tricky, suffering from the aftereffects of the big crash five years earlier, but eventually our house sold and I walked away with an amicably agreed £25k, the balance allowing my wife to buy a decent three-bed semi for her and the kids with no mortgage. Her father had left her some money, so that helped.

Jackie and I, on the other hand, knew we would have to support our mum as she was left with a basic widow's state pension and little else. She was still living in her council house and wanted to stay, so we put the wheels in motion to enable us to buy it for her, even though it was against her wishes. But she was in no state to fight too hard and it meant we could finally create something for her which would not be a constant drain.

My ex-wife and I had done well out of the Chippenham house, the modifications and extension doubling its value and allowing both of us to start again with a reasonable amount of money. Sorting everything out between us in an amicable fashion helped considerably. We didn't employ a solicitor for the divorce itself. Instead, we just waited until enough time had passed so we could file the papers ourselves without any contention. It cost around £20. Lots of heartache and money can be saved even when a relationship comes to an end by both parties adopting a pragmatic attitude and showing some flexibility and realism.

CHAPTER 19

THE ONLY WAY IS UP!

At the time of the house sale, I was thirty-eight years old. I'm told this is the age many in the UK are now buying their first home, yet despite splitting our assets in the marriage break-up, my ex-wife and I had each walked away with quite a substantial sum of money. My £25k (the equivalent of about £50k in today's money), considering where I had come from, felt like a crazy amount of money. No-one in my family had ever seen a five-figure sum in any form, and yet here I was with a lump of money sitting in my bank account. Was I finally on a straight road to riches?

Our ability to come out of this situation with this kind of dosh occurred despite the country going through one of the biggest property price crashes of all times and me having an extremely modest income (my ex-wife hadn't worked since our first child came along). It was still the case I had a lower income than almost everyone I knew. I didn't have the same inside knowledge of people's incomes as I had when working at the bank, but as I began to arrange more and more mortgages for clients, I became aware of what average incomes were for people in not dissimilar circumstances to myself. And yet, I seemed to be doing quite well in comparison to most of them.

I still don't fully understand why this was, though I've been pretty detailed about my penny-pinching attitude, sustained over many years. Perhaps this made the difference – if it did, then it's good news for all of you, as anyone is capable of doing it. As I continue writing, perhaps I will be enlightened more.

What is true is most people overestimate what they can do in the short term, but massively underestimate what they can achieve in the long term. Small savings made regularly over many years will make a huge difference to you. But if you think you're going to make a fortune with your new venture or attitude over the next two or three years, then you are likely to be disappointed.

My own property

Armed with my £25k, I took milliseconds to decide to invest in another property. I could have done all kinds of things with that money. I could have bought a flash car. You know I love cars. Had I bought a classic Ferrari, which I could have done with £25k, I might even be worth more than I am now. Or perhaps it would have bankrupted me. Whatever, I am happy I made the decisions I did. Property has been the key to my wealth and I still believe it's the best way for most people to move up the financial ladder.

So, I set about looking for somewhere to buy. It needed to be in Bath, where most of my clients were. I needed an area to work from home, hopefully not in a room which doubled as my living space. And I really wanted a garage to house the racing car I had recently acquired.

I also fancied the idea of buying something I could improve and therefore make money on, as I had before. But the market was starting to pick up and I struggled to find anything in Bath which I could afford. It's a very desirable place, so that previous sentence could have been written at any time in the last forty years.

At one of the networking events I attended, I often bumped

into a guy I regarded as a bit of a joke. He was supposed to be an estate agent, but he was always flitting from one job to another, with ridiculous stories about the big deals he was about to pull off. He had no credibility as far as I was concerned, but he would usually latch on to me at events, probably because I am a patient listener. I've always been able to build rapport with people by using my ears and mouth in proportion (two ears, one mouth), choosing to listen rather than download the contents of my brain on them, a somewhat rare attribute in my experience, with so many at the centre of their own universe. As he was.

This guy was what I would call, without putting too fine a point on it, a bull-shitter. I believed almost nothing which came out of his mouth. I still laugh about the £multimillion deals he was on the verge of completing, while he languished in his grotty little office by the railway station.

At one event, I told him I was looking to buy a property and he immediately launched into sales mode, telling me he had exactly what I was looking for. Apparently, it was a repossessed property. A detached bungalow with a large garden and garage on the south of Bath, it seemed reasonably priced at £79,000. I didn't believe this guy actually had it on his books, but it transpired he did and I was soon looking around it with my then girlfriend.

Typically of repossessed properties, it was needing some TLC to say the least. The previous owner was what you might call a 'character', supposedly a builder, though not the type you would want working on your property. There were half a dozen major jobs he had started and not finished, including cutting out half of the roof supports in the loft, perhaps with the intention of making a loft conversion. A marriage split and mortgage arrears had put a stop to all of that. We joked he had been trying to cut the house in two as his version of a divorce settlement.

None of the work fazed me. I knew it could all be sorted, and the most important aspects of the property were excellent, such as its position within its own plot, its potential to expand and its location. A deal was done. Although I was in a relationship, it was a volatile one and I never knew how long it would last, so I would buy the bungalow alone. This turned out to be a very good decision.

The importance of money management

Although part of my business was arranging mortgages for people, it was still not straightforward finding the finance for the bungalow. My income was modest. I was probably not clearing more than £15k a year, from which I was supporting my family. Nevertheless, I found a lender who thought I was a reasonable bet and off we went.

One of the most important things when you're trying to borrow money, especially if it's for a property, is to have as clean a credit record as you can possibly manage. Many underestimate how important this is and how easy it is to blemish your record due to something which may have seemed insignificant at the time, yet has huge consequences. Often these blemishes and consequences affect your credit status for many years, usually seven. Keeping yourself clean is mainly a matter of discipline.

Making sure you pay every bill on time is perhaps the most obvious way to improve your credit record. It's not about how much money you have, but how you look after it. **Budgeting** your finances by setting aside either real or notional pots of cash to account for bills or expenses which don't come monthly is at the crux of **money management**. For example, you know Christmas will come every year. If you want some money for Christmas, be realistic about what you will spend, divide that by twelve (or fifty-two if you are paid weekly), and set that money aside somewhere. Do that for every outgoing you have which isn't monthly (or weekly). What you have left after accounting for all that is what you have to live on. If you don't have enough to cover everything, cut something out or earn more money.

Sounds simple. It also sounds harsh, but unless you practise money management, you aren't going anywhere except down. People earning six-figure sums are on the verge of going under due to their inability to manage their money. And someone I know very well who has only ever earnt less than the minimum wage performs miracles with her money. She has savings, goes on holiday regularly and generally has a good life, all because she is meticulous in her money management and accounts for every penny.

If you are stable in your job and where you live, that will help your credit rating too. There are a few other things you can do as well, like having a credit card which you use and pay off completely every month. But paying your bills is top of the list.

Never give up!

The first task at my new property was to set up an office so I could continue working from home. The bungalow came with an integral garage which I had soon converted into a good-size office. The property was on a sloping site, so the former garage was below the rest of it. That was a bonus as clients would come into the drive and see my office right in front of them. The rest of the bungalow was up above, so out of the eye line.

I was able to employ someone to assist with my administration tasks. When I was in the flat, a couple of local ladies would come in now and then when I was out on business and tidy up. They did a good job, but I needed someone regular. I found a local lady who was reliable and conscientious and able to keep some of the admin side of the business together. This freed me up to do what I did best: finding new clients, talking to them and sorting out their needs.

The move worked well. I gradually started to feel I had a real business, especially after I ditched the time-consuming and unprofitable network marketing. Suddenly, all the effort I had been putting into that was channelled into my main activities, and I saw the results.

I was helped tremendously when I was introduced to a trainer, who worked for a company I had aligned with so I could utilise its products such as life insurance, pensions and investments. The sales training came as a bonus which we could access free of charge. He was an old-fashioned salesman, probably far too pushy for the tastes of today, who belonged to an American club for salespeople who supposedly earned more than $1m a year. I was trying to move my business away from pure sales and into the area of advice, but I was realistic enough to know I needed to talk to more people if I wanted to grow. Referrals from existing clients were my most important source of new business, but network marketing had given me the confidence to cold call anyone, so my fear of approaching someone with no connection to me whatsoever had been massively dissipated.

For many, fear of rejection is the greatest barrier to any kind of cold approach, whether it's to chat up someone who takes their fancy, ask for a discount when making a purchase or pitch to someone with a view to them becoming a client. Like most things, it's all to do with your mindset and how you view and react to the outcome of your approach. There are all kinds of techniques you can use to help, but something you can't beat is practice. The most successful people know this and use any opportunity to exercise their negotiating skills. It's why you see ultra-successful and wealthy people quibbling about the price of every modest item. It's a habit they have developed, and they want to keep themselves sharp by practising whenever they can, even if they don't need to.

Those who look on and have reservations about the ethics of this aren't going to have anywhere near the results of those who have the kind of mentality that knows the **art of negotiation** is key to so much success. When this concept was new to me, I was suspicious too. But I knew having an open mind was the only way to truly learn and progress, so I absorbed as much information about this subject as I could.

My trainer was effective in almost all areas of the sales process and had a charisma which drew me to him. I embraced everything he had to say, gleaning as much as I could, and then doing my best to apply it where it seemed appropriate.

Techniques and strategies are fine in theory, but like most elements of success, they are inextricably linked to effort. You can have the best sales pitch in the business, present impeccably and close your deals like the end of the world is nigh, but it all takes work. And true success only comes if you go the extra mile and call the next ten people on the list at 9pm, even if you are knackered, pushing and pushing until you have met the daily, weekly and monthly targets you have set yourself.

Did I mention those? Yes, sorry to tell you, but without **setting yourself targets**, you just aren't going to achieve the success you believe you want. And if you can't be motivated to set the targets and do everything humanly possible to meet them, then you don't want the success you think you do.

I'm not super human, so I can't say I worked night and day without a break, but I did put in far more effort than almost everyone I knew at the time. I got a massive buzz when I saw my efforts being translated into something tangible, and although I had huge amounts of rejection, I believed pressing on, keeping my head down and never giving up would pay in the end.

This reminds me of a quality snippet I picked up regarding sales perseverance: "What does NO stand for? Next One." Don't take rejection personally, just see it as part of a numbers game and move on. Eventually, you will strike gold if you talk to enough people and never, ever give up. **Persistence** is key.

A little contrast

However, we all need some contrast in our lives. And luckily for me, mine came in the form of another business.

My motorsport PR was booming, so when I felt burned out from the constant cold calling and rejection, or just the volume of work which needed doing in the financial business, being able to switch to something totally different was a release. People who knew me well often commented that they couldn't understand how I could switch from one discipline to another, and yet still keep control of what was going on. I can't explain it totally, but I was always good at multitasking, helped by enjoying everything I was doing, especially the motorsport side.

For a time, my heart wanted me to ditch the financial side and concentrate purely on the PR. Eventually, my head ruled. The main determinant was never meeting a journalist who was totally financially secure. Unless I made it very big, it seemed the most I could hope for was a modest living, mainly because leveraging my efforts in PR would be much more difficult than it is in financial services. If you want to improve your finances, gearing or leverage is one of the keys. Every decent size business must leverage in many ways in order to survive.

As my money started improving, so did the bungalow. My next job was to build another garage alongside the old one so I could store my race car. Having that at home was an absolute joy. Whatever else I have done in life, my original passion for cars has never waned, and being able to own and race a car was extremely important to me. The bungalow received lots of other treatment too, including a new kitchen and bathroom. I seemed to have unlimited energy for renovation work in those days.

But as the world approached the end of the twentieth century, I began to wonder how I could take the next step towards improving my lot...

CHAPTER 20

DREAMS CAN COME TRUE!

It's a Friday afternoon, the year 1999. I have been thinking about what I should be doing to progress my business and therefore myself. There are various ideas buzzing around in my head, but the pressures of everyday work don't allow me much time to contemplate. What to do?

At the time when most people were finishing their week's work, on their way home or already putting their feet up, I decided I should write another list of goals. It was about 5pm when I started. I remember it clearly as it became another pivotal moment in my life. Just as important as the wood-chopping epiphany as a kid or the pledge to save all my window-cleaning money when I was fifteen.

I liked the place I was living in. It had a large garden and a reasonably spacious garage, and I had the convenience of my office being downstairs from the kitchen. That also had its disadvantages. It was too easy to creep back down into the office to do a little more work, so I could never truly walk away from the pressures. And I just wanted to keep improving.

My business was becoming more sophisticated. I was concentrating on mortgages, pensions, life insurance and some investment business. I had done a deal with an insurance broker I knew in Yate, who would buy my general insurance book in exchange for a few shares in their business and a modest ongoing income. I could refer all my clients' car, house and business insurance needs to the broker, who would look after them, relieving me of the large amount of admin which went with such business. I therefore had more time to devote to my core activities.

In order to progress, though, I needed the credibility of a proper office rather than a converted garage below my house. Something had to change. I had a few conflicting ideas, so I decided to write down my most important dream requirements. It was a handwritten list on the back of some scrap paper (I have always used both sides of almost every piece of paper which comes into the office to save money and waste). Here is the gist of what I wrote:

1. I need a high street office, but I want it to be a short walk from where I live, as I like convenience and don't want to commute.
2. I've always wanted to build a house, so I would like to find a place with a plot of land to allow me to do this.
3. There must be space for garages to house my cars.
4. It must be in Bath as that is where most of my clients are.
5. I want to get into renting out property, so if there is a way I could do that at the same time, that would be good.
6. I don't want to sell my current place to buy the new one, to allow me to make the transition more easily.

I thought some of these requirements were potentially conflicting and finding one place to meet them all would probably be impossible, especially in Bath, where space and prices were (and are) at a premium. But essentially, they were *dreams*, designed to drive me forward over the next few years to achieve my goal.

Taking the first step

By now, it was 5:30pm. I almost put the paper to one side. But I remembered being told when you have completed a list of goals, you should do one thing, however small, to lead you towards achieving them. **If you aren't heading towards your goal, it's probable you are moving away from it** is a crucially important lesson.

What should I do? This was in the pre-internet search-engine days. I knew the kind of property I was looking for would only be handled by a commercial estate agent, but I didn't know any, so I did what most people did in those days. I picked up the now defunct Yellow Pages. For those who have never heard of it, yellow and huge sums it up. It was a directory of local businesses based around their telephone numbers, split into various categories, from plumbers to hit men. The latter section was quite small. But there were a number of commercial estate agents.

I decided to call one. I thought it would be too late to speak to a real person, especially on a Friday evening, but I could leave an answerphone message and at least I would have done something towards my goal. Perhaps the agent I chose was the first one I saw or maybe it was because of its location, bang in the middle of the city.

I rang and, to my great surprise, the call was answered by a guy called Geoff. I explained I had some property goals that were a bit of a long shot, but would he bear me in mind and let me know if anything came up? This was the kind of thing agents might do in those days.

Geoff took it all in. "We do have something in a small suburb of Bath, on the high street," he said. "It was the old Co-op, now rented out as a pine furniture shop. There's a yard behind, with some garages at the bottom, rented out to a charity for storage. And next to that, a plot of land is being incorporated into this sale. There's the potential for it to be a building plot. And the Co-op also has a flat above the shop, which is rented out."

My stunned reaction was something like, "Oh, right, how much is it?" Geoff explained the offer process was to make sealed bids by a certain date and the best would win. Pressed further, he thought the ballpark figure to work to was around the £200k mark.

That was way more than I could contemplate spending, but the place seemed totally perfect and, on the face of it, met my goals exactly. I was shocked to the point it seemed like a weird joke, but I said I would drive out there the next day and take a look. Which I did.

In real life, it seemed even more perfect. In terms of corresponding with my goals, anyway. It was all a little tatty and needed tons of work. The rear yard was in a poor state. Locals living in the adjacent properties had dumped their garden rubbish over the wall. The garages at the rear were run-down and half the shop had a horrible flat roof dating from the 1940s.

But I could see massive potential. The Grade II listed main building on the high street had lots of character and a long history, though I discovered much later this was as much a liability as it was an asset. The plot of land was in the bottom left-hand corner of the site, so was a good distance from the main road, but would only mean a twenty-second walk to work. All this was assuming I could build the house and turn the pine shop into an office.

I had to have it and something told me I would. I always advise my clients to do plenty of due diligence when buying any kind of property, especially a commercial one, but there was a deadline approaching for the sealed bids. The words of General

Patton came into play once again: *"A good plan violently executed now is better than a perfect plan next week."*

I didn't even have a good plan, just a few vague ideas. But crucially, I had a tremendous feeling of confidence. This was a place I must have, whatever it took. So I made a sealed bid of just under £190k, with no idea how I would raise such a substantial sum of money, and waited for the result.

Financial challenges

Things initially moved quickly. The phone call came from Geoff, who informed me I had been unsuccessful. There were two bidders who had offered amounts higher than mine. Not by a huge amount, but even if they had been £10 more, I would still have been the under bidder and I would have lost out, such are the rules in these situations.

Nevertheless, something would work out. I wasn't even terribly disappointed as I knew I would get the property somehow. If I had told anyone how I felt at the time, they would have said I was mad and suffering from Pollyanna syndrome (blind optimism), but this kind of feeling was not new to me. I didn't get it often. But occasionally, there would be a situation where I just knew the outcome would be OK, even though the odds were stacked against me. This was one of those situations. It makes no sense in many ways, but I believe when you are a possibility thinker and prepared to consider almost any opportunity which comes your way, your brain is trained to align with the once-in-a-lifetime ones.

Two weeks passed by and Geoff rang again. By then, I had built up a good relationship with him. I liked him and the feeling seemed mutual. It transpired the highest bidder could not raise the money and the second highest bidder had changed his mind. Geoff told me my bid was still below the minimum the vendors would accept, but if I could come up with just a little more, the property could be mine. This might sound like estate-agent sales talk, but I felt Geoff was genuinely honest. I have subsequently dealt with him for the last 20+ years; it has become clear my gut feeling was correct.

Without a clue how I could possibly raise that kind of money, I put in my bid for just under £200k. This was duly accepted and the task of raising the dosh began. This was 1999, when a nice three-bed semi could cost less than £100k. More significantly, mine was not a conventional purchase by any stretch of the imagination. It was mainly commercial, and therefore normal residential mortgages were not available. It had a plot of land on a separate title deed, with no planning permission. Indeed, planning permission to develop the entire site had been declined a couple of times. And there was no possibility of me selling my existing property to finance the purchase as I would have nowhere to live or work.

That would have been enough to deter most people without the cash in their hands. Not me. Arranging finance was part of my business, so if anyone could do it, then I could. Of course, I didn't let on to Geoff what a challenge awaited and he didn't question me too much about how I would be financing the purchase. These days, you need to be extremely resourceful if you want to pull off something outside the normal run of things, as agents are much more inquisitive and want lots of proof of your ability to proceed before they will even talk to you. This is where involving a professional can make a huge difference. Your ability to create any kind of wealth, particularly involving property, is directly related to your ability to raise finance.

We've already talked about how the days of having a relationship with a lender have disappeared. What you need instead is a great relationship with a financial adviser or mortgage broker who understands this kind of situation inside out and is prepared to think outside the box. If you can forge a relationship with a similarly innovative solicitor, that will help too.

Unfortunately, these people are not easy to find. There are plenty who will tell you they can do all sorts of things for you, but in practice, many advisers are little more than salespeople, looking to hook you up to something which requires the least effort from them for the maximum reward. This is where **learning as much as you can about finance** will pay dividends. If you put yourself completely in the hands of a professional when you have no knowledge of that world, it is difficult to know whether you are getting decent advice.

What makes this yet more tricky is even good advisers will differ in their approach, so if you start shopping around, you will inevitably get conflicting advice. And you will need an element of shopping around in order to find your future financial guru, but just like the dating game, if you are playing the field too much, you are likely to end up pissing off everyone and getting nowhere. Cost is something it's easy to get totally hung up about if you don't appreciate the value which is often inherent in a good adviser, though not always obvious.

It's vitally important to find professionals you can establish a long-term relationship with. It will make such a difference to what you can achieve. No one is perfect, but again like the dating game, when you find someone you feel comfortable with, you'll overlook the small imperfections for the benefit of the long term.

I had no-one to turn to except myself. Not for raising the finance, anyway. On the legal side, which was going to take on an unusually significant role in allowing me to buy this place, I was fortunate. From my early motor sport reporting days, I had formed a good relationship with a solicitor based in Bath, one of two brothers running the family firm. We served together on the committee for the RAC Rally when it came to Bath, though our interactions were mainly regarding his success on the race tracks, where he was a fast and competitive pilot. His brother, who was also a motor sport nut, handled the property side of the firm, so when I bought my second house in Chippenham, it was to him I turned. I used him and his firm for every property transaction after that, until the brothers retired and the firm was absorbed into a larger outfit.

When I was working through the puzzle of how I would finance the purchase, it quickly became obvious it would be impossible to find a lender who would stump up all the money. I had enough experience to work that out without putting too much effort into a thankless task. Instead, I focused on how I could divide up the property and use different methods to finance each part. The building plot was already separate, but had no planning permission. A couple of declined planning applications on the whole site was not much help either. So I didn't think I had much chance of raising any finance on it. It was down to me to come up with the funds. Luckily, it was a relatively small part of the transaction, around £25k. I could probably raise this by emptying every piggy bank, putting my hand down the back of the sofa and selling anything which might have some value.

I also had my existing property, which I had improved considerably so its value had increased quite significantly. As I had done before, I remortgaged it to extract as much equity from it as I could.

Remortgaging

In case this sounds like jargon, it's possible (subject to you meeting various criteria) to find a lender, either your existing one or a new one, who will allow you to borrow a certain percentage of the value of your property which happens to be more than you currently owe. The difference comes to you.

This is a strategy which is absolutely essential to build any kind of property portfolio. It's at the very heart of everything I've done in the last thirty years, both for myself and for my clients. My simplistic explanation makes it sound easy and there have been times in the past, particularly in the late-1980s and the mid part of the 2000s, when it was. That's a big part of why there were subsequent financial crashes. It's not something to do lightly and it's important to fully understand, as well as you can, what the implications are and how it affects the big picture of your finances. Every penny you borrow has to be repaid at some stage, so make sure you know exactly what you are doing and why. The government's health warning "YOUR HOME MAY BE REPOSSESSED IF YOU DO NOT KEEP UP REPAYMENTS ON YOUR MORTGAGE" is there for a reason.

Remortgaging a property to extract money from it has inevitably attracted negative connotations. Like any tool, it's how you use it which makes the difference. If a remortgage is suggested to you, it's important to understand the context in which you will use it. Things which potentially grow in value are a far better bet to buy than things which almost instantly have no value. If you are planning to remortgage to finance a holiday, however much that holiday enriches you emotionally and even spiritually, it does nothing for you financially.

If you are extracting equity from your existing property to buy another one, there's a second strategy which can sound equally dodgy until you understand it. It's the practice of merely covering the interest on the mortgage, rather than repaying the capital you have borrowed as well. The latter is commonly known as a repayment mortgage, because it does exactly as its name suggests. If you are building a property portfolio, unless you have oodles of cash, your ability to build that portfolio is directly linked to your ability to borrow

Dreams Can Come True!

money. So repaying money you have just borrowed when, at some stage in the future, you will want to borrow again is counterproductive.

Often, repaying interest is all that is viable anyway, but even if a repayment mortgage is affordable to you, it's usually wiser to use the money you would be giving back to the lender to create a pot towards your next property. Or to spend on your current property, enhancing its value so you can extract more equity later on. I raised some useful funds towards the deposit on my new purchase mainly because I had bought my existing property at a good price as it was in a poor state. I then spent money on it to improve it, enhancing its value, which I was able to extract cash from.

A mass of complexity

That still left the matter of funding the main part of the property. The next bit to chip away at was the flat above what would become my office. I knew I could raise a buy-to-let mortgage on it with a modest deposit, but the flat was part of the same title deeds as the shops, yard and garages.

This was where more negotiation came into play. I, or rather Geoff and my solicitor, needed to persuade the Co-op to allow the title of the flat to be split at the same time as me buying it. This would be prepared and readied in advance, and on the day of completion, the mortgage proceeds would be received, the title would be split and the flat would be mine. All this had to happen at the same time as my purchase of the other parts owned by the Co-op.

The word to describe this happening is contemporaneous. I like to learn a new word every day. It was pretty complex, especially when I tell you how the other part of the purchase was funded, but it was essential to me acquiring my dream property. My solicitor told me at the end it was the most complex property

197

transaction he had ever been involved with. His bill reflected that.

From my days working at the bank, I had a pension fund, which was just about the only thing my former employer was reasonably generous with, though my low pay was a strong counter to that. Another example of LUD: take a high-paying job with no pension or a low-paying one with a good pension.

It's possible to purchase commercial premises with a pension fund. In fact, it is a strategy many people use, turning what you might see as dead money into something which will work for you. It's necessary to transfer your pension funds into a different kind of wrapper called a self-invested personal pension (SIPP), which is as the name suggests. You decide where the money is invested (within limits) and take control of your fund.

All sounds fine and it can be, but since this option has been available, many people have lost all or most of their hard-earned pension funds by investing in all kinds of spurious schemes, usually involving property (some not even real). Criminals in suits set up traps which appear plausible, but the only positive outcome is the lining of their own pockets.

For your own business, where you are in control, SIPPs can make the difference between being able to purchase a property and not. Which was the case with me. I came up with the idea, thought out exactly how it would work, and then presented it to my solicitor for him to effect. I won't bore you with the intricate complexities of how this was done, but it was not the work of a moment. This was where having a good relationship with the agent made a huge difference as, by keeping him in the loop, I enabled him to reassure his client and make sure the transaction stayed on track. Another of the many examples in life where the human side is extremely important, if not essential.

Despite the complexity, the legal and financial work was completed far more quickly than we have become accustomed to in the UK. In the recent property transactions I have been involved with, delays of six months have not been unusual, even for the purchase of a single residential unit for a first-time buyer.

New beginnings, new challenges

While the legal and financial side was being processed, my thoughts turned to the practical aspects of the site. The planning permission for the build of my new house was the first major challenge. I had been bold enough to take a risk on a site which had already been declined, but the previous schemes had been much more ambitious than what I had in mind. All I wanted was to build one nice house for me, which would be next to a row of garages I could use for my own cars. The plot wasn't huge and my plan would leave me little outside garden space, but I wasn't into gardening so that was not an issue. It was to be a house for life for me, with no thought I would ever sell it, so it only needed to reflect what I wanted.

It all seemed very straightforward, so I decided to book an appointment with the planning officer for the area. I told him exactly what I wanted to do and without hesitation, though with the usual caveat that nothing can be guaranteed, he told me such a scheme ought not to present any problems. It was the closest I could get to a yes without actually making a planning application.

Tick.

Alongside everything else, I then began designing in my head the kind of house I would like to build. But one step at a time.

There was also the matter of the tenant occupying the shop. Or rather, shops. The high street element consisted of what had been two separate shops which now had access between them. There was a part to the rear with a flat roof, and running along behind, almost hidden by everything surrounding it, a large store, spreading from one side of the shops to the other and underneath the flat. It was all far too much for me, but I wanted some of it for my new office.

I made contact with the guy who owned the business and it transpired he had other premises too. Fortuitously, he was open to reducing what he was renting to one of the shops as, reading between the lines, the site wasn't a vast money maker for him. So we easily made a deal and I had a shop to move into.

There were a couple of other existing tenants for me to deal with too. The first was simple. A charity shop was renting some of the garages for storing larger items and had already decided to move on when it found the premises were for sale. I only had my own road car and one race car at the time, so my garaging requirement was modest, but I needed some income to justify the purchase and help pay for what I had planned.

Out of the blue, I was approached by a man in something of a predicament. He had been running a garage business in Bristol, had split with his wife and was about to become homeless and without anywhere to work from. He was aware of my premises and asked if I could help him.

On one end of the row of garages was a building which had been a slaughterhouse over 100 years before and had an upstairs room, running water, a loo... and not much else. This guy asked if it would be possible for him to live in this somewhat primitive area and for his kids to stay with him there at weekends. Just as importantly, he wanted the adjacent garage so he could continue making a living.

It seemed like a disaster waiting to happen, but I wanted to help him. And the modest rent I agreed with him would go towards the finance cost. He installed a ramp in the garage side, which I still have and use to this day elsewhere, and started his car repair business. It wasn't the ideal thing as part of my property's outlook, but I had no issue with it as overall, it was giving me the money I needed.

For my own use, I sectioned off the garages closest to my building plot, giving me a substantial area, far bigger than I had been used to. Interestingly, the boundary I chose for the new wall I built became very significant in later years in a way my conscious mind had never been aware of. Perhaps deep down, my brain was telling me this would be a good place to make the division. More on that later.

Finally, I had the flat above the office to deal with. The less said about that, the better. I was unable to inspect it prior to purchase as the tenants weren't amenable. I soon discovered why.

Despite the rent being modest, there were difficulties paying it. This was not revealed to me when I became interested in buying, and to be honest, even if I had known about the problem, I would probably still have gone ahead as the overall deal was so attractive. Nevertheless, it was something of a shock to be told just before completion about their rent arrears, which I would inherit with the purchase.

Yes, it sounds crazy, but apparently a buyer inherits any arrears of a tenant in situ at the time of purchase. I found it hard to take, but there was nothing I could do about it if I wanted to go ahead. So I had no choice other than to look even deeper into the sofa crevices and come up with a few hundred extra pounds.

Although the sisters Dave, Adrian and I had rented the flat to in Bath ten years earlier had struggled with their rent, this was a whole new ball game for me and was a harsh introduction to the realities of being a landlord. I've since done well from letting property, but the journey has been tough and it's certainly not an easy way to make money. But there are no easy ways to make money, especially when you're starting from nothing. Whatever you choose if you want to do more than scratch a living, you will face challenges. And scratching a living is also hard. It's how you deal with the challenges which determines the outcome.

So, towards the end of 1999, I finally became the owner of my own shops, yard, flat and plot of land. My dad had died six years earlier at a time when I was, in his opinion, at a very low point, living in a little flat in Bath, seemingly having lost everything I had worked so hard to build. He and my mum found it difficult to accept I had gone from having a large detached house on a desirable estate, a good job and a lovely young family, to living like a student. To them, I had achieved the ultimate in life, far beyond their wildest dreams, and then let it all go.

Six years later, my life had flipped again. I had another detached house, almost as good as the one I'd left in Chippenham, and what amounted to a small estate with enormous potential. But my dad would never know about it. I only ever wanted him to be proud of me and I guess he was, but it would have been so much better if he could have seen me on the rise instead of leaving me as I had fallen.

CHAPTER 21

NOW WE ARE MOTORING

Finally, thirty years after my first commitment to myself, I was in a place where I could do something and make a big difference to my life.

There was still a long way to go. I was financially exhausted, but the incomes from my independent financial advice (IFA) and PR sources were reasonable, and now the new premises were mine, I had the rents coming in to help finance all my borrowing. In every case in my life where I have taken a big risk and borrowed a relatively vast sum to finance something I knew would be beneficial, the early days have been a bit sphincter tightening. It's also been true that once things have settled, my mind has grown accustomed to the amount of debt and it becomes normalised.

This concept is part of learning to **expand your comfort zone** and it's very important to understand. It is another lesson that's vital to success. If your habitual way of living is only to do things you feel comfortable with, your comfort zone will gradually shrink, which is a scary thing.

The size of your comfort zone
Imagine yourself sitting in the middle of a circle the circumference of which you can reach by stretching out your arms. If you live your life within that circle, over time, it will reduce in size to

the level it sees you reaching out to. It becomes smaller. Then you feel less comfortable with things you used to be OK with. So your reach shrinks again and the circle retracts even more. Eventually, there is almost nothing you can do which doesn't give you some anxiety or worry.

The opposite is also true. Absorb the discomfort which comes from reaching outside of your circle and the circumference will grow accordingly. After a few painful stretches, the edge of the circle has expanded, but is easily within your grasp. If you keep doing this, you will be amazed what you will attempt – things which once would have scared the pants off you. No pain, no gain. So simple, so often true.

Take a moment to look at those around you whom you know well and have done for some time, say at least ten years. Think about the things they used to do when you first knew them and the kind of life they live now. How did they used to be as a person then and how are they now? As we have been talking about those who shrink their comfort zone, let's focus on those you see as having become less adventurous. You should be able to see a pattern and a trend.

We all know those who have allowed their lives to shrink to the extent where even simple challenges have become a problem. Like much which determines our levels of success, it's the tiny things which make such a difference when seen in the context of ten or more years. Language is one of the most important of these tiny things. Those who tend to say no to things develop different characters to those where a yes is the default response. Guess how much of a difference this makes to the size of the comfort zone.

One of the main reasons this happens is due to the way our subconscious mind wants to prove to us how correct our conscious mind is. George Zalucki[9], one of my earliest

---

9   https://georgezalucki.com/

inspirators, calls the conscious mind the 'thinker'. This is the place in our brains where we tend to believe we get everything done and our emotional state exists. Our subconscious mind is the 'prover'. It is constantly monitoring our conscious and trying to show us ways in which we are correct.

So, if John is regularly using words like 'horrendous' to describe the normal things which occur in life – the weather, for example – his subconscious will say, "Ah, John thinks this rain is horrendous, so it must be. The next time it's raining and he is wondering whether to go out or not, let's make sure we tell him it is horrendous, so it would be better to stay inside." If you are that way inclined, your tendency will be to only do things you are comfortable with. Over time, your comfort zone will shrink and your beliefs about the weather, and many other things, will deteriorate with it.

On the contrary, if you are constantly taking risks, even small ones, and your inner dialogue is more "It will be OK" than "That's a bit dangerous", then your subconscious will learn to prove you are correct. And guess what – the more you take risks, the more you try new things, the more chances you take, the better you get at managing or dealing with the outcomes and the bigger the life you will lead.

This life lesson is so important, I urge you to read this section again to make sure you have fully considered and understood it.

A new business proposal

Let's get back to my story. As if buying a huge property was not enough, something else significant was going on in 1999. You likely remember I had an association with a broker business which I sold my general insurance book to earlier that decade. The man behind it, Mike, traded as Ford & Co. As well as his general insurance business, he also ran a successful letting agency for rented property, though his main business was that of an IFA (Independent Financial Adviser). This was similar to me, except Mike had been fully independent for some years, whereas my business had been closely aligned to one financial services provider. But I was gradually making the move to full independence, which was where I saw the market going.

After Mike acquired my general insurance business, we would regularly speak on the phone and we got to know each other quite well. Our conversations would often end with Mike asking me to come and work for him so I could be a true IFA. I was determined to be in control of my business, so it was never of interest, but Mike kept trying every now and then.

Like me, Mike would work very long hours and it was not unusual for us to chat at 7:30 or 8pm while still finishing up for the day. Up until you reach a certain age, it's not only possible, but somewhat critical to use these extra hours to really establish your business. If you are contemplating self-employment, this is one of the most important reality checks you need to undertake. Ask anyone who has ever succeeded in business. They will all tell you the same. The only way to get anywhere is to put in the hours. Those with an employee mentality might find this somewhat unpalatable, but there is always a price to pay for everything... LUD.

One evening, out of the blue and as a complete surprise, I received a call from Mike asking me if I wanted to buy his business. A pensions review had been part of a witch hunt by the governing body, intended to wheedle out bad eggs from our business. Unfortunately, the good eggs like Mike were massively affected too, with huge amounts of work required to justify business which had often been written many years before and satisfy the regulator's requirements. Mike is a good record keeper, like me, but even so, those were very stressful times, especially as he had a young family who probably saw him much less than they would have liked.

My immediate reaction was, "I can't afford it". I didn't know a massive amount about his IFA business, but I knew it was successful and would have a decent value. The offer came at a time when I had just committed to buying the new premises.

Mike wasn't fazed by my reaction. Instead, he surprised me again by saying he didn't want anything for it other than an ongoing way to benefit from it. We agreed to meet, and then began a series of discussions where we both dug deep into each other's businesses. As this progressed, we were both surprised to find out how similar we were in a number of ways.

After much deliberation, we agreed I would take over the handling of all Mike's IFA business. In exchange, Mike would receive a monthly percentage of the income I received from my now much bigger business. We would employ a new adviser, based in Mike's office in Yate. Luckily, he already had someone in mind. The adviser would look after Mike's old clients for their life insurance, investment and pension needs. We would, in theory, sort out their mortgage requirements as well, though in practice, almost none of that business came our way, mainly due to the location of the clients.

A couple of years or so prior to this, I had taken an adviser under my wing. After her husband's retirement from being an adviser, she was looking for someone to work with as she did not have the confidence to go it alone. So we made an arrangement where she carried on working from her own home office, but traded under my business's name, Edison Associates. So, I was already used to having an adviser to manage.

The world of financial services had become heavily regulated during the time I had been involved. Compliance matters were the elephant in the room, so taking on another person for whom I would be responsible was not to be done lightly. Luckily, Mike knew the new adviser very well and was totally sure he was trustworthy and reliable. When you are looking after someone else's money, this is obviously hugely important.

While these arrangements progressed, I was also busy making plans to convert the old pine shop into my office. Luckily, the owner of the pine shop business referred me to an excellent guy who did all his building work. The builder did a great, inexpensive job, changing the space into what I needed, with an open-plan area at the front, a separate small office for an adviser and a larger office for me at the rear.

Recommendations such as this are extremely valuable. As you progress in life and business, you will need the services of all kinds of people and it's vitally important you choose the right ones. It's as much an art as it is a science, but practice makes perfect. Or rather, practice should make you better. If it doesn't, then you have probably perfected the skill of being a poor judge. A rethink might be an idea.

Edison Ford

After much deliberation, Mike and I agreed it would make sense for all our businesses to trade under one name. Entrepreneurs can be very possessive and sensitive to such changes, partly because of ego, which can be a powerful driver but also an inhibitor for many things. Whenever you encounter something which makes you feel uncomfortable, it's always worth running an ego check to understand why you are feeling the way you do. **If you can put your ego to one side, you are much more likely to get a positive outcome to any situation**.

In the course of this ego contest, we finally decided on Edison Ford as the core name for all our businesses. The Ford bit was obvious – Mike's surname, which he understandably wished to retain. The Edison part came from my grandfather – Granfer Moon, the guy who had taught my dad to be impervious to anything the world threw at him. I had been given Edison as one of my middle names and although it had led to some ribbing at school, I'd always liked it. It was unusual, so it made me feel special. Did it help me progress with confidence? Who knows, but I believe nominative determinism is powerful and it's interesting how many successful people use it when naming their offspring.

The only downside to the Edison Ford name was its potential to be confused with a Ford motor dealership. This was in the early days of the internet, when people would still call directory enquiries to search for a certain type of business, and the call centre people would often suggest Edison Ford as a garage in the Bristol and Bath area. Once accurate search engines on the net became the norm, the problem disappeared.

On that subject, I'm proud to say I was one of the first people to list their IFA business on the internet. I had no idea how to build a website and had no budget to go about it, but I managed to find a group of young students studying IT at the local university and gave it to them as a project. They did such a good job, Edison Ford would appear on the first page of any Google search for financial advisers nationwide, and for a year or two, we were second in the rankings. It would cost a fortune to replicate that now, but then it cost me nothing, apart from my effort.

As well as signifying the start of a new millennium, the year 2000 marked a momentous time in my life. I had the premises, Edison Ford IFA moved into its first proper office and the planners had approved my new house. By July 2000, it was ready to move into. Looking back now, I don't know how I achieved all this in such a short space of time. I'm not sure I could do the same today, but I'm probably underestimating the power and energy which come from a drive to succeed or achieve. I certainly haven't lost that, but I don't need to go the extra mile these days. My wife probably wouldn't agree as she sees me

embark on yet another project I can't help getting myself into...
like writing a book.

My dream house becomes reality

Towards the end of 1999, I had already commissioned an architect
I had got to know in the network marketing business. Once again, I
was extremely lucky (or was it skilled?) to find such a brilliant guy.
I had designed a lot of the house myself. I wanted a super-efficient
building in terms of space and energy usage, and realised a perfect
square gives you the best use of both with no wasted areas. The
architect took my design, added a few tweaks, including a brilliant
roof light which cast natural light down into the hallway, and
handled what turned out to be a fairly straightforward planning
application. What's more, he was managing complete building
projects for clients using subcontractors he had worked with for
many years. It was an easy decision to engage him, especially
as I had seen examples of his previous work, as he was also the
retained architect and building surveyor for the Castle Combe
Circuit, my second home.

It was January of 2000 when the work started. My architect
and I had decided on a timber frame internal design, the main
advantage of which was the ability to get the skeleton of the
house up in a few days, allowing it to become watertight very
quickly. The frames were built off site and craned into place,
creating an almost instant building. The external stonework
and the plumbing, plastering, electrics and finishing could all
be done at the same time. Even I was astounded when I had a
house I could move into seven months later, despite what could
have been a catastrophic fire. It was only discovered by luck
before it had spread too far.

What is even more astounding is how I found the money to
build it. Having exhausted myself financially just a few months
before, I had no funds, apart from my ongoing income, for any

kind of property build. But with planning permission, my plot had probably trebled in value in the short time I had owned it. There was no mortgage on that piece of land, so it was available for raising finance on. This would give a lender a large buffer of security upon which to rely, so they'd be comfortable to lend me some starter capital, and then ongoing chunks of money as the build progressed and the value increased further.

Someone I had been talking to about the situation mentioned a bank which had been very helpful to him, so I contacted the local office. One of my old tutors when I had attended night school twenty-six years earlier was a lending manager there, so it was he I first approached. Property finance was not his thing, so he passed me on to a colleague who was happy to help.

I was surprised how quickly and easily the bank agreed to finance the whole project. It required me to remortgage the new house to repay the debt once I had completed it, as the bank wasn't into long-term mortgages at the time, but that was not a problem for me.

I saved as much money as I could by being innovative with the fixtures and fittings. I wanted a traditional designer-style kitchen and saw the perfect example in an advertisement on the rear cover of an upmarket French magazine on one of my regular trips to France with my then girlfriend. The manufacturing company's pricing was way beyond anything I could contemplate. It would have added 30% to the overall build cost of the property. So I set my mind to thinking of ways I could replicate this amazing furniture at a fraction of the cost.

France has a nationwide chain of *brocantes*, which are warehouses selling second-hand items on behalf of owners. It's like a real-life Ebay, though most of the stuff is furniture, much of it from old, traditional houses inherited by children who want something modern. We scoured these *brocantes*, looking for things which could be repurposed or used in the new house.

On one visit, we spotted a wonderful old French dresser. Its style was exactly like that which I had seen in the magazine. The dresser was old, had some damage (which I was sure I could repair) and was a little unloved. But it was the right shape and size, and with some renovation and new paint, it would become the base around which the rest of the furniture could be styled.

I also found a large solid-wood kitchen table, eight chairs and various other lovely items which would make it a special house, with a little imagination. This was at a time when the pound was very strong against the euro, so even with the travel cost, I acquired all these pieces for tiny amounts of money. Moreover, I discovered plumbing supplies were much cheaper in France than at home. I could buy bathroom fittings of very high quality and unusual design for far less than ordinary items were available in the UK.

It's fair to say, creating the new house went far beyond my wildest dreams. I only sold it a few years ago, but I see it every week and I'm still as impressed by it as I was when it first came into being. It was built in Georgian style to resemble many of Bath's traditional buildings, with liberal use of the local stone. An indulgence which was an addition to the original design was a porch fronted by two substantial stone pillars. It gives the house an imposing look, back then a little out of kilter with its place in my courtyard which was still quite a mess. The old garages at the bottom didn't help, but I was thinking long term. I didn't have any particular plans for what I might do there, I just knew this was to be my home for life. I had created a wonderful dream home and nothing would ever make me want to leave it.

But things change...

Tenants

Having retained my existing property with the office underneath and managing to get this far, handling all the finance costs from my various bits of income, I decided it would be sensible not to sell it as originally planned, but keep it as a longer-term investment. By now, I was pretty much convinced property would continue to increase in value, despite the occasional blip, so if I wanted to build my fortune, this was the way it would happen.

It was one of the goals I had set myself on that fateful Friday afternoon. I had started to acquire a number of clients who were also building property portfolios, and in helping them with their financing needs, I had strengthened my belief in what they, and I, were doing. Of all of them, two in particular have done remarkably well. Over the years, they have become much more than clients and their friendship is far more valuable to me than any other relationship I have enjoyed with them. Perhaps the main reason for this is what we have in common, having shared a very long journey to achieve something out of the ordinary.

So, my previous house was handed over to a letting agent and filled with a tenant as soon as I had moved into my new place, christened Mulsanne House. Those who follow motor sport will recognise the word Mulsanne from the long straight of the same name at the Le Mans 24 hour circuit in France. I gave the house that name because of a wonderful story told to me by a neighbour when I first acquired the site. The person who told me had no idea of my motor sport interest.

The story was that many years ago, a local man attended the Le Mans race and brought back an acorn, which he then planted in the courtyard. That acorn grew into a large oak in front of where I built Mulsanne House – it's still there to this day. I had no idea if this was true, but recently, the guy who planted the acorn contacted me out of the blue to tell me the same story!

When you are involved in lots of things, stuff like this is more likely to happen to you. If you really want to make something from nothing, doing nothing is not the way to help yourself.

Start doing something, anything, open your mind, and you will be amazed how many interesting things will happen to you. For me, stuff like this is every bit as fulfilling as all the money I have made.

Anyway, my old house was let. The rent wasn't great and I know why now, though I didn't want to listen to the letting agents at the time. I had been living there with my then girlfriend who was a talented artist and painted various murals in the house. While they were impressive in their own way and I couldn't bear the thought of hiding all those hours of work, the agents were right when they told me not everyone has the same taste and advised me to paint over the murals. It cost me money to have that view, and eventually they all disappeared under a few coats of emulsion anyway. Ego getting in the way again. Another lesson learnt.

One of the main challenges of building a property portfolio and therefore becoming a landlord is handling your tenants. Not every tenant is perfect. Let me tell you, landlords hardly ever evict tenants for no reason. Every landlord I have known (and I have known hundreds) wants to keep good tenants and would never evict them as long as they live like any reasonable person would.

I mentioned before how I had inherited challenging tenants when I acquired the flat at my new site. I dealt with it as well as I could, but it wasn't easy as I was relatively inexperienced in this kind of thing. So I did what seemed sensible and natural, and gradually got to know the tenants better. Initially, the woman on the tenancy agreement was very reluctant to have any kind of conversation with me, and as I found out the true reality of her situation, I discovered why.

Everyone lives their life slightly differently to everyone else. The choices you make early on make a huge difference to how your life evolves. Some choose to aim high, others to live for today – LUD. Here was a young woman with two or three children, living on benefits and enjoying the pleasures which apparently come with such a lifestyle, including smoking various substances. She was not unintelligent and her father was a successful builder who, coincidentally, built the dividing wall in my workshop. Paying the rent was not one of her top priorities, but we struggled on, trying not to let it get too out of hand. At least some of it came my way every month.

I was always as kind and helpful as I could be, and eventually, I was allowed into the flat, mainly to deal with some issue the tenant was having. I already suspected there was a man on the scene and it transpired he was the father of the children and lived there permanently, but as far as the benefits office was concerned, she was a young single parent, living alone and therefore entitled to enhanced financial help. In reality, the father was working and bringing in a decent enough wage. I got to know him quite well and we always had a good relationship, but I found knowing this scam was going on under my roof unpalatable, to say the least.

Their inability to manage their finances was not the only problem. Add to that the tenants' inability to clean and keep the place tidy. I'm not talking about a little bit of dust here and there, but unimaginable filth. It's safe to say, no cleaning had taken place there for many years. Nor had anyone thought to pick up anything which had been dropped on the floor, including faeces from their pets. The stench was gut wrenching.

Moreover, the amount of clutter and junk meant their living conditions were cramped, with the kids sharing a hovel of a room, even though the premises are spacious. Something had to be done. There was not a chance in hell of them renting a different place from another landlord, so social housing was their only answer, though the waiting lists were very long. But at that time, if a family was made homeless, the local authority rehoused them immediately. Unfortunately, the system was such this would only happen on the day the tenant was physically evicted.

So, we reached a practical agreement. Their arrears were plenty for me to obtain a court order for eviction. They wouldn't oppose the order, but would stay until the very last minute. They advised the local authority this would happen and, on the day, they would be swept up and re-housed. A good arrangement all round as it meant I got the property back and could refurb it before letting it to someone more viable, and they got the home they needed. I would just have to stomach the rent arrears.

That is exactly what happened. My former tenants were very happy with their new home in the same area, but there was one factor I had not accounted for. Not a financial one, but something which affected me far more deeply. I hadn't been the most popular person in the area since acquiring the site, partly because no-one likes change and partly because my site had been convenient for the locals to use as free parking and a rubbish tip. When I caught someone in the act, the typical reaction was "Well, we've always done it". As soon as I insisted they would do it no more, I became the man they loved to hate.

It transpired my old tenants had explained their eviction to the neighbours in a somewhat disingenuous manner. They twisted the true reason into a story of me wanting the property back to renovate. The rent arrears and shockingly filthy state of the flat were conveniently omitted. When I was confronted by one of the neighbours expressing disgust at the way I had treated this poor young family, I was taken aback. It was one of my first experiences of this kind. As the sort of person who naturally likes to live in an open and honest manner, I found the lies my former tenants had told shocking. I probably should have known something like this would happen, but I guess I was naïve, believing others would act in the same way as me.

I've spoken before about the words we use on a day-to-day basis being important to the programming of our brains. It therefore stands to reason if we regularly bend the truth, we will programme ourselves accordingly. It explains why some people feel happy about telling outright lies when faced with something which isn't going their way. This is why I really don't like it when people exaggerate or twist the truth to make stories sound exciting.

In your quest to improve your life, be aware that not everyone will be honest and not everyone will be on your side. It helps if you are prepared. We will talk about how best to do that later in the book.

As soon as the property was back in my control, over the course of a few months, I cleared it out, renovated it from top to bottom and eventually let it, choosing to rent each room individually. Room rental is a lot more work than letting the entire property, but made sense for the layout of the flat. I still have the property and it provides a good income, as well as being a source of capital a few years later when I undertook my next huge property project.

Moving with me to Mulsanne House was my girlfriend, who had been with me in the previous property. We had been together a few years, but the relationship was volatile to say the least. It deteriorated to the point where she had effectively become a lodger, though my friends described her more as a cuckoo. Either way, it was time for that chapter to close and eventually, after some turmoil, I had the house to myself.

I was ready to enter another phase of my life and get everything working in harmony...

CHAPTER 22

RELATIONSHIP GOALS

For some, the idea of seeking out a specific kind of person for a future relationship may sound somewhat ruthless and calculating. I can see why those looking for love, especially when they're first starting out, might feel something special has to be in place for them to fall for the dream person.

You hear the word 'fate' being used in this context, but this makes me feel a little uncomfortable. The idea some external force is determining what happens to you in life must mean you are, to a greater or lesser extent, seeing yourself as a manipulated puppet.

If you take a focused approach to love, it doesn't mean something special cannot happen to you. Traditionally, and certainly before the rise in internet dating, meeting someone was a totally random experience, so your chances of finding the perfect mate was as much luck as anything else. In my parents' time, it could be so difficult to maintain communication with anyone, it was not unusual for a couple to marry the first person they had any kind of romantic encounter with. A little different from these days of swiping on to the next one.

In the early 2000s, it was my turn to start looking. Initially, I had nothing long term in mind. I didn't want to have a series of one-night stands, but neither was I looking for a partner for life. But as time went on and I experienced more of the world, I started to see things in greater perspective.

After a number of relatively short-term relationships, all of which gave me a benefit in one way or another, I realised there was something missing. Although men who talk about the importance of a partner's physical attributes are often called shallow, in reality, I'm sure everyone has a preference for how they would like their other half to look. Just as important, in my view, is mental or intellectual compatibility. This is the cement holding a relationship together long term. Without it, I believe relationships cannot be truly happy, at least not for any length of time.

As my goal setting for my financial life seemed to be working pretty well, I wondered whether the same principle could apply to relationships. After some thought, I decided I had nothing to lose, so I would 'design' the sort of person I would love to have in my life. I wrote this down and the attributes were specific.

I've discovered the more specific you are with goals, the more likely you are to achieve them. For example, stating you want to be rich is meaningless. Stating you want to have £1m in ten years' time is much more powerful. I'm not telling you exactly what all my requirements were, but someone with ambition was important. As with the other goals I had set, I didn't refer to them constantly, but I knew they were there and trusted my subconscious would take the necessary action to attract the right person to me.

Speed dating pays dividends

One day, one of my employees mentioned a speed dating event he thought would be fun to go along to. This was in the early days of such things and I wasn't exactly sure what to expect.

Thirty guys and thirty women would sit in a circle in a room and have two or three minutes one to one with each other. They then moved around one space, so by the end of the session, everyone had met. I found it great fun, didn't take it seriously, but got on extremely well with one of the last women I spoke to. So much so, we are still married...

It took us six months of seeing each other as friends to form what might be called a proper relationship, and from then on, we didn't look back. I've discovered someone I find physically attractive, but just as importantly, she's someone I can converse with on an equal level and ambitious enough for us to work together to achieve our goals.

Would I have found this person without my goal setting? Who knows? Quite possibly. More importantly, knowing my goals made me take the necessary actions to pursue Jane over all others, even though when we were just friends I had few signs the relationship would ever be anything other than platonic. I'm hesitant to refer to the title of this book in this context as in some ways, it does not seem at all appropriate. But it is. I had no-one in my life I could be with for any length of time, so I started from nothing. I decided to change that, took some actions and have found myself in what I see as a perfect situation. Something very significant has come from nothing.

With the correct mindset, this is something anyone can do. It's often been said to me how lucky I have been. My auto response is, "Yes, and the harder I work, the luckier I get".

Working hard is not just about the number of hours you put in. If that were the case, many people living at the poorer end of our society would have a much better life. Making your brain work hard is even more important. The thinking, mental exercises and analyses I have been through have made me realise this is actually the hardest work there is. Which may explain why so few people do it, another reason why one of the greatest barriers to your success can be the people you mix with.

Your friends and family may be well meaning, but

fundamentally, people want those they mix with to be just like them. When something is presented to them which threatens that, their reaction is often negative. "Too risky", "Too much work", "You have to know the right people", "Not enough time" are just some of the typical responses you are likely to hear when you start talking to others about your plans to improve yourself. You might already have heard them.

Meet someone like minded and things are very different. It's why I knew I could never stay with my first wife, lovely person though she is, and why I have achieved so much since meeting and marrying Jane. During the time I knew Jane just as a friend, she acquired her first property, bought with a colleague from work. This colleague was at the speed dating event and also married the guy she met there!

This showed me Jane was ambitious and innovative. She was relatively new to the world of work, having studied her geomorphology profession extensively for many years, gaining a couple of degrees and later becoming a scientist. She wasn't entrepreneurial, but she had a professional job, albeit in an industry which paid relatively poorly for the level of skill required to work in it. I could relate to that...

Buying a house on her own was not possible, but by clubbing together with her friend, she got on to the first rung of the ladder, offsetting all the rent she would have been paying to someone like me. Once they had that achievement under their belts, it opened the doors to many possibilities. We have already seen examples of some of these possibilities and will expand on them as we move forward.

For many relationships, the financial ties which inevitably form are the strongest of all those holding a couple together. Or, indeed, splitting them apart in a painful way. I've always been very conscious of making sure I don't get myself into a situation where I feel powerless. This stems from my childhood, where

I was aware my family was one tiny step away from disaster. When you live on the edge of poverty, even small things can tip you over the edge and the consequences can be dire.

This is why I am habitually **analytical about where I am in life, what my risk factors are, and what I should do and not do to make sure I can control my destiny**. It sounds ruthless and in some ways it is. It also means I've never been put in a position where I have had to rely on someone else to bail me out, whether the state, family or friends. The thought of having to consider doing that has been my life's greatest fear. It's probably what has driven me more than anything else.

Analysing a relationship for risk

Entering a new relationship with someone is a life event where risk analysis is vitally important. (This is the point where you might decide this is far too ruthless a thing to be doing!). But there are far too many examples of partnerships ruining someone financially, so I'm convinced you should treat a personal relationship with the same level of caution you would a business one. It's why I didn't want to buy a house with my French girlfriend.

Establishing someone's attitude to money is a good first step. Some people are born spenders, some are born to be careful. It could be fine to be with a spender if that person is a very high earner or from a wealthy background with plenty of assets (though that can still be disastrous as many former millionaires have discovered). But if they are already deep in debt, have limited earnings and nothing of substance behind them, that's a big warning sign life is going to be challenging. If everything else about them is perfect, it's easy to brush this trait aside and live in hope you can change them. But leopards tend to keep the same spots they've had for a while. It's why so many people lurch from one financial disaster to another, blaming everything and everyone while ignoring the one common denominator which remains throughout – their attitude.

Such people can be great fun to be with. But in the long term, they will drain you in more ways than one. Of course, there are levels to this kind of behaviour and we shouldn't condemn anyone for having a modest tendency to be less in control of their finances than others. It's important to honestly consider how life could be with this person when you are weighing up a long-term commitment with them.

Because I have been in the unusual position of having intimate knowledge of people's personal finances since I started working in the bank at age sixteen, I've built up a huge mental database of habits, attitudes and effectiveness, relative to how they go about their money management. It's easy, therefore, for me to see through the mists of obfuscation which people can use to disguise their true financial position. When you have had access to huge amounts of data over a very long period of time and the same patterns emerge over and over again, your ability to make fast judgements about someone's financial standing is much enhanced. I would like to help you to enhance your judgement in this area, but it's as much an art as it is a science. Being observant and consciously analysing the habits and experiences of others, will help. But because people's true financial situations tend to be kept well hidden, it's often tricky even for those in a close relationship to know what's really going on. As with many things, the more you practice and think about this stuff, the more you are likely to improve.

Being able to make speedy judgements is helpful when you're assessing a potential transaction with someone new, or even someone you think you know well but have never crossed paths with financially. And the financial ties which grow in a relationship can be the most painful to unravel, as many divorcees will tell you. In my case, I quickly knew both my wives would be the sort of people I could have total trust in financially. The first because of her extreme caution and the second because of her habits and desire to better herself. So soon into our relationship, I was looking for ways to help Jane improve her lot.

A partnership in more ways than one

The home Jane had bought jointly with her friend had risen in value with the market. Their earnings increased as they progressed in their jobs, so it was soon viable for them to sell that property and each buy one of their own. Jane was spending lots of time at my house, but was still not quite confident enough to move in with me altogether. She thought the best compromise would be to buy a house within walking distance, so we could see each other whenever we wanted, but she would have her own space.

It was a great idea. She bought a lovely little cottage two streets away, kitted it out nicely and spent about four nights there before moving in with me and never going back...

This provided an opportunity. We could rent her house out to provide extra income. So we did. And I felt confident I could dive into another venture with Jane which would benefit us both.

With most of my property portfolio within sight of where I lived, I appreciated the value of having investments close at hand. A new client who lived a few paces down the street came to me for help, having become entangled in a complex situation involving buying property in Spain off plan (you might remember I got burnt by buying off plan in my early days).

This kind of thing was all the rage in the early 2000s. I regularly had new and existing clients seeking my advice about whether to get involved with such schemes. In reality, most of them were merely seeking validation for a decision they had already made. Fooling oneself is a very common trait. In every case I told them to steer well clear. I remember almost begging someone not to proceed with what they had in mind, but to no avail. In every case they lost money and, in some cases, all of it.

This was certainly the case with my neighbour who had been duped by the celebrity involved in the marketing of her dream home and found herself with nothing to show for her investment. As she had very little income, her only option was to sell the house she was living in, but there was another problem. It was unconventional to say the least, with many quirks and foibles, split over a couple of levels. These days, developers will snap up anything going. At that time, the market was a little less bullish and she knew her place would be tricky to sell, having already tested the market.

But I could see possibilities. There was a downstairs space which could be converted into living accommodation with a new entrance, while the upstairs could also be a self-contained unit. It would not be easy, but having negotiated a good price, I just had to find a way to buy it.

This was where Jane came in. I proposed we do this project together. Although in full-time employment, she could devote time to it in the evenings and at weekends, and her regular income would assist us in obtaining finance.

The value of Mulsanne House was by then far more than the money I had borrowed, so I had another opportunity to raise cash to use as seed capital to buy more property. This was the key to the creation of my future wealth, and if I could do it with the person I loved, it would be perfect.

After some consideration, Jane agreed to go ahead with me. Although we weren't married at that time, this transaction was important in terms of binding us together. I saw it as significant in that regard as I was sure this was the right thing to do with someone who would be with me for the duration.

Mortgage finance was at a point where lenders were feeling generous, so we borrowed as much as we could, in the hope that after we had finished changing the property, we could re-mortgage it, release some money and do the same again. We retained the guys who had worked on my flat to do this job and, although it took a lot longer than we had anticipated, eventually we had ourselves two rentable units. As with the flat, we decided renting individual rooms would be the way to go. And so, Jane jumped into the world of property rentals, handling the letting and many other aspects.

At the time, there was a boom in people coming to the UK from Poland and a few of them became settled tenants, one of whom stayed for eight years. I still have tenants who were linked to this guy some twenty years later, showing it pays to look after people and think long term.

CHAPTER 23

INVESTING WITH OTHERS

A year or so after Jane and I bought our first property project together, another opportunity arose. When you make a decision to become involved in something, it's surprising how opportunities which never seemed to exist before come out of nowhere. This has happened to me so many times, it's impossible to say it's a coincidence. I have my own theory on why it happens, but we'll visit that later.

This project was even more daunting than the last, but I could see the potential. The landlord of a small shop was thinking of selling the freehold because he was looking to retire. It transpired the property actually consisted of two shops and three flats, and it would be sold with the tenants in situ.

This substantial building came at a cost far in excess of anything I had looked at before. An inspection made it clear all of the flats were tired, having been renovated over twenty years before and hardly touched since. The shops took care of themselves as the tenant had leases which required them to keep the premises in good order, as is usual for commercial lettings.

I ran a few numbers and could see the potential in buying the place, renovating the flats one at a time, and then remortgaging the whole lot to get back the money invested. I would need the help of the seller to achieve this, but I sensed that might be forthcoming as he had no-one else interested and was very keen to sell. Initially, I put the proposition to my investment club (more details on this club later in the chapter), but most of the members were unable or unprepared to invest.

I thought that might be the end of it, but then decided to see if there was any way Jane and I could do it ourselves. Our first property was up and running, the value had increased, and so it was possible to raise some money on it to go towards the renovation of the new place. But we still had to buy it. Arranging a mortgage for 75% of the value was easy. Finding the other bit needed some ingenuity.

This was where the seller came in.

A mutually beneficial deal

When people negotiate a purchase of a property, one of the things many overlook is the circumstances of the seller. With any property I have ever purchased, I have always dealt directly with the seller. This has paid massive dividends for us both.

When you're buying property, it's vitally important to find out as much as you can about the situation the seller is in. In this case, I had a number of meetings with the seller, sitting down with him at his home where we got to know each other. This was equally as important as the other elements of the deal. I would need him to have trust in me if it was going to work.

Having discovered the seller did not need the money from the sale, but just wanted less hassle in his life, I came up with a plan which still gives me a sense of pride today. The seller would lend Jane and me the money for the deposit on the property. As security, we would give him a second charge on the title. A charge is another word for a mortgage. Many people say things like, "We have a mortgage of £200k on our house". Actually, it's the lender who has the mortgage. It is their legal charge on the property which secures the debt the buyer owes. What people should be saying is, "We have a loan outstanding on our house of £200k", but that is more of a mouthful, so they use a euphemism instead.

So, the seller would have the charge on the property. He would receive 75% of the sale price on completion, and we agreed we would pay him so much a month towards the other 25% he had lent us. We would renovate the property, and as soon as it was finished, we would remortgage it and repay him everything.

With the large amount of money involved, this was a risky thing to do for both of us. A property crash or a problem with the renovation could have put us in serious trouble. But the seller was a very switched on and successful guy, and his confidence in us gave Jane and me the confidence we could do it. So we did. And it worked. Again.

Some months later, with our regular guys engaged to do the work, we found ourselves with a couple of nicely renovated flats and a third one still to do. The increased value was enough to allow us to re-finance. The new mortgage was for almost as much as we had paid for the property, so we ended up with an investment bringing us an income into which we had sunk very little of our own money. Just the sort of something from nothing I like.

I don't want to understate how difficult all this was to do. It was tremendously hard work, requiring a lot of thinking and determination. Additionally, the mortgage market had fewer restrictions in those days than it does today. Most lenders will not now allow the kind of arrangements we instigated, but by the same token, very few people would have taken the risks we did.

We weren't quite finished yet, though…

A stressful deal

The limiting factor for Mulsanne House was the size of the plot it sat in. Although it looked out on to a spacious courtyard, it had no rear garden, just a small strip of land and a reasonable-size patio to one side. The way to enhance its value would be to allow the house to sit more centrally in a decent-size plot, but living there on my own, I had been quite happy with it as it was.

Jane was much keener to see if we could expand the garden. Beyond my tiny strip at the rear of the house was a substantial garden, running along the entire length of my courtyard and the Mulsanne plot as part of the curtilage of a house on the high street. The garden could only be accessed through the house, which was Grade II listed, so it had few development possibilities. If I could acquire two-thirds of it, the difference to my house would be substantial. It would make the place exactly what it deserved to be.

This would never happen without me taking a bold step. The initial owner had sold the property not long after I had built Mulsanne and at that stage, acquiring the garden was the last thing I could contemplate. I got on well with the new neighbour and we had become friends. He was also a client I helped with various bits of advice. Overall, he was a good guy and I was pleased to have such a pleasant neighbour.

He wanted to sell the property, and so the only way Jane and I would acquire the garden would be to buy the whole place. We would then take some of the garden and add it to that of Mulsanne, selling the original house with a much smaller garden.

So, that's what we did. But not without difficulty. The biggest issue was my neighbour being fully aware I was in no position to do much negotiation. He knew the difference the garden would make to my property, so his asking price was pitched accordingly. I would be paying too much, but for once in my life, I was in a position where I just could not afford to say no. My usual method of negotiating was to decide in advance I would walk away if the deal wasn't what I wanted it to be. In this instance, that would be the wrong thing to do in the long term. If the property was sold to someone else, the opportunity to expand Mulsanne's garden might never present itself again. So I agreed to pay the somewhat ridiculous asking price and set about making it work.

As usual, I had to find a way to buy the place without any money to put towards it. Having acquired the last property using the seller's help, I saw no reason not to try the same again. I knew my neighbour had a good job and was in a position where he didn't necessarily need all of the money from the sale straight away. So, he would lend us the money for the deposit. Jane and I would raise a mortgage on his property so we could buy it and the neighbour would take a second charge on both the property he was selling us and the first property Jane and I had bought together. He needed this extra security as we would be stripping out a lot of the garden from his house. We would also be undertaking refurbishment which would take time and could leave him exposed. The market was still rising, but he (and we) had to hope we could remortgage the house and raise enough cash to repay him. Another very risky deal which kept me on my toes for many years.

The problems began with the refurbishment. My regular guys were busy elsewhere, so I was recommended a builder by an old friend and client of mine. He had used this builder successfully for many years, so I thought I was in good hands. But things can change and the job turned into a minor nightmare. It took much longer than we had planned and the workmanship was poor. I was still sorting out his mess bit by bit years later.

Worse than that was the timing. Right in the middle of the renovation came the start of the biggest financial crash the world has seen, culminating in the so-called credit crunch. I saw what was happening and realised we might never sell the property and raise enough to repay our former neighbour. Especially since we had annexed a large part of the garden.

Thankfully, the full effects of the crash took a while to hit, buying us just enough time and leeway to get the place revalued and remortgaged to repay the second charge held by the previous owner. It was a real skin-of-the-teeth job. Only a week or two later, it would not have been possible as lenders retracted most of their mortgage deals, to the extent there were only a handful of buy-to-let products left from a market which formerly had hundreds, if not thousands.

Although the house was not ideal for letting, we had no choice. It was a lovely old property, full of character, but not really durable enough to take the battering which letting inevitably brings. It was a constant battle trying to keep it in good shape. We must have repainted one of the kitchen walls more than twenty times over the years we had it. And when we eventually came to sell, Covid had struck and everyone thought property prices would collapse. After all the work and effort, we only just broke even on it.

There was also a huge upside. We had completely transformed how Mulsanne House was presented in its plot.

A serendipitous speculation

Just after the credit crunch, I became seriously ill, a combination of far too much work and stress. No-one knew exactly what was wrong with me, but the major worry was two separate tests indicating my body was in an incredibly low state of wellness. On both occasions, I was told it was almost impossible for me still to be walking around. I had no choice but to take three months off work.

So, what did I do? I switched my mental work into physical work and spent every day in the new garden, levelling, landscaping and sculpting it into a seamless and attractive part of Mulsanne. Nothing beats physical activity for improving your mental state. It was a huge amount of work, made easier with the help of a mini digger lent to me by a good friend. I shifted around 50 tons of earth to create a small semi-underground room below the lawn, with steps leading down from the main level to a large patio. It transformed the house and created a spot where Jane and I enjoyed many lovely evenings and weekends with friends, family and just the two of us.

Meanwhile, there were other property projects which had been rolling along, almost as an aside to everything else I was involved with. Once more, when I look back, I don't know how I managed to juggle all these different things at once. It's no surprise my health suffered.

Amongst the many projects going on over the course of the 2000s was a property company set up with Mike, my business partner from Edison Ford. We bought and sold a number of houses in the area, and then set our sights further afield when we believed the local market had reached its peak. In hindsight, this was a major mistake. Although we made what we thought were nice profits at the time, if we had kept our local houses, we would have been sitting on a goldmine now. Instead, we speculated in areas of which we had no experience, costing us a lot of money. Most of the profits we made in the early days were offset by the later losses. But it was all good experience and made me even more sure how important it is to stick to the markets you know.

There was one purchase which is memorable for amusing reasons and is another example of how opportunities crop up when you are proactively engaged with the world. Mike and I attended an auction in London at which a small estate of ex-US military properties near Kettering was being sold off. The houses were well built and substantial and close to a very desirable area. We did our due diligence, which took many hours, arranged our finance and turned up with a view to buying one, two or even three properties.

We quickly realised we wouldn't be buying one. The opening bid on the first house was already above the price we had decided to pay, so that was that. Although we had spent lots of time and energy prospecting these houses, we both put it down to a learning experience. Our mindsets were in sync at the very moment we knew we wouldn't be making a purchase. Obviously, we were disappointed and probably uttered some choice words, but within a second or two, we had moved on, thinking about how we could maximise the day some other way.

We sat through all the other lots, suspecting there would be no overlooked bargain amongst those we were interested in. Then after lunch, we decided we would head home. We got up from our seats just as a new property in another area was starting to be auctioned. In unison, we turned to look at each other with identical expressions as we heard the opening bid: £20k. We had no idea what this property was, but we returned to our seats, found it in the catalogue and agreed to bid.

It was a small flat in Bournemouth, not too far from the sea. The South Coast resort is generally a desirable place, so small flats at bargain prices shouldn't carry too much risk. We were successful bidders and paid something like £28k for it, which hardly seems possible now, but this was just before the big property boom of the mid-2000s. And the property needed refurbishment.

After a few moments of contemplation, kicking around various ideas, we decided we didn't have the time to spend on a renovation project, so perhaps the best thing to do would be to put the place on the market with a local agent at an optimistic but potentially achievable price, and see what happened. We didn't visit the flat or even hold the keys. They went straight to the agent.

Within a day, I'd received a call from a client who lived near London. He was a keen property investor and I had been helping him with various acquisitions over the years. He told me he had found a small flat in Bournemouth which he wanted me to arrange finance on. And yes, you've guessed it – the client wanted to buy our flat! I have no idea what the odds are for this kind of thing to happen, especially given the geographic span between the West Country, London and the South Coast. Nevertheless, this is exactly what did happen.

He bought the property from us at more or less the asking price, we made a nice profit and everyone was happy. A perfect transaction.

Investment club

If you can't manage to do a deal on your own, find trustworthy likeminded people you can do it with. At the same time as running my property company with Mike, I also started acquiring properties with other people, my sister being one of them. Our first project was to buy the house where we grew up for our mother to live in. I've already described how anti our mother was to this, but Jackie and I went ahead anyway as we knew it would be for everyone's benefit. We were then able to undertake some refurbishments which made the place so much better for her, which would never have been the case when she was a tenant of the local authority. As she grew older and less able to manage a house, we were in a position where we could sell and move her to a nice manageable bungalow, within sight of her old place, where she enjoyed many happy years.

Another group of people I began buying properties with is still going strong as I write. One of my very earliest clients, dating back to the late 1980s, had become a good friend who introduced me to many of his friends. They in turn became clients and friends of mine, and eventually a group of seven of us formed a small investment club in the 1990s. We did reasonably well from some stock market dabbling, but most of the funds we built up over the years came from the small contribution we would each put in every month.

Eventually, we had enough for a deposit on a property, so we bought a student let in Bath already owned by one of the members who wanted to reduce the size of his portfolio. Between us, we had enough skills to acquire, improve and manage the place and, in line with increasing property prices in the 2000s, we created a decent equity.

Then, using my tried and trusted method of remortgaging to release some of the equity, we bought another place. And then another. One of those was a second student let in Bath which we've subsequently sold. We've had a lot of fun along the way, learnt from the experiences (for example, we would have made a huge amount more on the student let if we had kept it) and are currently selling the last of the properties to help some of the guys with their retirement.

CHAPTER 24

THAT ELUSIVE SEVEN-FIGURE GOAL

We talked about the importance of knowing your net worth in Chapter 10, so you likely won't be surprised to learn I expanded this concept over the years. As I gradually and painfully clawed my way from destitution into a more positive situation, I also raised my sights.

In Part One, I recounted how I helped start a local motor racing club and used all my spare cash to get the car I'd always longed for. By the time I was twenty-two, I had acquired a car I could only have dreamed about a few years earlier. It was an Escort RS2000, one of the best performance cars of its day and still revered. Values now are probably 20x what I paid for mine in the late 1970s. I was very pleased with myself, especially when I showed up in it at the Autograss club. Most of the guys there were much older than I was, but had nothing to compare with this vehicle.

I was already getting used to being on the receiving end of comments such as, "It's OK for you, working in a bank, earning a fortune". Little did they know my wages were a pittance. I just didn't spend much. But there was one positive comment which has stuck with me until this day.

One of the members was an unlikely supporter of the club. He was the manager of a business which wrote manuals for ships, so his skill was that of a technical author. He had already complimented me on my writing skills and I liked talking to him as he was intelligent and full of insights which I didn't come across too frequently. When he saw my car, he congratulated me on being able to acquire it. And then he spoke the memorable words.

"Now you've reached that goal, you think that's it. You have the car of your dreams and you can just enjoy it. But if you have the skill and tenacity to reach that goal, what's to say you shouldn't reach for an even higher one? Why not think about the next car up the ladder? It might be a stretch, but **if you plant the idea in your mind now and start working towards it, there's no reason why you shouldn't reach it.**"

Who wants to be a millionaire?

When I read those words now, they seem completely obvious to me, yet at the time, they were an amazing revelation. Although I had been goal setting from a young age, I had been doing it without realising what I was doing. Finally, someone had told me there was more to it than a thing John Moon had in his head.

There is an argument which says continually wanting more just makes us unhappy or perpetually discontent. Some say it's at the heart of many people's problems. We want a product, item of food or experience, get it and the dopamine hit which comes with it, and minutes later we want something else. But there is a key difference between wanting another cake or sweet drink and saving up for weeks, months and years to buy something which has a value. I know cars depreciate, but if you buy carefully and treat them well, you should still have something to show for it when the time comes to change. Continually buying cakes and cola will only help you achieve a bigger waist.

So, I enjoyed and appreciated my RS2000, but I also knew I wanted something else. Which, as you know, was a property of my own. I now own around nine cars (it changes frequently) and I'm fairly content with them, but my goal setting mentality is still there and probably will be for life, so there is always something else to go for.

A goal I set in the 1990s was to spend the winter indulging in my second passion of skiing. It took a long time to achieve that one, but for the last four years, Jane and I have spent many weeks of the winter in the Alps. It's one of our most important pleasures and one we will continue to enjoy.

My most significant goal (to date, anyway) was something which is still unimaginable to many. The word millionaire will conjure up different things to everyone. The value of £1m is much diminished since I was first aware such a thing existed. Many people are millionaires these days simply through owning a nice house (the definition is having a net worth of more than £1m). When the word first came into my consciousness, most stately homes were worth less than £1m, so the prospect of ever entering that elite club seemed ridiculous. Inflation has meant billionaire is probably today's equivalent unachievable goal, though £1b is still a far more valuable figure than a million was in my early days.

To put the two in perspective, a million seconds equates to eleven and a bit days, while a billion seconds equates to over thirty-one years. It's just one letter different, but what a difference. Nevertheless, at least 2,500 people have achieved the feat of becoming a billionaire, so it's certainly not impossible.

The thought I could one day have a net worth of seven figures began growing as I built my property portfolio. All of it was built on debt, but the equity would surely increase as the years went by, so I ought to make it eventually.

Some things are in one's own control; some, such as property price inflation or deflation, are not. But there was something I could control and had been doing for a while, and that was renovating and improving the properties, bit by bit.

Another thing I had been doing was keeping detailed records. Spreadsheets have been a godsend to me and I've used them to monitor everything to do with my properties and other businesses. I also started to use one of the sheets to keep a record of clients' properties and in many instances, I had/have a better record of what they have and how it is doing than they do. And yet they made no effort to try to understand how spreadsheets worked, which always surprised me.

So, it was easy for me to know exactly where I was heading and when I would break that seven-figure barrier. I won't tell you when I hit that milestone exactly, but it wasn't in this decade or the previous one. Obviously, I was very happy, but I was also realistic. Life doesn't suddenly change when a number on a screen becomes one digit longer than it was. I've never been one to celebrate successes too much, or to be too miserable about my failures, so life carried on as normal.

When your net worth is more than £1m, it doesn't mean you instantly have lots of money in your pocket. In my case, it was the opposite. All my wealth was tied up in property. All of it was mortgaged, usually for the maximum I could squeeze out of it, and all my spare cash went into developing my existing properties. I still had to be careful and couldn't/didn't want to spend what I saw as silly amounts of money to get a temporary dopamine hit. With the debt I had, I was taking a big risk, so there was a way to go before I could be sure I wouldn't end up back at the bottom of the pile. So, it was work, work, work for another ten years at least.

Holiday lets

We haven't mentioned the old garages and buildings in my courtyard recently, but while all my projects were going on, I was simultaneously developing my little enclave. I started by turning the former slaughterhouse which the mechanic had made his home in 2000 into a very nice two-bed cottage. Then I knocked down half of my office and rebuilt it into two flats with a small cottage behind. Another couple of cottages at the bottom of my courtyard evolved and I created a nice, clean new garage for my cars next to Mulsanne.

It was a huge amount of work which went on for over ten years, so it's not surprising I didn't endear myself to my neighbours. The end result was something I am extremely proud of and has made a huge difference to the area generally. My net worth was ever increasing and despite more debt, my bottom line doubled within a year of hitting the first £1m target.

Just to keep me on my toes, I decided to start a holiday lettings business. This was despite me running the IFA and motorsport PR businesses, developing my properties and looking after all my own lettings. For many, just one of those would be a full-time job.

The holiday lets evolved from some success Jane and I had with Mulsanne, where we would swop houses with other people in various destinations around the world. The house swop system meant we got free accommodation *and* someone to look after our place while we were away. We enjoyed some fabulous stays in the USA, Canada, the Alps, Paris and Spain, and learnt a lot about what people like and don't like when they're staying in a place other than their own.

We started with the smallest of the cottages, styling, equipping and decorating it to a high standard. It was hard work as we did everything ourselves initially, but we had to prove it would work. We were then able to outsource a lot of the tasks like cleaning and laundry. As I developed the courtyard, we added more holiday properties to our portfolio and had a very successful business. I became chairman of the Bath Self Catering Association which I helped to move into the online world to stay abreast of the competition such as Airbnb.

Expanding the holiday let business and with property development a constant, I needed full-time staff. It would be impossible to do everything myself, so just as I used borrowed money to gear up a property business, I used employees to gear up a conventional business.

Employees come with advantages and challenges. Unfortunately, a less-than-positive experience with a staff member upon whom I relied took the edge off that period of my life, and for my own sanity I had to massively reduce the size of the holiday let operation. Eventually, I closed it, having learnt a tremendous amount.

Escape to the country

At one of the times when I was at my most pressured, something unexpected happened.

My wife's passion is horses. It is as strong as mine for cars. After she had moved in with me, she would spend one or two evenings and most weekends at my sister's where there was plenty of room for her to keep her horse. It wasn't an ideal situation, with the travel taking up more than an hour each time, but we lived with it and thought that was the only solution.

I had always said Mulsanne was my house for life. It seemed to be everything I wanted, especially with the lovely new garden. Then Jane started dropping the odd hint about houses in the countryside which might suit us one day. We never did much more than look at them briefly online and there was no question of us going to see one. I wasn't moving, so there was no point.

Then one evening, Jane pointed out an online listing for a bungalow in a small village I had hardly heard of, some thirty minutes north. The listing was extremely poor, not helped by a grainy photo of a plain 1970s bungalow. The interest was the 7 acres of land it came with, along with where it was.

It transpired the village was well known to Jane, who used to ride a horse there on a loan arrangement from a distant relative. She told me how beautiful the area was and how rare it was for such properties to come on to the market. The asking price was ridiculously high for what the place appeared to be, but to appease Jane, I agreed to drive up to the house and look at it from the outside the following weekend.

That agreement turned out to be life changing…

As soon as I drove into the lane, I knew this was an extremely special place. There was a former farm at the very end and no through traffic. The lane itself was an offshoot of another dead end, so even better. I've rarely if ever found a quieter place and the views of the Cotswolds were some of the most beautiful I had ever seen, and remain so today. Yet it was only ten minutes to both the M4 and M5 motorways.

Just like when I had first seen my courtyard site, the same kind of mental click occurred. I knew this would be a wonderful place to create a dream home where both of us could be equally happy, and I had to find a way to make it happen.

The story of that project could fill another book, but let's just say it took ten years and was by far the most challenging period of my life. Even buying the place was a challenge, every bit as difficult as when I bought the courtyard. I had very little liquid money. I couldn't sell Mulsanne as we needed somewhere to live while we changed the new place into what we wanted. And I had everything else going on in my life as well. But with lots of refinancing, juggling and seemingly never-ending toil and struggle, we eventually created an amazing dream home, with stables, garages and everything anyone would want from a grand design. I couldn't and wouldn't have done it without Jane who has a wonderful eye for detail and has helped create something extremely special.

Every day, I'm grateful, impressed and joyful about living in such a wonderful place. The community has been incredibly welcoming and friendly, and I felt more at home in my first two weeks of living there than I ever did at Mulsanne. And contrary to what I had always believed, I sold Mulsanne. Luckily, the new owners are very nice people, which is important to me as I still have the other properties in that area and it's great to see friendly faces when I go to my office.

Which just about brings me up to date. I've stepped back from many of the things I used to be convinced I had to do and my stress levels are a fraction of what they were. I could give up everything and put my feet up, but I know that is not something I will ever want to do. I enjoy being engaged in projects, challenges and opportunities, so my time is always filled with something. But now it's on my terms. I do as much skiing and motor racing as I like. If I fancy going to a festival or having a few days away, then it happens without me feeling guilty about it.

Perhaps I'm finally living the life of a millionaire. It hasn't been easy, but there is little I would change. My goal now is to help others do as I did. It starts with my own family, but I also want this book to provide inspiration and a guide to those who might otherwise see such an achievement as impossible.

Part Three of the book will give you a few specifics about what is needed to make it happen.

Part Three

SKILLS WHICH COST NOTHING BUT GIVE YOU SOMETHING

CHAPTER 25

COMMUNICATION

Learning from others is one of the most rewarding aspects of setting out on a journey to improve your life. It helped me to develop certain skills, which in themselves have contributed to my successes.

When you develop a learning mindset, the uncanny thing is you gain momentum. The more you want to learn and develop, the more opportunities to do so reveal themselves to you. And when it comes to side effects, an improvement in your financial position is an attractive one.

The title of Part Three implies all the skills we will cover here come without cost. Sorry to say, that's not true in the strictest sense, as everything we do in life has a cost. If it didn't, then LUD would not be a thing. But assuming you are interested in the monetary costs rather than the not irrelevant cost of your time, I can say my heading is accurate.

There is so much you can gain by adopting the right kind of mindset and observing closely what is going on around you. With time, you will be able to make distinctions which will transform the way you look at the world, react to what comes your way and **communicate** effectively.

To get the most out of anything, it's important to start off in the right way. You need to work on developing certain attributes which will encourage the right kind of thinking to allow you to learn effectively. The first one we will look at is **communication**.

More than words

If I had to choose one attribute which has contributed to my successes over all others, then by a small margin it would be communication. As I'm sure you are all aware, breakdowns in communication, from personal right up to inter-continental, are the cause of much of the world's ills. Even as a child, I was surprised how conversations could so easily become distorted between the transmitter and the receiver, simply because one or two words were misinterpreted. This is happening on a constant basis, every second of the day, all over the world.

Why are we humans so poor at communicating? Like many of the challenges within this book, I don't proclaim to have the answer. All I can do is tell you what I do and have done, and you can see if that helps you. My exposure to the written word from a very young age helped me enormously. For all my mum's imperfections, I owe her a great debt for spending so much time reading to me.

You may not have had such an advantage. If that's the case, all I can say is please put that right. Not only can you develop a habit of reading books that will help you towards your goal (you've made a great start by choosing this one), but if you are ever in a position to do so, be sure to read to your own children, nieces, nephews, grandchildren etc. Exposure to words, the subtleties of language, the context of the situation and the calming effect of a kind human voice cannot be underestimated.

One of the things we often forget is communication is about much more than just the words. For spoken communication, words only make up 7% of the package.[10] The rest is taken care of by intonation and body language or physiology.

---

10 N Belludi, 'Albert Mehrabian's 7-38-55 Rule of Personal Communication' (Right Attitudes, 2008) www.rightattitudes.com, accessed 22 April 2024

You might find this hard to comprehend. You might also believe that in a written communication, the words will account for 100% of the message. If you do believe that to be the case, then read this next sentence and tell me what it means.

I didn't say she stole the money.

Now try saying the sentence again, but accentuating the word in **bold text** in each of these six examples:

I didn't say she stole the money. (Someone else said that.)
I **didn't** say she stole the money. (I deny saying she did.)
I didn't **say** she stole the money. (Perhaps she did, but I didn't say so.)
I didn't say **she** stole the money. (Someone else did, not her.)
I didn't say she **stole** the money. (She didn't steal it – but she could have lost it.)
I didn't say she stole the **money**. (She may have stolen something else, though.)

One sentence can have at least six different meanings, depending on how we intonate. If we can create so many meanings from just seven words, it's not surprising difficulties and conflicts between us arise from miscommunication.

I can't even begin to scratch the surface of the skills and strategies you need to become an effective communicator. That has been done 1,000 times in numerous books, including the excellent *How To Win Friends And Influence People*, written by Dale Carnegie in 1936.[11] Despite its longevity, it still contains some pearls which are relevant in today's vastly changed world. But finish reading my book first, please.

---

11   D Carnegie, *How To Win Friends And Influence People* (28th edition, Vermillion, 2006)

How do you become an effective communicator?

Like with many skills, some people seem to have been born with inbuilt advantages when it comes to communicating. This may be true of you, but it is what you do with what you are given which counts. You can perfect a skill to become above average if not brilliant at it if you practise enough. But to have the will power, tenacity and energy to become good at anything, you need to be interested in it to the extent you are prepared to do what most will not.

If you spend your life without the attributes of awareness and curiosity (we will look at these in detail in the next chapter), it's unlikely you will be a great communicator. If you speak to people with your mind elsewhere or if you are predominantly a transmitter, constantly spraying your own thoughts and words over others with no honest interest in what they are saying or thinking, you are probably not a good communicator. I'm sorry to say you're not the kind of person I want to have dinner with either.

If you work in a sales role, your ability to communicate effectively will be one of the main parameters determining your success. If your target buyer doesn't fully grasp what you are saying, they might still buy from you (for various complex reasons), but it won't be a purchase with any sense of commitment to you. To succeed in sales and in business, you need to build long-term relationships. This is extremely important and, without great communication, that job is a lot harder.

So, back to the practice. If you can develop an interest in improving your communication skills (just keep thinking of the benefits), then you need to use every single opportunity to observe, evaluate and learn to understand what makes great or poor communication. Unless you live alone on a desert island, you can begin practising right now. Even if you have been such a poor communicator up to now, you have no friends and no job, you can start methodical observation of people communicating with each other in countless situations and stockpile mental or physical notes of examples which resonate with you. Just go out into the street, shopping centre or anywhere with lots of people and start observing.

When you come across examples of poor communication, break down exactly where the shortfalls are. More often than not, it will be intonation closely followed by facial expression which you will notice making a difference. If you get on a bus, the driver can tell you the amount of the fare with a grunt and a grim face, which adds nothing to your day (or theirs). Or they could say the exact same thing with a smile and a pleasant lilt in their voice, which lifts your spirits (and theirs). This is so obvious, I almost feel embarrassed having to write it, yet great communication is such a rare skill, it's clear most either don't get it or can't be bothered to take notice of what is going on.

The good news is it doesn't take too much effort to improve and begin to stand apart from the crowd. We may live in a world of billions of people, yet the competition to be a good communicator has relatively few participants. If you are learning from what you observe and putting it into practice, this should give you the confidence to do more and rise to another level.

While this is all very helpful, you should also be aware of some of the pitfalls, especially if you have been someone who traditionally struggles in this area.

The pitfalls to watch out for

The biggest trap you can fall into when you're trying to communicate in a situation which is especially important to you is speaking too much. If you are naturally a transmitter, this will be an intrinsic part of you, so becoming more of a receiver may be especially difficult. A quick way to keep on track is to remind yourself of the ears to mouth ratio, ie you have two ears and one mouth, so listen twice as much as you speak. Only when you have mastered this will you be in a position to move forward.

Even if you are not naturally a talker, saying too much can still be a problem. Until you have the confidence to chat naturally and effectively with almost anyone, it's better to say too little than too much. By showing interest in the other person with your attentive body language and asking short questions which you genuinely want to know the answers to, you build up **rapport** (see Chapter 26) without saying much at all.

It's telling how people will believe you are pleasant and interesting, even when you have said very little and allowed them to do all the talking. Although I have spent a lifetime being interested in communication and am happy to speak publicly to large audiences with little or no preparation, I still find it better to keep my words to a minimum when I am in the early stages of getting to know someone I have met on a one-to-one basis. This is all part of **establishing my reputation early on**.

Often linked with saying too much is the trap of trying to appear too clever. I know several successful people who have achieved great things, despite the seeming disadvantage of a not particularly high level of intelligence. They've made up for that with hard work, being streetwise and not saying much. It's better for people to find you something of an enigma or hard to read than to think you are an idiot. If you don't know or understand something, others will respect you far more if you say, "Sorry, I'm being a bit thick here, could you explain that to me, please?" as opposed to pretending you understand when you clearly don't.

That leads me on to another pet skill of mine. I told my wife about it years ago and now she notices when I do it and even finds it slightly annoying. But it helps in many situations, especially sales.

It's the old nugget of never answering a question unless you have got to the bottom of what the questioner is really asking you. Let's say you work in a shop selling lawnmowers. A person takes an interest in one you have on display. Potential buyers always go through a mental game of ping pong where they find ways to both justify and veto their possible purchase. For a tin of baked beans, this contest in the brain takes milliseconds because the consequences of getting it wrong are relatively tiny. In the case of a bigger purchase, like a lawnmower, the contest can go on for minutes, days or even weeks.

So, when a customer is in front of a salesperson, they will often feel they have to ask some questions. This is usually just to give them time to think – they don't really need to know the answer to most of the questions they ask. An experienced salesperson can easily spot the important questions and differentiate between them and the fluff. An inexperienced seller will bombard the potential buyer with unwanted and unnecessary information, which will more likely dissuade than persuade.

Sales is a game of cat and mouse. Or more accurately, mouse and mousetrap. Although most cats are effective at catching mice, mice run away at the first sign of a cat. People tend to be like that with sellers who move too quickly towards them. My technique is to be like a mousetrap (or a skilful cat). It's better to lie in wait, patiently observing, keeping your bait in tip-top order, and time your move to the optimum moment so you entrap your prey. All done in the nicest possible way, of course.

Back to the lawnmower shop. A typical question might be, "Does this model come in red?" An inexperienced salesperson might spend unnecessary time trying to find out. Or they might know it doesn't and assume the worst if they say so, trying to overcompensate for the lack of what they believe must be an important aspect for the potential buyer.

The experienced salesperson will simply say, "Do you want it in red, then?" More often than not, the reply will be something like, "Oh no, it's OK, I just wondered. I quite like the green, actually."

When a person's question is complex or off the wall, it's even more important to find out if it's a real question or just a barrier for some other objection. Here, you need to keep asking questions about their question until you have got to the bottom of what they mean. This is not intrusive or rude, unless you make it so. Your body language and intonation will determine whether you are being helpful or just awkward.

In a situation where it is necessary to ask questions, perhaps personal ones, the worst thing you can do is be apologetic about it. When you start your first job, this can be difficult as you may never have had to ask anyone anything personal before. This has given rise to a phenomenon where people are so embarrassed about the questioning, they cannot even directly ask a person their name.

For example, I want to book a table in a restaurant. The waiting staff need my name to confirm the booking. I prepare myself for the almost inevitable.

"What was your name?" they ask. My name has never changed, it's always been John Moon. Why don't they just say, "May I have your name, please"? It cannot be anything other than impressive to find a person, especially a young one, who asks questions directly, clearly and politely, rather than using the ridiculous euphemisms society has invented to prevent the 'pain' of having to do so.

Call me old fashioned, but another trend I find incredibly annoying is the overuse of superlatives, coupled with ridiculous amounts of mock politeness, which leaves the transmitter nowhere to go when genuine praise or kindness is required and justifiable. One example is the word 'perfect'. This seems to have become the default response to even the simplest request.

Going back to the restaurant, the staff member has asked my name (in the past tense). I state my name, avoiding the temptation to tell them it was, is and will continue to be John Moon. The usual response?

"Perfect."

Do they mean my name is a perfect example of how someone could be identified? Or perhaps the way I stated my name was perfect. Lovely intonation, meaningful body language, no mumbling and in the present tense. What kind of response were they expecting? How badly would I have to say my name for them not to say perfect? What word would they use if they actually found a situation where someone had done something perfectly?

My daughter would tell me I am now sounding like a grumpy old man, which is probably true, but I also know I am not alone in thinking this. So if you speak in clichés, please stop. You will never be admired for your eloquence otherwise.

Dealing with conflict

I understand many people struggle with expressing themselves verbally, and in some cases this is due to shyness, which can be hard to overcome. This is particularly challenging when such people are faced with awkward situations, for example where there is an element of what they see as confrontation. They will often do everything they can to avoid situations where they feel the communication will be uncomfortable.

This can create a downward spiral where their comfort zone for such situations diminishes as time goes on, which results in them doing everything they can to ensure they avoid even the slightest element of discomfort. Unfortunately, this often leads to a limited life where the fear of having to step outside their comfort zone prevents them doing all kinds of things.

Progression comes with challenge. If you want to do better

and improve your lot, it's inevitable you will have to face such situations and you will need to learn how to deal with them. The more you avoid them, the worse your ability to deal with them becomes, so it's essential you face up to your fears and overcome them.

Like most of the skills in this book and in life, the best way to do this is to practise. Luckily, everyday life gives you plenty of opportunity. I'm not suggesting you go out looking for arguments or difficult situations to become embroiled in, but what you must do is find your own way to deal with people when you encounter a situation where there is some kind of disagreement or mild conflict. Simply being aware you are in a situation where you can learn is half the battle.

When you face difficulty or conflict where you know it's important to stand up for yourself, rather than just making a point for the sake of it, say what you feel as soon as the thought comes to you. The longer you wait to express yourself, the more difficult it is likely to become. It will often reach a point where you talk yourself out of saying anything and the painful feelings just sit there in your mind, percolating. This is another LUD example.

A good tip to enable you to say what you think while taking the heat out of the situation is to speak as if your brain is a third person involved in the conversation, for example, "I hear what you say and right now, my brain is telling me xyz." Then see how the other person responds. At the least, you will have broken the ice around the subject and it should lead to a more relaxed dialogue.

Using the third person to talk about things in your head is extremely beneficial in many situations, especially stressful ones. I'm sure you know how easy it is to give advice to your friends, and yet when you are presented with similar situations affecting you, you get brain fog. Talking to yourself as though you are a third party allows you to distance yourself from the problem and see it more clearly.

Another way is to have a mental mentor. Choose someone whom you have great respect for. It can be someone you don't know, even no longer living such as Steve Jobs. You could ask him what he would do in this situation. It's incredible how much help you can get from these mentors in your head – they give you wise words, even though it is your brain making them up. Assuming your mentor is a decent and successful person, of course. Choosing the wrong one can be as disastrous as a good one can be invaluable.

When you are thinking clearly and with awareness, it's easier for you to face up to any conflict you have been putting off. It doesn't matter how you achieve that clarity, but it will help you so much when you have it.

So far, we have focused on verbal interaction. We mustn't forget how the written word has gained importance in the communication hierarchy with the ever-growing rise of electronic interaction. Is this at the expense of verbal skills? It's given rise to the keyboard warrior where even the meekest and most mild-mannered person can become pathologically aggressive when using the written word. Could this be part of a downward spiral where avoidance of face-to-face conflict has created frustration which has to be released somehow? If so, it gives us another reason why learning to interact effectively face to face with others is so important.

Internal and external dialogue

There is another part of communication which I haven't spoken enough about so far. Internal dialogue is so important as over time, the words we repeat on a habitual basis form neural networks which become hard wired into us. It doesn't matter whether these words are in our heads or if they are clichés or patterns of external communication. It's what we say and how we say it which makes a difference to how we evolve as people over a reasonable period of time.

The sad thing is, the words we say and the way we say them in the early years of our life is often seen as endearing, especially to those close to us. In the community of my childhood, there was (and still is to a degree) a tendency for the males to react in an ironically negative way to most interactions. This was seen as cool or manly amongst the young males and cute amongst the females. There are tons of examples. One you might recognise is a reaction to the weather – a favourite non-contentious way of opening a conversation for the British.

Someone says, "Lovely day today." The sort of response you might expect from those I'm highlighting would be, "Yeah, but I bet it'll rain this afternoon when I mow the lawn." This kind of response seems innocent enough. And if it's said with a smile or a certain intonation, it can be amusing. But if the semi-negative response becomes your default pattern of speech, the damage it does to you over time is incredible.

Like with many habits, it's easy for the transmitter to be totally unaware of what is happening. The slow, inexorable, marginal build-up of neural pathways which eventually become steel cable-like can turn that person into someone it's not so nice to be around. A younger person's idiosyncrasies which we initially love them for can evolve into unappealingly negative character traits which culminate in even their loved ones becoming tired of them.

The good news is this can be prevented by being **aware and honest** and monitoring our internal and external dialogue (more on awareness in the following chapter). How we greet people is a good place to start. In the area of my childhood, it was traditional to say "Alright?" as the standard greeting. It's still pervasive today in many tribes and is a lazy way of saying "How are you?" In such tribes, it's generally cool to keep anything which might seem caring or nice to an absolute minimum. The standard response to "Alright?" is "Not too bad" or "Could be worse".

I remember one guy. When I met him at age sixteen, I thought he was very cool because he used the immortal "Fair to middling" as his response to "Alright?" The sad thing is he was probably correct. If he has carried on using such language, I would guess that's what he still is right now. I hope I'm wrong.

Your subconscious wants to give you all the reasons it can to ensure you are correct about what you are saying and thinking in your conscious mind. If you constantly say everything is a bit shit, then guess what your subconscious prover will do. It shows you all the ways life is a bit shit. Although I am not a religious person, there are some useful phrases in the Bible. 'Seek and ye shall find' is one of them. In other words, you get what you are looking for.

This is why you have to be so careful with your dialogue. It's also why those who love conspiracies will find all sorts of 'evidence' which proves they are correct. What they don't realise is their subconscious prover is constantly researching on their behalf, based on the words they are using in their everyday lives. The prover will seek out anything it can find, however ludicrous, to back up that person's conspiracy. Scary, eh?

Since my unaware days came to an end and certainly in the last thirty years, I have loved studying and analysing the things I hear from others. It's interesting to notice tendencies and patterns within groups of people, especially those about to learn or take part in a new skill. I get this opportunity with both my skiing and motor racing. I spend a small amount of time each year helping at the racing school at Castle Combe, as well as teaching circuit driving techniques on a one-to-one basis, so I interact with a lot of people. The words they choose prior to their experiences are good indicators of the attitude they will bring with them to the car. It doesn't necessarily predict how well they will get on, but it does give an indication of how well they will learn, which usually translates to their performance on track.

Some people are great to be around and others seem to drain us. I call the latter fun extractors. If you know any fun extractors (you surely will), monitor their words and intonation, and you will quickly understand how their habitual programming is giving them their negative aura. It's likely the worst offenders will be older people, because their neural networks have become stronger and more well-established as the years have passed.

Another factor to consider is your store of dopamine declines with age, so the older you are, the less pleasure and excitement you derive from your activities and lifestyle. This is why it's so important to do everything you can to give yourself the best possible chance of a positive mental state as you age. Diet and exercise play a vital role in this, and so do the people you communicate with. When you meet a skilled fun extractor, sadly, it's best to move on. Unless you are incredibly strong, they will drain you. Look for people who add something to your day rather than being dragged down by those stealing your energy.

CHAPTER 26

AWARENESS AND RAPPORT

This is another big subject, perhaps needing a book's worth of explanation to explore everything involved in being fully aware. Fundamentally, you need to develop the ability to criticise and evaluate yourself in as objective a manner as you possibly can.

So many of us walk around in a kind of trance. We notice little, and yet there is so much to take in. When we bury our heads in our phones, it's simply not possible to be truly present. And therefore, we can't be aware of what is going on, where our focus really lies, what limiting beliefs we are constantly reinforcing, what negative patterns of behaviour we are becoming adept at developing, what wonderful things are in front of us and around us.

When you start to discover your awareness factor, you might not like what you find. But unless you have completed the process of moving from being unaware you are unaware, through the phase of being aware you are unaware to being aware you are aware, you have no hope of improving yourself or learning from others. By spending time working on this, you can ultimately enter a state of being where your awareness is automatic. In other words, you will be unaware you are aware. Then, one of your biggest challenges will be dealing with those who exist so much in their own heads, all they are interested in is themselves.

This is such a common trait, you might well discover you are one of those people, which is why becoming aware is not always a pleasant process. It is relatively easy to find out if you have this flaw. Just monitor yourself in conversations. If you are doing most of the talking, see if there is a pattern. When you ask someone a question, are you already preparing your own speech about the subject you just asked them about? Do you dismiss their reply as fast as you can so you can blurt out the thing you can't wait to get out of your head?

If you don't do this, then good show. It means you've probably noticed others who do this all the time. It's tiring, boring and rather rude. If you have no awareness of what you are doing, habitually, it's a trap you can fall into. You will never learn as well as you might with that kind of mindset. Use your ears and mouth in the 2:1 ratio.

Before you can be fully aware, there are two traits you will need to develop: honesty and curiosity.

Honesty with yourself is a fundamental attribute you require to become aware enough to learn from others. If you can't be honest about your own shortcomings, then you will find it tricky to gain anything by observing others.

Our ability as humans to deny the grim reality of the things we are less than optimal at is one of the biggest reasons we don't move forward. If we can fool ourselves for long enough, we will eventually reach a point where it doesn't matter to us that we can't do something, and then we give up trying altogether. Being honest about our own behaviour opens us up to learning so we can improve and make ourselves (hopefully) better people.

Monitoring your own conversations is part of being honest about how you perform in certain situations. There is no point kidding yourself you listen to others when in reality, you are doing anything but. The quality of honesty about ourselves is absent in all of us to a greater or lesser extent. Being objective about yourself is one of your greatest challenges, but it's worth spending your valuable brain power on it.

Now let's look at **curiosity**. You may find others interesting or annoying, but perhaps the best way to deny yourself the chance to learn from them is indifference. If someone's behaviour winds you up, then using awareness and honesty, you could develop a curious mindset to find out what is driving this emotion. You may be surprised at what you find.

It's said love and hate are often close bedfellows. Many of you will know from your own relationships how true this can be, but perhaps the worst thing for any relationship is indifference. Counter it by being curious and aware, and then honest about what you find. There is no point in being super aware, vacuuming up lots of external input, and then doing nothing with it.

By asking yourself questions about what someone has said or done, you can learn much more than you will by just being attentive. If you are lucky enough to have someone you can talk to about this kind of thing, it will help you. Talking and exploring with a likeminded person creates a synergy where you both gain more insights than you would in your own heads.

Couples often do this. They discuss what one of their friends has said to see if they agree on what was meant. The main problem with this is such conversations can have a tendency to focus only on negative things. It's important to expand your ability to analyse anything which might help you grow your skills of understanding and communication.

Rapport

This is a skill which cannot be underestimated if you want to do just about anything with your life. And like most skills in this book, it costs you nothing to acquire, apart from your own time and energy.

Almost everything you want to achieve is going to involve engagement with others in some way or another, so if you aren't good at forming connections, then life is going to be harder than it needs to be. While it's possible to gain rapport through the written word, here, we are going to concentrate on face-to-face communication, as I believe this is the area where most progress can and needs to be made.

Rapport is another huge subject in itself, so I can only scratch the surface, but anything is better than nothing. This small insight may prompt you into further research and developing your skills.

Surprisingly, rapport with others is not essential to succeed. So, why is it important?

I see many examples where people have gone through life gaining very little rapport. Some still manage to achieve a kind of success, but in the main, it's at the expense of personal relations. You may know of people who have risen to senior management positions, yet command little respect from those they are supposedly managing. This kind of situation is more likely to occur in large organisations where 'difficult' people are often promoted just to get rid of them to another department. It sounds ridiculous, but it happens. It's one of the major causes of failure in such organisations.

Lack of rapport is much more of a handicap if you work for yourself. It's tricky to succeed on your own when you are unable to build good relationships with others. So, let's agree rapport is something you need. But what is rapport and how do you achieve a decent amount of it?

Defining rapport eloquently is as difficult as achieving it. When you have established it with another person, you will know, and it will be different with everyone. A dictionary defines it using expressions such as harmony, mutual trust and understanding. You could say it's when you click with someone.

If you are aware of how you are communicating, being honest with yourself and authentic with others, and taking a genuinely curious interest in what is going on, then it's likely you are already pretty adept at gaining rapport. Otherwise, you probably at least know some of the fundamentals of rapport building.

First impressions are important, so if you have a weakness here, it's something you need to work on. Shyness is one of the biggest handbrakes, as it's often confused with indifference or superiority. It is so sad when a shy person is desperate to make connections, yet appears to be someone who wants to do the opposite.

I don't have any magic answers to overcome being shy, even though it is something I have suffered with myself. There have been few occasions in my life when I have admitted to this. I struggle to remember any prior to writing this book, though one or two perceptive people have spotted it. Most who know me will say this is ridiculous, but I can tell you my fundamental default option from childhood has been introversion. It's still there now in certain situations, but because I was so desperately determined to overcome it and I seem to possess a certain tenacity, I forced myself to operate out of my comfort zone and to do and say things I felt really uncomfortable with. This is a good example of what you can do with the skill of **persistence** (which we'll cover in the next chapter). With a passionate interest in trying to change something, coupled with practice on a daily basis over a long period, you can overcome almost anything.

Strangely, my limitation is restricted to one-to-one situations with people. I've never had a problem in addressing large groups, yet in the past, a face-to-face encounter, especially with someone I perceived to be superior to me, used to scare me terribly. When I worked for the bank, there was a senior HR manager at the area office who petrified me. I found it difficult to say even one word to him in the early days, but by the time I was twenty-one and had progressed to the much bigger environment of the Bath Old Bank branch, I was a changed person.

Recognising and respecting personality types

As words are only a small part of communication, it's logical they are also only a small part of gaining rapport. Body language or physiology is extremely important and an intrinsic part of understanding personality types. Another huge subject – read some books on it, it's fascinating.

Although there are numerous ways of classifying people (Myers-Briggs is the most well-known) and I have studied most of the main schools of thought on the subject, I believe we all break down to four broad types, though the majority of well-balanced people will be a mixture. The tricky ones to deal with are those who are ensconced in their chosen quarter.

The thing to remember here is trying to gain rapport using a style that works for some will not work with others. And perhaps this is the secret to rapport. Being chatty with certain personality types will get you nowhere. Being a chameleon and matching yourself to the personality in front of you is important, if not essential.

If this concept is new to you, you may find it somewhat difficult to accept or comprehend, perhaps even deceitful. But it's all about intention. If your motive for gaining rapport is to take advantage of someone, then I agree, it is deceitful. If you believe gaining rapport is about making others feel comfortable around you so you both achieve something worthwhile from the interaction, then what is the problem? In sales, we would call this a win-win situation. As many wins are just a feeling we have in our head and time can change our perception of them anyway, all we can do is act honestly and authentically at the time.

Let's take a look at the four main personality types. Imagine a matrix divided into four sections. On the top left is the engineer type. Top right is the entrepreneur type, bottom left is the sensitive, motherly type and bottom right is the party animal. Those on the bottom of the matrix tend to make decisions based on their emotions. Those on the top do so based on facts. On the left-hand side are the slow decision makers, on the right-hand side are the more extrovert fast decision makers.

So, the sensitive on the bottom left is a quiet, warm type who values family and friends as the most important things in life. They like dealing with nice people who aren't too loud. The engineer type speaks for itself. They may or may not have leather patches on their sleeves, but they will definitely carefully consider how they enter into any transaction. Neither of these two will like being sold to. You have to befriend the motherly type and impress the engineer with facts.

Top right is the go getter/entrepreneur who wants to succeed beyond everything. That type will appreciate great sales skills and will want to work with you to get a satisfactory outcome, but you'll need to speak fast, get to the point and waste no time. Bottom right is the loud socialiser type who likes to head straight to the pub with their mates after work and thinks all paperwork is pointless.

If you are naturally an outgoing character with extrovert tendencies, using lots of gestures and speaking quickly, those from the opposite side of the matrix are likely to treat you with suspicion. You could find it difficult to break down the defensive barriers they might erect. If you interact with an engineer type who carefully considers every word, you are not likely to gel with them unless you keep your conversations factual, perhaps avoid too much eye contact (this kind of person can find that suspicious or intrusive) and stress how important it is to be accurate about details. Loud party animals who flit from one thing to another and find admin dull tend to struggle in these situations.

If you want to play with this, act out (without speaking) how the four different personality types would perform a simple interaction such as going into a jewellery shop to buy something on display. Imagine how each type would enter the shop. The two on the left might not even go into the shop, but would buy online. The engineer would do hours of research, the sensitive type would trust the recommendation of friends. Top right would want a deal. Bottom right would want to enjoy the whole experience and not be too bothered if it costs more, as long as they feel great about what happens.

Now think about what you would do to give the impression of being each of the four types. You may not be adept at acting, but you can imagine how a shy, introverted person might look, with head down and sloping shoulders, moving hesitantly. Then imagine if the shop assistant was a bottom right, greeting the sensitive with big demonstrative movements and launching into a jolly spiel about how wonderful the product is. Probably wouldn't work too well.

Think about how you act and react when confronted with each different personality type. You might say, "This is how I am, they can take it or leave it, I'm not changing." That's absolutely your right. All I am saying is if you want to follow a smoother pathway, make more of opportunities which may be hidden in plain sight by getting to know someone you otherwise wouldn't, then what is the harm in changing your behaviour slightly to fit the circumstances?

I've angled most of this from the context of a sales environment. The same principles apply in almost every situation as pretty much every new human interaction involves a kind of sale. If you meet someone new and want to have some kind of ongoing relationship with them, a sales process takes place, whether you are aware of it or not. You gain a first impression, one party decides they wish to continue the interaction and begins their 'sales pitch', which may be nothing more than standing there with a silly grin. At some point, the other party decides whether they wish to devote any of their time to this interaction and behaves accordingly. Sometimes, this process can be over and done with in a millisecond. In other instances, it can go on for years. Like it or not, rapport will be at the heart of most of these situations.

Authenticity

A strange aspect of rapport is how authenticity plays a part. I'm happy to nail my colours to the mast by telling you how important I find the quality of authenticity. I instantly like some people and the determinant is almost always how authentic they are. Yet it's important to align yourself with others by changing your method of being with them. How can that be authentic?

Most people I would call normal have elements of all the personality types and, with practice, can learn to accentuate or minimise each of them according to the situation before them. This doesn't mean they are being unauthentic, they're merely focusing on different aspects of their characters according to the circumstances. The truly unauthentic live their lives acting as if they are someone they are not. Ego plays a large part in this.

There is a tendency for many to try too hard when they're meeting new people and go overboard with bullshit. They believe they need to big themselves up for others to like them. For me, the opposite is true. Understate and over-deliver is much more preferable. Having said that, I don't mean you should focus on your weaknesses in the mistaken belief others will like you or feel sorry for you as a result.

All this depends on the situation, of course. In a highly combative situation, the grand masters of battle might claim weakness where they are strong and strength where they are weak, in a ploy to outwit their opponent.

If I meet a totally unauthentic person, I will simply move on to those I feel are more genuine. Similarly, I believe unauthentic types seek out those who are like them. That might explain the loud groups you can encounter in public places, oblivious of the impact they are having on the outside world. The fascination is those firmly on the left side of the matrix are likely to feel those completely on the right are unauthentic, while those on the right feel those on the opposite side are boring. In the relatively rare situations where an intrinsically extreme top-right person interacts with an extreme bottom-left type, it's more than likely things aren't going to work out.

In your early days of trying to make a success of your life, you may sometimes feel it is necessary to bite your tongue and deal with those you have nothing in common with. If this really is the case and you aren't simply being lazy by failing to be curious enough about them, then you have a dilemma. If you are desperate for a sale of whatever type, it will be so tempting to devote huge amounts of energy to making this interaction work, as you feel you can't afford to let anything go. The challenge is while devoting your energy to pushing water uphill, you will miss the nice stream running alongside which you could naturally tap into.

Giving up on something when there appear to be few other opportunities is difficult, especially if you are inexperienced in these things. People do it with personal relationships more often than they might want to admit. Business relationships mirror this, and a valuable lesson in both is to know when to say no and walk away. You don't need to create rapport with everyone – but maximise it with those for whom it is worthwhile.

If none of this makes sense to you or you don't have the patience to take it all in, then just appreciate most people aren't interested in what you have to say. Their own story is much more important to them. If you want to build rapport, simply feigning even a small amount of interest in them and listening while they download themselves on to you can achieve surprising results.

CHAPTER 27

PERSISTENCE

It matters not whether you possess any of the skills I have mentioned so far. Without persistence, you will under-achieve compared with those who stick at it.

There is so much evidence to show how simply refusing to give up when confronted with a challenging task is the way to eventually conquer it. A quick study of any of the world's most successful people, whether they have achieved in sport, entertainment or business, shows the main attribute which contributed to their successes was the ability to just keep going until they mastered whatever they were trying to do.

In Chapter 5, I referenced Matthew Syed's book *Bounce*, which shatters the myth of talent and shows how huge success so often comes from huge effort, in most cases at least 10,000 hours of practice. There is also the now ancient story of how Thomas Edison initially failed to invent the lightbulb, but kept on trying until he succeeded. The true facts seem lost in time and estimates vary between 700 and 10,000 failed experiments. Either way, Edison realised he had to find many ways to fail before he succeeded.

In this age of instant gratification, discovering you have to put some effort in and keep at it when you feel like giving up might be the biggest shock of your life. Sorry. I'm sure it's possible to provide examples of people achieving great success with little effort, but that's either luck, fluke or dishonesty. And the success is often transient. If you want to achieve long-lasting success, then there simply is no substitute for putting in the hours until you have found a way to get your particular ball rolling.

There are some caveats to this, though. The biggest challenge to persistence is contained in the contrary quote often attributed to Albert Einstein: "Insanity is doing the same thing over and over again, but expecting different results." Edison didn't continually repeat his same methodology hoping for a different outcome. He either changed something each time or became more skilled at the processes he was aiming to perfect.

If you keep doing something badly without being **aware** and add in a touch of **dishonesty** to help you justify your poor results, then success is likely to elude you. And you will never be able to put this in context unless you are very firmly aware of what your **goal** is. The work you put towards the goal, ie the act of persistence, can be likened to a journey. What you are striving to achieve is the destination. Without knowing exactly where your destination is, how can you modify your journey when it looks like you are veering off course? If you don't know where you are going, how do you expect to get there?

With any goal or destination, the path won't necessarily be straight. Veering offline is expected and likely. The main thing is to make sure you are heading in the right general direction. That's why it's important to keep going. It's so easy to give up, but the destination might be just around the next corner.

While you need to know what your goal is, sometimes the journey will give you greater insights and a different perspective on what it is you are seeking to achieve. So, while persevering is important, that doesn't mean you should disregard alternatives, as long as you are choosing them for the right reasons. Switching to something easier to manage is OK if your original goal was ridiculously unachievable and the alternative is potentially as fruitful, but if you are taking the easier option just because it's easier, then you need to seriously examine that. The most important thing is having a goal which will put you on a path to making your life better. Let the journey be as fulfilling as the destination and it's possible the goal will become superfluous.

To stick at it, perhaps for months, years or, in my case, decades, you have to enjoy what you are doing. No-one is going to put in 10,000 hours of table tennis practice if they prefer playing football, which is where choosing your goal is important, ha-ha. Seriously, you need to like what you do if you are to have any kind of long-term commitment to it.

The goal could be something monetary such as being a millionaire in ten years' time. If you have a strong enough desire to be a millionaire, then you might be able to stick at doing all kinds of things you don't particularly enjoy as you know they are taking you closer and closer to your destination. But such a goal has to be deeply imbedded in you for it to drive you towards it. And you will need to work on keeping it as the most important thing in your life if you are to have any chance of reaching it.

If you have a passion for something which is strong enough to aim you towards great success, then you are both lucky and cursed. Lucky to have something you can latch on to, but cursed with the commitment and sacrifices you will need to make to get there. Your attitude to that will exactly determine how far you will get.

I believe you have an above average persistence ethic. You've got this far in the book, so that's good enough for me. Many would have given up long ago...

A good work ethic

What I really mean by this is you must work hard. But I didn't want to scare you off, so I chickened out and used a euphemism instead. You won't succeed if you don't have persistence, but vying for the top spot in the skills stakes is hard work. Sorry again. The difference between persistence and hard work is the amount of effort you put into the time you spend on it. Fooling yourself by spending hours supposedly working yet avoiding doing the necessary things is pointless.

Here is where LUD comes into play once more. Do you tread water and do as little as you can get away with because life's too short? Or do you give everything you've got to achieve something for the future, albeit with a sacrifice today?

You should now know there is no correct answer. All I can do is refer you to my story and what worked for me, with examples of where hard work made all the difference. This will either inspire you to do the same or put you off as it sounds like too much effort.

There is little chance of getting a business to anywhere beyond Mediocre Alley if you are only prepared to work normal office hours. What makes the difference between ticking over and going somewhere is the extra time you put in.

It seems to work like this. In a work day of, say, seven to eight hours, you spend most of that time doing the normal stuff to keep the business going, rather like an employee does. If you want to make the business properly successful or stand out, the vital after hours are where it all happens. This is where you start putting the icing on the cake.

When I was building my IFA business, I spent the normal office day dealing with the work from clients. In the extra hours, I was prospecting, marketing and doing anything I could to get more business. It was often extremely demoralising. The sales game is a lesson in **persistence**. It's normal to have low levels of success compared with the effort you put in while you are in the learning phase.

One of the things I would do is cold call by telephone – perhaps the most difficult sales approach of them all. I forced myself to keep calling, regardless of how many nos I received. I just would not allow myself to stop until I achieved some kind of positive result.

As a one-man band operating from the flat in Bath, I regularly fell asleep at my desk as I kept working until I dropped. I've already told you how, when I moved to my office, I would often talk to my business partner Mike at 7:30 in the evening while we were both still at our desks. I rarely made it back to the house before 8pm. It was normal and necessary for both of us if we were to grow to where we wanted to be.

If ever there was a prime example of a workaholic, it has to be Elon Musk. As well as being a genius, he has an incredible work ethic, apparently averaging sixteen hours of work a day, seven days a week. He demands similar from his employees, so I hope they are well rewarded. I guess they must be, as I could never work that hard for any length of time for someone else.

The need for a good work ethic is why you must do something which is more than just a job. The word 'passion' is a much overused cliché which organisations will sprinkle around to convince their employees or future employees they are in a very special place, when in reality they are just being brainwashed into working long hours for little or no extra reward. You might say Elon Musk's businesses fall into this category, though his employees might say they *are* rather special. And perhaps they are. I guess if you buy into Elon's vision of the future, you might enjoy making a job the centre of your life.

But it's also important to know when to stop. When your decision is to live for tomorrow, it's a good idea to understand when you will know 'tomorrow' has arrived. Some might say it never does. Hopefully, your goal setting will have been specific enough for you to have some idea of when to throttle off as you reach the required altitude.

In my experience, however lofty the original goal, once it's achieved, it's tempting to brush it aside as if it meant nothing and to set an even bigger goal. People often say success breeds success and it's true that once tasted, success can be addictive. But you should be very careful you aren't carrying on just because of the addiction or the habit. Take some time to be **honest** about your true motivation. There is no point in being the richest person in the graveyard, so if you can give yourself time to devote to other things (like writing a book!), then do whatever it takes to do so.

If you are at the start of your journey, what I have just said might seem irrelevant and crazy, but so many successful people will tell you it's almost as difficult to stop working hard as it is to get yourself going in the first place.

Reliability

Being able to trust in arrangements is a core part of a civilised society. If you compare various countries around the world, you can see how those where people have such trust are generally more pleasant to live in. And vice-versa. Arrangements can vary from simple things such as basic financial transactions to more important stuff like the absolute right to own property without fear it will be taken away from you.

Whatever your view of the UK, we who live here are lucky in being able to take for granted many arrangements which others cannot. Our systems for such things as property rights were established many, many years ago and over time have built into a strong and robust set of rules. Although clever fraudsters are always trying to find ways around them, there is rarely a situation where someone buys a property in the UK and later finds they do not own it after all.

What does this have to do with reliability? Like many things, what you experience in day-to-day life is to some extent a reflection of what happens at a higher level. If your country's leaders are corrupt and you never know whether you can trust a transaction you might get into, then it's not surprising if your attitude to making arrangements on a day-to-day level is similarly affected. But people love dealing with those they consider to be reliable and trustworthy. Even the most deceitful of people would prefer to deal with someone honest. So, when you are trying to establish yourself in the world, it's important to acquire this attribute which almost everyone is going to appreciate.

This book is all about gaining advantages from things which cost nothing in monetary terms, but make a difference. Reliability as a core attribute is one of those things. Even if you are lacking in almost every skill imaginable, have no talent and limited intelligence, you can still make a good life for yourself if you are 100% reliable.

A musician friend who is part of the comedy band I formed in 2006 (yes, another thing squeezed into my busy life) believes the most important attribute for anyone wanting to join a band is to be reliable. You can be the best guitarist in the world, but if you don't turn up, you may as well be the worst. Showing up, keeping your word and doing what you say you will do will send you a long way down the road of success while you develop other traits to put you on an upward trajectory.

My much-admired late cousin worked for forty years for the same company, delivering milk – a tough job which included working on a Sunday morning. He never once took a day off sick. Not one day in forty years.

Read that again. A hard act to follow, but one which many might find beneficial to emulate...

CHAPTER 28

FINANCIAL MANAGEMENT

In all my years of having an insight into people's finances, there was one factor which stood out beyond all others. It may seem hard to believe or comprehend, but apart from a few exceptions at the extreme ends of the scale, I've realised it is not what you earn that makes a difference to your financial state, but what you spend.

How can this be? Life must be far easier when you are earning £150k a year than if you are earning £15k.

Of course, potentially it is, but that does not stop high-earning people from making a complete mess of their finances and going bankrupt. Nor does it stop abstemious and thoughtful people on minimum wage from saving reasonable sums. There is an old saying about cutting your coat according to your cloth. In other words, only buy things you have sufficient money to pay for (appreciating assets excluded).

By managing whatever money I have had very carefully, I've been able to achieve things which those earning much more than me have not. This still applies now almost as much as it did fifty years ago. I look around at my contemporaries and realise I do more and have more than most of them, yet often that has been achieved despite me earning far, far less. The scale of my earnings has moved up somewhat over the years, but the principle still applies.

Do I have some magical method or formula? Have I made a pact with the devil so I will pay the price under LUD? Do you want me to tell you something exciting? Sorry, but I'm going to give you a boring answer. Most of what I have achieved is down to a thing called **budgeting**. I've talked about it before. It should be taught in every school as an essential fundamental. It's crazy it isn't.

The concept of budgeting is so simple and obvious, I feel condescending even including it in my book. But I also know a huge number of people who should practise it don't. So here it is:

The goal of budgeting is to help you achieve financial stability by ensuring you have enough money to cover your regular expenses, set aside some funds for unexpected expenses, and ideally amass some savings.

How to budget

To create a budget, you first need to determine your total monthly net income, ie what goes into your bank account after all taxes and other deductions. Remarkably, so many have no clue what it might be. This net income includes all the money you receive from your job, any benefits (childcare for example) and other sources. Once you know your accurate total net income, you can start allocating it to various categories which need to be paid every month, eg rent or mortgage, debt repayments, utilities, groceries, transport, entertainment etc. If you are self employed with a variable income, then work out what your average income is and use that.

It's important to be realistic about your spending habits and allocate your funds accordingly. When I go through budgets with clients, those who struggle with their finances will often ignore small things which they believe make little difference, yet add up and help create the problems they are faced with.

Coffees, magazines, subscriptions, haircuts and pet costs are some of the classic examples.

When you have a total for that lot, you can compare it to your income figure. If your monthly outgoings exceed that, then you are in trouble as there is plenty more to add on yet. This is akin to a company's gross profit position. Your comparison needs to show enough of a profit for you to go on and deduct all your other ongoing expenses from. If it's already showing a deficit or only a small margin, there are two answers. Cut down on those expenses or find a way to generate more income. It sounds harsh, but there is **no other option** which will help you in any way.

If you have a healthy enough profit margin, you need to set aside money for non-regular expenses. Again, you must be thorough, realistic and honest. Car repairs, holidays, birthdays, annual insurances, an allowance for unexpected house repairs (assuming you own a property) are all essentials for many. Just because an expense is not pressing now, doesn't mean it won't come along one day. You need to make provision as far in advance as you can to lessen the pain when the expense does arrive.

For example, car insurance is due every year, so a year is the longest time you can take to save up for it. A dream holiday might happen every five or even ten years, so you would divide the expected cost by either 60 or 120 months respectively (and don't expect to have the holiday more frequently or sooner than your budget has allowed for). If you run a car, it will need replacing one day. If you think it will last another three years, divide the amount you expect to spend in three years' time by thirty-six and put it in the budget. For example, if a new car is likely to cost an extra £3,600 in three years' time, then you need to save £100 a month between now and then to allow you to buy it.

It's important you spend enough time on this to include *everything* likely to need expenditure at some stage in the future. If you don't do it thoroughly, then you are just fooling yourself.

Because it's crucial to ensure you don't fall into debt when non-monthly expenses arise, you must total them up and put that fixed amount into a separate budget account each month. That way, when the time comes to make the payment, you should have the funds set aside and won't have to dip into your regular spending. You might be unlucky if one of the big expenses comes around before you have had time to build up the funds and this is the one time a small amount of debt could be allowed (eg use a credit card or go into an overdraft). But it's essential you put this right quickly or the whole point of budgeting will be lost.

Ideally, start budgeting well before you really need to, then you will have enough time to build up the funds. Thinking ahead will help you more than most things you can do, and budgeting is simply that. Long before a painful bill comes in, start preparing and the pain will be a whole lot less.

There aren't many things in life which are truly unpredictable, so take responsibility now, rather than letting the challenges of life control you. If you are fifteen years old, start now. If you are twenty years old, start now. If you are fifty years old, start now. It's never too late, but it's a hell of a lot easier if you start at fifteen. Budgeting is a valuable tool for managing your income and ensuring you can not only cover your regular expenses, but also set aside funds for the non-regular stuff. By creating a realistic budget and sticking to it, you can achieve financial stability and peace of mind.

But we haven't quite finished the process yet. Once you have a total of all your likely expenditure, including the day-to-day, monthly and less frequent outgoings, you can deduct that grand sum from your total income and see what the difference is. If you are lucky, there will be a surplus of some kind. This is where you could allocate some for regular saving.

After all that has been taken into account, you may have an amount left over which is your spending money. It's the only money you have which hasn't been allocated to something else and it is as the name suggests. You simply cannot spend any more than that on unplanned purchases.

For many/most people, their spending money is a random figure which has not been tracked, determined or monitored. They spend money regardless of the effect it will have on their cash flow and overall monetary situation. So it's not surprising when they end up with money management and debt problems.

An example of a spreadsheet I use with my clients is given on page 284. It's quite easy to recreate in Excel, or I will send you a copy if you ask me nicely:

You can make the difference
You might say, "I just don't have enough income to account for all those things you have said I need to budget for." Welcome to the real world. Very few people have the income they need to do all the things they would like to do. Some are in a position where they have insufficient income to take care of even basic necessities. And by that, I mean feeding themselves, not whether they keep the Sky TV subscription going.

This is why this book is particularly important for those starting out in life. The sooner you begin planning and ensuring you don't make life decisions which back you into a corner, the more likely you are to survive and even thrive. If you are further down the road of life, then it will be more difficult to start planning ahead, but better late than never. Not knowing the extent of your income deficit compared to your expenditure is not going to help you improve your situation. Avoiding the task won't make things any easier. You have no hope of ever

NET MONTHLY DISPOSABLE INCOME CALCULATOR	Me	Me	Partner	Partner
Net regular monthly income				
Net other income (earned)				
Benefits				
Total Net Monthly Income (x)		£0.00		£0.00
MONTHLY REGULAR EXPENSES				
Mortgage payments or rent				
Food and Drink				
Utilities (gas, electricity, water, etc)				
Council Tax				
Phone				
Internet				
TV subscriptions, Sky, NetFlix, Prime etc				
Car fuel				
Car road tax				
Public transport				
Social/Leisure				
Childcare				
School Fees				
Personal care, hairdressing, beauty etc				
Clothing and Footwear				
Loan repayments				
Catalogue repayments				
Credit card repayments				
Lottery/gambling				
Life & Protection Insurances				
House insurances				
Pension payments				
Pet food				
Pet insurance				
Prescriptions				
Tobacco/vaping				
Sub-total Monthly Expenditure		0.00		0.00
Surplus/deficit to monthly income		0.00		0.00

NON MONTHLY EXPENSES	IRREGULAR EXPENSES (Annual figures)	Divided by 12	Partner's IRREGULAR EXPENSES (Annual figures)	Divided by 12
TV Licence		£0.00		£0.00
House repairs		£0.00		£0.00
Ground rent		£0.00		£0.00
Tax (if self employed/non PAYE)		£0.00		£0.00
Xmas		£0.00		£0.00
Car repairs		£0.00		£0.00
Car replacement		£0.00		£0.00
Holidays, (annual and short breaks)		£0.00		£0.00
Medical/dental expenses		£0.00		£0.00
Birthdays		£0.00		£0.00
Pet care		£0.00		£0.00
Other (always insert a contingency amount)		£0.00		£0.00
Regular Savings/Investments		£0.00		£0.00
Total Non-monthly Expenditure (y)		0.00		0.00
Total Monthly Disposable Income (x minus y)	(A)	0.00	(B)	0.00

Total Joint Disposable Income (A) + (B)		0.00

(If expenditure is a joint commitment complete applicant 1 only)

An example client spreadsheet.

being financially stable unless you get this part of your life under control.

At this point, a reaction I often hear is, "Well, it's not my fault. The government should stop prices rising/tax the rich more/give me more benefits/make my employer pay me more/ etc". While some or all of those points may have some validity, the grim reality is you are the only person who can make a real difference to your situation, whatever injustice or inequity you feel is being placed upon you.

We have spoken before about choices and decisions. Generally, if you are an adult, you are where you are now because of the myriad decisions you have made. If you drill down enough, you can almost always go back to a decision you took which brought you to the circumstances you now find yourself in.

There are lots of things people believe it is their right to have and to do, such as starting a family, regardless of where they are in life. Doing so with nothing behind them and relying on the hope nothing will go wrong or someone else will pick up the tab is, in my opinion, at the least apathetic and at worst grossly negligent in their role as a human being and a parent. When someone says they can't afford to feed their family, this can only be due to things they decided to do or not do in the past.

Making inadequate provision in case things turn against you is not the greatest strategy for having a successful life. You might say, on this basis, hardly anyone would start a family. Given the planet's current trajectory, some might say that is not a bad thing.

There is currently much talk in the UK of food banks, unaffordable utility bills and many other hardships affecting people. I'm not going to say life was any more difficult for us as a family when I was a kid, but it certainly wasn't any easier. There was no question of buying fast food to take away, going to a pub, having any kind of phone, least of all a mobile one, or calling a taxi to take us shopping. Yet in today's world, some consider these as essentials, even for those classed as living below the poverty line.

Reality is perception. It is not my wish to offend you. Life can be tough and sometimes the realities are hard to accept. If you are an adult, it will be your choice as to how you react to my words. I can't dictate how you will feel about something I write. I'm not in control of your brain. But rather than being offended, you could be better served by devoting your energy to doing something to improve your lot.

Budgeting is a good place to start.

CHAPTER 29

CHOOSE POSITIVE INFLUENCES

Anyone who has gone through life for a few decades and made a reasonable go of it will likely not need much persuasion to agree with the theme of this chapter. The influences you have around you in your formative years make a huge difference to how you turn out.

The key words in that last paragraph are 'formative years'. These are the years which will determine how you spend the rest of your life. They aren't always the obvious ones, and they will be different for everyone. Some will find their attitudes, beliefs and behaviours are inexorably formed in their early years. Others may not see their pathways set until much later in life.

The unfortunate truth is some young children can be subjected to all kinds of horrors in families which are dysfunctional, but that doesn't necessarily mean they will turn out to be less than decent people. Sometimes it's quite the opposite. We often see those who have had difficult early years going on to have an amazing life due to a transformative moment which changed their mindset and put them on a new path. What is common to many of these scenarios is change came about because of an outside influence. However it occurred, that person became open to something they weren't open to beforehand as a result.

I've written a few times about how important influencers have been to me. I'm lucky enough to have recognised the ones who are positive and why (probably more subconsciously than consciously in my early days) and luckier still to have some of them around me to this day.

While parents are often our main influencers when we're children, by the time we reach the dreaded teenage years, most of us have decided we will do anything rather than take the advice of those who brought us into the world. This is quite sad when in most cases, our parents only want the best for us. So why are we so reluctant to accept their help and, in the worst cases, we get involved with those who are only going to drag us down? It's not a question I'm qualified to answer. I just hope it's not a situation you find yourself in.

So, when are your formative years? It will be different for everyone, but in many cases it will be early in life. For me, while a young child and teenager, I was subject to negative influences at home as far as success was concerned, even though my parents meant well. Yet as soon as I had a small amount of exposure to a positive influence, I was drawn in that direction.

Some might see this as due to pure luck or coincidence. Or we could look at it another way. Even when I was ten years old, my decisions determined who I mixed with and listened to. Thankfully, I didn't mix too much with those who saw no future in trying hard and preferred mischief. Probably because they were beating me up, a good example of not looking only at the short-term outcomes. If I had been accepted into the gang of bullies, who knows what might have happened to me? Sometimes being a victim is a good thing, even though it makes our lives a misery at the time.

Not everyone wants you to succeed
One of the most difficult things to do when you are trying to

better yourself is to realise not everyone wants you to succeed. Actually, that's not exactly true. It's not necessarily the case that your acquaintances or friends don't want you to succeed. It's more that most people want those they mix with to be in a similar position to them. It's so obvious, and yet that barrier to success isn't always recognised.

This is why tribes are so powerful and so popular. They are everywhere and we are all part of at least one, whether we like it or not and whether we think so or not. Join any club, organisation or association, and inevitably the core of it will be likeminded people. Those in the Women's Institute tend to be slightly different to those in the Hells Angels.

In some cases, the reason for the negativity from our family, friends or contemporaries when we profess our desire for success is because they don't want to see us hurt if we try something different. If we suggest we are starting a new business, there will always be someone who will tell us about the person they knew who did so and failed miserably. And they don't want us to end up in the same position.

The other main reason also comes from a place of caring. People who like you simply don't want to lose you as a friend. If you belong to the Women's Institute and say you are going to a Hells Angels meeting, some of your contemporaries will fear you might find the allure of oil-stained denim more appealing than that of freshly baked scones. Their negativity comes from them wanting to keep you close to them. This is why it's so difficult to pull away from any tribe, as part of the appeal is knowing you are wanted. Cults use this to great advantage and, in extreme cases, can exert influences so powerful, they determine whether or not someone chooses to continue living.

If you feel you have no positive influencers in your life, how do you go about getting some? Like many things, it's nothing more than a numbers game. The more people you meet and talk to, the more chance you have of finding someone who will assist you rather than hold you back. Every single person you interact with is a potential key to unlocking something which will help you. Discount no-one. Even the biggest losers might give you an introduction to someone worthwhile. That doesn't happen too often, so I'm not advocating you seek out losers, quite the opposite. But if they are all you have available at the time, be vigilant to see if they have any connections which might be worthwhile.

I often run through in my mind how I met a certain person – I find it fascinating. I enjoy recalling the tree of connections, for example I met A through B and B through C and so on. Often the person at the root of the tree has no significance in my life anymore and I might hardly remember them. Yet the person at the top of the tree is a valued and worthwhile connection, and usually a good friend.

When I look at people I have known all my life, much of their success, or lack of it, has been determined by how much they engage with others and seek connections. Those who savour and value every new interaction with a human being have generally done well. Those who don't and just let the moment go have not.

Interestingly, as you rise the ladder of achievement, you will likely discover the more successful and balanced the person you meet, the more they will encourage you to succeed. This can come as a shock to those like me who, in their early years, had little contact with the world of successful people. I was told by my mum those who were 'above' us wanted to keep us down in 'our place'. When I discovered those very people were happy to give me good advice and encourage me to do well, it was contrary to everything I had been told.

I'm sorry to say the opposite is also true. The worst place to seek advice about climbing the ladder of success is from those who are on the same rung as or below you. This should be obvious, yet it doesn't seem to be. We wouldn't dream of being taught how to ski or drive a racing car by someone who hasn't done it before or who hates the sports. Yet we seek the opinions of those in a similar position to us about things they may never have attempted. Is it any wonder the inertia of the tribe is so powerful?

If you don't believe me, try a little experiment. Tell your tribe about this book and ask what their reactions are. They may not be what you'd hope for. Or perhaps deep down, you know the answer already and won't even ask.

In my case, I have always felt it is better to say nothing about my plans and aspirations and just get on with them, even when I wasn't consciously aware those around me might not be positive about what I wanted to do. This lesson was reinforced in my network marketing days. I remember a few who made massively optimistic predictions to their mates and prospects about how rich they were going to be. It didn't help them recruit many into their network and lost them a lot of credibility when it all went wrong, as it did in every case.

I recently heard of some research which gave a reason not to tell your friends about ambitious goals, even if they happen to be the type of people who will be supportive and positive. Apparently, the dopamine hit you get from receiving encouragement after you have told them is similar to that you get when you achieve a goal. So subconsciously, your brain will already have been partly satisfied and won't push you to the lengths it might if you had kept your plans to yourself. Conversely, if you get a negative reaction, you might be spurred on to achieve, but I guess that will depend on how tough your mental armour is.

If you decide to test the water with your tribe and the reaction is less than positive, then you could have a challenge ahead of you. At least it's a fast way to find out who is going to be the kind of person you want on your journey to a better place.

Temptations

Let's say the friends you have are less than thrilled when they discover you might be on a path to bettering yourself. Some might be openly anti, while others will be more subtle.

Then, the challenge really begins. Sometimes, it's the latter group which is more difficult to deal with. At least you know where you are with those who openly express their disapproval of what you are doing. Your friends with the hidden agenda will wait until a moment you're appropriately vulnerable before revealing their true feelings.

A common negative will be around the question of time. You know you will have to spend some time doing whatever you need to achieve your goal. You tell your friends you can't make it to the pub or wherever and the mind games begin.

The most common and obvious will involve LUD. It will go something like, "What's the matter with you? You only live once, come along and enjoy yourself." It takes a strong will to resist social pressure such as this, but whether you do or not will start to determine your habits and if you really are committed to improving the rest of your life. As with all of the challenges contained within LUD, it's not for me to say what you should do. That's your dilemma.

What is important is to recognise your true valuable friends and cherish them. While they may or may not be rooting for your success, your true friends will usually want to make sure you are at least OK. Sometimes, you need someone who knows you well to put you back on the right track.

We often understand the problems of others, even if we don't always have the right solutions, while we can't work out what our own issues are. And it works the other way too. The skill is in recognising those you should seek advice from. In most cases, looking inside yourself and being **honest** about what you are hearing will give you the answer.

There is another huge influence which is likely to determine your attitude to LUD. I've touched on this before. The temptations and inducements all around you are designed to make you spend your money as quickly as possible and live for today. This seduction comes in many forms, and you must be aware of them.

The most obvious is big business and only slightly less subtle is the government of your country. Big business wants you to buy its products and uses all its skills to make your mouth water and your brain crave dopamine. It has decades of experience to its advantage, and it has been extremely successful at influencing most people to believe true happiness lies somewhere between another cup of coffee and a holiday in Spain. A nice new car on finance and a wardrobe with a few labels, and your life is complete.

This is not a great organised conspiracy by a group of shady connected businesspeople, but the result of years of experience, refining methods and perfecting ever more clever ways to extract our money from us. It has worked brilliantly (for them), but by most metrics, consumers in developed countries are no happier now than they were in the 1960s when the only way to drink coffee for the majority of people was to open a jar of instant.

Assisting business along the way is the government. For many years, our leaders have been obsessed with gross domestic product (GDP), which is the total value of all of the goods and services sold in the country. There are a few reasons for this, and tax revenue is at the heart of them. The more a country's businesses sell, the more VAT the government earns. The more employees businesses need, the more income tax the government receives. And on and on it goes. It's like a merry-go-round at a funfair. It has to keep spinning or we will have nothing to ride on.

Do you think your government's policies are more or less likely to influence you to live for today? Is that why budgeting is not taught in schools? It's not a totally straightforward question and those with strong political views at either end will probably take issue with it, so it requires yet another book for me to explain this fully. In general, just bear in mind these big picture influences. The ones which are all around us on a daily basis and are most likely going to steer us into the path of today's temptations at the expense of a better future.

These next two skills are only tenuously linked to the overarching theme of this chapter, but they are important. I have mentioned them before in various parts of the book, but there's a risk you will be overwhelmed if I go into too much detail about them. So I'm keeping them short and sweet and I will leave you to investigate them more. Or I might write a book about them...

Develop visualisation

Your subconscious or the proving part of your brain will do all it can to bring you evidence to support the things you see in your mind. So it's really important you visualise yourself achieving your goal. This is so powerful. It is almost impossible to achieve something if you can't see yourself doing it in your mind beforehand.

Try it with something small and see what happens. If you play any kind of ball game where you practise a particular move, imagine yourself hitting/kicking/catching the ball. Develop the scene in as much detail as you can and see how your hit rate improves. Or if you do stretching exercises and you can't quite reach a certain point, see yourself achieving it. My bet is you will if you can see it clearly in your mind.

It's pretty incredible to experience that.

Optimise everything

This is almost the theme of the book. If you have little, you must make the most of what you have. Extract every tiny bit of potential from each thing or situation which comes into your path. Successful sports people know the value of this. Especially in motor sport where every minute element can contribute to success or failure.

For example, you may have little in the way of time, money or resources, but you can vastly change what you eat, drink and do with your body every day, just in the course of living. There is a ton of information already available about this, so unless you ask me nicely, I'm not going to write another 100,000 words detailing my habits. Suffice to say my healthy lifestyle has massively contributed to my success and the wellbeing I have in my life now, and there's no reason you shouldn't follow that same path.

There's almost always a way to make more of what you have. But you have to use all the skills I have talked about in Part Three of this book, and perhaps a few more besides. That's how you make something from nothing. And money is at the heart of all of this.

It's safe to say I could not have achieved a fraction of what I have without understanding and taking advantage of the power of optimising my money. In other words, I've turbo-charged the power of the cash I have by borrowing to invest in something which has given me a far greater return than I could have generated just using my own money. You know my favoured choice for this is to invest in property, but you can also optimise the skills of the people around you if you develop a scalable business in conjunction with finding good staff.

This also needs another book. I'm going to be busy, aren't I?

CHAPTER 30

YOUR PURPOSE

Three decades ago, when I was heavily into the world of personal development, I came across the concept of establishing your life's purpose. In other words, what is the one thing deep down which drives you more than anything else? It's not always easy to find this out, but question yourself enough and it's possible. When you know the answer, it can be quite a revelation.

When I discovered my purpose, it explained many of the things which had happened in my life, both positive and negative. It also explained one of the big drivers for me writing this book. It transpires the main thread running through my life has been my desire to make people happy.

Your purpose is not necessarily something you think about consciously for any length of time, but when you look back and examine your decisions and motivations, you can often see what has driven them. This is easy to say when you have made a success of your life. If your major concern is making sure you have enough dosh to pay this month's electricity bill, your purpose is probably low on the list of your priorities. I'm hopeful you will not be in that position, or at least not for long.

Whatever your purpose might be, it almost always involves others. You know mine, but a favourite for many is 'making a difference'.

A common mistake when people are asked to reveal their purpose is that they do not drill down to the roots of what it really is. When they state their purpose, people will say things like "Making a success of my career" or "Contributing to my community". These are commendable goals, but they are a level up from what your true purpose actually is. When you present what you believe is a purpose, if you are still able to ask yourself the question "Yes, but what will achieving that purpose give me?" then you haven't truly established exactly what your purpose is.

For example, someone says to me, "My purpose is to contribute to my community." I would say, "So, how do you judge when you've achieved that?" They reply, "When someone tells me what I did helped." I would then say, "OK, so could it be true that what you did in the community was the means and not the end? Isn't your true purpose your desire to make a difference to people's lives?" When I uncover a person's true purpose, it's amazing to see their eyes light up as if there has been a great epiphany. Perhaps there has.

Why is this important?

It would be a tragedy to go through your life and not be fully aware of the one thing which means more to you than anything else. You might say you have a family which fulfils that need. If you genuinely feel your family is the most important thing in your life, then perhaps the reason that is the case is they are enabling you to fulfil your purpose. There will be things you do with and for the family which are totally in line with what your purpose is. If you are lucky enough to feel this, then you might wonder what all the fuss is about and how relevant purpose is. You have probably found your purpose, but not realised what it is in your conscious mind.

We also have to remember not everyone is in a happy family

situation. This can be due to all sorts of complex reasons, but if someone has a purpose which is out of kilter with family life, it's not surprising if things don't work out.

Because you now know awareness is important, isn't it logical you should have some idea of your main driving force, even if it has been kept well-hidden until now? I'm not going to say discovering your purpose will change anything radically for you, at least not instantly, but it might well explain some of the decisions you have made in the past which have either worked well for you or to the contrary. For me, this was the most revealing part of discovering my purpose.

Like any attribute, there will be pluses and minuses attached to your purpose. When I was lending other people money as part of my job, my tendency was to help wherever I could. Being a possibility thinker and wanting to see people departing feeling happier than when they'd arrived, I found it very difficult to say no when presented with a loan application. Since becoming aware of my purpose, I have been able to understand how it impacts my decisions and I can react accordingly.

This is one of the reasons why I don't directly lend money anymore. I prefer to act as a middle man where I can still help people, but I allow third parties to make the final decision. It's also why I enjoy writing, presenting and commentating as I can see and hear my actions having a positive effect. And I get somewhat depressed if people don't like what I have presented to them, so please, please like this book – my sanity depends on it ☺

A word of warning
Purposes should come with warnings. If your purpose is something positive which you believe will make a difference, it may come as a shock to find out many people won't share your enthusiasm. Refer back to the previous chapter for more on this.

I used to believe one of the ways I could use my purpose to make people happy was to show them how to improve in the areas I know something about. I wrote this book partly to do just that. I'm now realistic enough to know personal improvement is not something everyone has a desire for. Those people probably won't have made it this far into the book. If you have persevered, it suggests you are one of the relatively few people genuinely open to learning and improving. So it's important for you to know not everyone will share this attribute. And it's best not to waste too much energy trying to convert those who don't. You will not only annoy them, but you will also make yourself unhappy in the process.

There are only a small number of skills I have which I would consider using to make a difference to people's lives. I'm not the kind of person who wants to ram everything I know down someone's throat. I tend to be more of a receiver than a transmitter, which is ironic given my experiences in speaking/performing to large groups of people.

Aside from the stuff I have documented in this book, I've become pretty accomplished as a race driver and skier, and I love to teach people those skills. And the most surprising thing I have learnt, which is common to both those sports and probably many others, is a huge number of grownups are not at all interested in doing what it takes to improve themselves or their skills. They may say they are, but when it comes down to it, even young adults have already settled into their comfort zone. There are a number of explanations for this, but the main culprit is ego. You can read lots about that elsewhere.

Occasionally, I will meet someone with a genuine desire to do better and learn. The difference between helping them and someone who pays lip service to the idea is vast. Perhaps there are no secrets to success, but if there is one, then having the desire to learn and improve as part of your DNA could well be it. I realise I have a habit of telling you all sorts of things are keys to success. That's probably because they all are...

I used to believe everyone must want to learn. Is it not logical to have the desire to improve? Yet I've seen time and again how people will use all kinds of excuses, explanations and reasoning for their lack of performance in life, on the racetrack or the ski slopes, while being adamant they don't need any kind of tuition or help to improve. There's probably another area where that applies. An old saying tells us, "Every man believes he is a good driver and a good lover". I know from my own experience only a very small percentage of the population can be classified as good drivers...

Does this mean I should stop trying to make people happy? It's crossed my mind, but like many things, it depends on the context and the execution. If you are aware and fully conscious when you engage with someone, you should be able to detect when you are making no progress. Just as in sales, an important skill is knowing when to give up. Rather than wasting huge amounts of time trying to change the mindset of one person, you're often better off moving on and finding someone more receptive to your purpose. Perseverance is an important part of all success, but you need to know where to apply it.

CONCLUSION

LUD is the challenge of making a decision about whether you do something to indulge yourself today or sacrifice today in exchange for a better tomorrow. You could call it living for today or living for tomorrow, though it's a little more complex than that.

But it sounds easy enough to understand. Surely there must be more perplexing things in life than this? In my experience, the fundamentals of how we live our life, and therefore what kind of life we have, distil down to how much we are prepared to give up or put in or delay now in the hope we might achieve something better in the future.

Are you prepared to sacrifice things many feel are essential in order to have something better in the future? What choice could be more important or tricky to navigate? You have to make assumptions about your future, and then take some tough decisions about what you do or don't do.

There are clearly degrees of how far to go with this. I've outlined some examples at various junctures in the book. Yet even what may appear to be small and insignificant examples of LUD will contribute to the training you are giving your brain, and therefore how well you will be able to deal with some of the bigger challenges and temptations which may come along from time to time. Whether it's eating the things on your dinner plate which you don't like first and keeping the best bits until last or giving up a safe job and a family to create something for yourself, LUD is at the heart of almost all decisions you have to make. Even if you don't realise you are making such decisions or interpret them as something significant, the reality is that, consciously or subconsciously, you are.

Do you buy that Creme Egg cookie and get a massive sugar rush or save the cost and put it towards something worthwhile? Do you save up for a car or buy one now on credit? Do you go out for meals every week or save the money and have a fantastic holiday? Do you chat up that gorgeous and seemingly unobtainable person you fancy and deal with what you believe will be the embarrassment of rejection? Or do you wait until someone/anyone comes along who you don't need to make much of an effort with? Do you work those extra hours to afford something you really want or do the minimum and go without? In the last case, if you allow credit to take the place of work, you will still pay the price. It's called interest and too much of it equals bankruptcy – perhaps the ultimate financial price.

All of these things involve making a decision. Some will find one option so obvious, they won't even see it as a decision, let alone a dilemma. Their live for * (*insert today or tomorrow as appropriate) mentality is so strong, there is no question of them doing things any other way.

Was it worth it?

It's completely natural for those starting life's journey to want to live for the moment and I would never argue against it. If you talk to someone with this mindset, they will probably have no concept of a life other than one to be lived right now. In reality, right now is all any of us have. Next week, next month, next year, or the next minute may or may not happen for any of us. We don't know until tomorrow if what we predicted yesterday happened today.

It's obvious this is the case, but many assume it's a given

they can go on holiday next year or put off seeing someone they love as they are too busy right now. Or start saving for their future when they get a new job.

Taken to extremes, living for now is more than likely to see you end your days with no more financial stability than you started life with. If there is a choice between working and having fun, then it's understandable many believe fun will win. I've met people who've decided life is too short, so they treat every day as if it's Christmas. In most cases, they degenerate to a point where they are almost or actually homeless. The fun lasts until reality kicks in.

The odds of dying young are far lower than the probability of running out of money, friends and sympathy. I believe there is some evidence to show those who tend not to worry too much about anything and live for today die from both disease and accident at a younger age than the worriers who think and care about the consequences of what they are doing.

The other extreme is as sad, though. The live for tomorrow person will be the kind who denies themselves everything so they can accumulate every last penny in order to have a better future life. So far, it sounds a lot like me in my early days, ha-ha. I like to think the difference in my case was knowing where and when to stop.

There are those who die in hovel-like properties, wearing rags, and yet they leave huge amounts of money in their estate. They tend to have few if any friends, because to add to their miserable existence, they have missed out on party time. Although my tendency in the past was to favour my future over the present, thankfully, I was aware enough to realise when I could start enjoying some of the fruits of my early struggles. Since then, I have gradually allowed myself to live more and more for now, to the extent where I do almost anything and everything I have ever wanted and there's truly little in my life

I feel is denied to me. But that is only possible because of my earlier sacrifices.

For this reason, I would change nothing about anything I have ever done. It has worked, so why would I change it? But was I just lucky? I have the benefit of hindsight and the fact what I did worked for me. It might have not worked for someone else setting out with the same mindset and making slightly different decisions.

So, was it worth it? Given where I am right now, it's easy to say yes. But it could have worked out completely differently. Part of the dilemma is we will never know how an alternative approach might have worked.

Proud to be different

I've already spoken about how decisions are one of the key determinators of your success. With just one different choice, all my years of toil and depriving myself of things others see as essentials could have been wasted.

You don't always have to sacrifice the present for the future. You can have your cake and eat it. You just have to make sure you like the right kind of cake. I remember very few times in my life when I felt I was missing out because I had chosen to do something which would benefit me more in the future than today. Even when I lived a life of the utmost frugality, denying myself most of the things the majority take for granted, I didn't feel as though I was missing out. I just reframed the experience in my mind, found a way to enjoy what I was doing and kept the faith in my belief that one day I would not have to make as many compromises.

The compounding effect of my actions over the years has put me in a place unimaginable in the back garden of my parents' council house in the 1960s. I have everything and do everything I want. The irony is I now chop wood in my garden and love doing it. Being outdoors and doing physical exercise to achieve something is about as good as it gets. I can afford to buy as much wood for our stove as we would ever possibly need, but the pleasure I get from finding and creating a pile of logs from nothing apart from my own physical effort is beyond a price.

What may seem a chore in one context can be a pleasure when seen in another. That's reframing. Some will complain about expending huge amounts of physical effort as part of their work, while others will choose to take part in the annual Marathon des Sables in the Sahara, enduring the punishment only the equivalent of running six marathons could provide. Perhaps the only difference between enjoyment and hatred is an attitude of mind.

The power of what can be achieved with consistent effort over a long period of time is wonderful. The trick is not to expect much to change in the short term.

A lot of things I have done in the past have not been terribly conventional. Particularly in my early years, from the time I was able to have some input into my future by starting work at fifteen, I lived in a way most would or could not contemplate. It may be difficult to appreciate the context of where I was at that time, but it seemed clear to me the only way I was going to find a way out of the kind of life my parents led was to do things few others were prepared to do.

Whether life has dealt you the worst or best hand in the pack, what you do with that hand will determine the kind of life you will lead. If you are dealt the kind of hand I was and don't do anything about it, then it's highly likely you will end your life in much the same state as you began it.

What I chose to do was to pay the price early on. I went without, sacrificed many things and was ruthless yet totally focused on getting enough money and/or resources to help me move up life's economic ladder. Apart from my stalwart buddy

Dave, I have no friendships which carried on from school, and the only friends I made afterwards were linked to my car-related hobbies. From outside my group, I was probably regarded as a somewhat sad or strange character, doing none of the things the majority of those my age chose to do. Yet this was exactly what I wanted.

Once I had left school, I didn't have a miserable life. I found ways to entertain myself which not only cost nothing, but eventually earned me a little something too. I turned being different into something I was proud of, as I could feel it was moving me in the right direction, albeit glacially slowly. I'm not sure many would have the patience to hang in there for thirty years.

As it transpired, everything worked out incredibly well for me. I paid a big price at the beginning and my rewards now are beyond anything I dreamed of as a teenager.

I've been speaking about LUD mainly in the context of your attitude to the monetary side of your life, which will also affect other aspects, such as your health and relationships. If you grew up with plenty of money available to do anything you wanted, it's understandable if that's exactly how you live. Spend, spend, spend. Live life to the absolute max. Have a ball. Sounds great – or does it?

How do you think that might end? If you have access to multiple millions or even billions, you can lead that kind of life for a long time, if not for ever. But unless you are an exceptional human being, you could lose any sense of value, thereby guaranteeing this decadent living will affect the kind of person you are. As Nicole Shanahan, the hugely wealthy ex-wife of Google co-founder Sergey Brin, admits, "It's nearly impossible to have mega wealth and be deeply grounded."

When you've had a dozen meals at Michelin-star restaurants this month, the thrill will wear off. It's logical you might become fussier and fussier and start demanding ever more ridiculous levels of service or distinction to give you the same buzz I got when I had my first Chinese takeaway at age nineteen. LUD has cast its spell on you. If you live for now, even if you can afford to financially, it may be at the expense of what this will do to you in the long term. So LUD applies to everyone, whether you acknowledge it or not.

How will you interpret LUD?

It's said money doesn't buy you happiness. But you can drive around in comfort looking for it, ha-ha. What is true is money is one of a small number of goals which people believe will bring them something they don't currently have.

Hand in hand with money are power and fame. All three will be useless at bringing you happiness unless you have it already. They are merely amplifiers. If you are someone who behaves like an arsehole, then money, power or fame will help you become an even bigger version of what you are now. If you are a kind and loving person, it's likely you will become an even kinder person if you one day find your bank account overflowing. This is why (assuming you don't want to become an arsehole) it is important to find out your **purpose** early on in your journey upwards. Establishing your purpose as 'making people's lives better' is probably going to make you much nicer than 'being the richest person in the universe'. And it's easier to modify your purpose early on than to let it become so much a part of you, it's almost impossible to change.

Assuming you are in a position where you decide to become consciously **aware** of such things as your purpose and are presented with LUD, what should you do? I have no definitive answer. That's why it's the ultimate dilemma.

There is no doubt I was prepared to sacrifice instant gratification in favour of the future. In other ways, I made sure, by acting both selfishly and selflessly, I was able to do exactly what I wanted to do in the here and now. But giving up a promising career in a bank is hardly the act of someone who lives for the future. Living for tomorrow isn't always the way to go.

Having said that, it's arguable I was doing the right thing for my future, both when I turned down promotional moves with two banks, and then left the industry altogether. But those actions could be interpreted as me prioritising my feelings for today at the expense of tomorrow. There was also an element, deep down, which told me I could never stay long term in such a career. I just needed to stick it out until I could break free and do something else. It's complicated, isn't it?

However you choose to interpret LUD, you must consider some of the side effects which come with that effort. Like most things in life, it's more about how you do something than the thing itself. Even if my efforts had not given me the financial rewards I now enjoy, I have gained so much from my mindset, I'm pretty sure I would still choose the same path again. Not only because I wanted to achieve certain financial goals, but also to fulfil my purpose, which is to make people happy. My feeling is I have generally managed to achieve both. But there is an element of compromise in anything. I'm sure if I had been more ruthless, I could have built bigger and better businesses and made more money.

But other things were more important to me and still are. Which is why I believe the balance I have achieved is absolutely right for me. Contentment is another way of defining success and I have to own up to not being content for the majority of my life. Most of the other successful people I know are no different. It's what drives us to do more, to get up when we've been knocked down, and it gets us started in the first place. But it comes with a price. While I've been busy making money and others happy, I've spent far too long being dissatisfied with my own lot. So how can we claim to be successful if we aren't content? All I can say is I would prefer to be not fully content driving my latest new car to a lovely restaurant than riding a moped in the bitter cold and rain to work all day for a pittance.

Writing this book has helped me put things into a much better perspective, so for the first time since I can remember, I am reasonably content. I know I will never be fully satisfied with where I am as I have spent too long developing a different mindset. At least I can now see where I am and objectively rationalise my gratefulness for having benefited from such a wonderful life.

The future

If I was a teenager today, in the same kind of position I was in in the late 1960s, I'm not sure I would have the same attitude as I did then. Right now, my major concern is the state of our planet as we as a species do our best to destroy everything which is important about it. I'm with David Attenborough (and many others) who think most of the world we currently regard as civilised will become uninhabitable in the next fifty years. Which means in the years prior to that, life for us will become increasingly difficult.

In fact, that is the situation we are facing right now. I haven't noticed the world becoming a better place recently, nor one which is getting any easier to live in.

We tend to blame politicians, other countries, big business or (if we are a certain kind of person) a mythical global elite for the challenges of higher energy prices, inflation and social care for the ageing population. In reality, all of these things are inevitable consequences of our decision as humans to live in a civilised world. I don't have the space here to go into this in any depth, but for a brilliant account of how we have arrived where we are now and how to put almost everything you know in perspective, read *Sapiens* by Yuval Noah Harari.[12] I believe it's one of the most important books ever written.

Obviously, if I was a teenager again now, I would not have the decades of knowledge, research and reading which have contributed to my current way of thinking and my negative view of the prospects for the human race. My dad used to say the most successful people he knew were not particularly bright, but just went headlong into things without being held back by considering all the facts and pitfalls. This could apply equally today. I might still set out on my path, blindly assuming the world will stay pretty much as it is now, choosing to be unaware of the huge challenges facing our existence. But I would need to be pretty blinkered to have that kind of thinking. After all, it is younger people who are currently actively protesting and bringing awareness to the issues brought by climate change. Many of my generation are still wondering whether any of it is real, despite the overwhelming evidence.

But being blinkered and unaware is a big part of what is needed if you really want to make a success of yourself. I've already spoken of the importance of being able to distance yourself from the inevitable negativity you will encounter if you decide to do things differently. You will need the same mindset to ignore the onslaught of negative news about what is happening to our world. Or even better, embrace the issues and find a way of profiting from them as the world changes.

Or you could do the opposite. Live for now. Don't go to university or get a traditional job. Find out what you really like doing and find a way to be the best at that. If it's skateboarding, teach it. If it's online gaming, become the best gamer you can be. If it's getting drunk, perhaps consider another option. Becoming a wine taster is probably not the way to go.

------

12   Y N Harari, *Sapiens: A Brief History of Humankind* (Vintage, 2015)

The great thing about today's world is it's possible to live for today without descending into the depths of the gutter, even though that will happen if you take that concept to its extreme. Nevertheless, living for today while avoiding becoming homeless requires a lot more effort than simply enjoying yourself without thinking about what you are doing. You have to be as savvy and adaptable as the person who is pinning everything on tomorrow. One could argue, to be a success at either option requires many similar skills. I told you it was complicated.

Success is an interesting concept. The most common measure of success is the impression we have of how much stuff others possess and how much money we assume they must be making and/or have in their bank account.

Those we see as singularly unsuccessful have actually perfected ways of being extremely successful in a particular way. The skills they have become great at may not appear to be attractive to us, but they nevertheless take a level of commitment. Becoming so obese you are no longer able to move under your own steam is not my idea of success, but nevertheless, the person who has achieved that has made an extreme commitment to put on huge amounts of weight. In a contest for the heaviest person boasting an attractive prize fund, the winner might see themselves in a different light. What we see as a loser in one context becomes a winner in another.

It's why I find the world so fascinating and interesting. And it underlines that you can learn something from almost everyone. Even if it's a lesson in what not to do. Life gives us lots of opportunities to learn for free, almost every minute of the day, which might even be the ultimate example of something from nothing.

The more I learn, the more I realise there is so much I don't know. To be able to learn from almost any situation, you absolutely must have the right attitude and develop the skills and attributes required. Making something from nothing is about much more than creating a pile of cash. Success comes in many guises. Just learn how to recognise it when it's bashing you on the head. Keep that reality, optimise everything and you can do it.

Thank you for sticking with me. It's been quite a journey. Good luck.

ACKNOWLEDGEMENTS

The more I progressed with this book over the last five years, the more I realised it had taken most of my life to write it. And so many people who came, went and stayed along the way, contributed to it. What has been revelatory to me is realising how important and significant some of those people have been, to not only the book, but my life.

If you have got this far, you already know about both the obvious and less obvious characters, but in case my gratitude hasn't been shown directly already, let's start with the unknowing contributors.

My parents, Des and Barb, are where both the book and I began. They always wanted the best for me, even though their aspirations had been limited by their own lives. Knowing someone is rooting for you, even though they may have limited resources and skills to help you move forward, is vitally important. Despite any limitations they may have had in that area, I now understand I am probably where I am now because of them.

There is a small group of people who have been with me for longer than anyone else on the planet. Chronologically, these are Jackie, Dave, Adrian and Maurice. They are also unknowing contributors, from whom I learnt without them teaching me and with whom I have shared a life filled with fun.

I thank my daughters, Rachael and Sarah, for keeping me grounded and on my toes with their honesty and insight and helping me to stay aware of who I am. I hope my own parents' sense of wanting the best for their offspring has passed through me, to them.

Jane's unwavering support for everything I do is so intrinsic, it would be natural to take it for granted. But I do not. Five years of patience while I spent so many hours at my desk, writing and re-writing to try to achieve the perfection I am cursed (or is it blessed?) with. I cannot thank her enough.

My thanks for the most valued practical help in achieving publication go to Leon Hunt, Debbie Young, Glynn Harper and Alison Jack. Debbie and Glynn for pointing me in the right direction and Alison for her genius with the written word. Holly Ainger's valued marketing advice may be why you are reading this or perhaps it's because of the great cover design by Adam Wiltshire, the son of one of my friends from the council estate.

Finally, to the countless individuals from every encounter, big or small, who knowingly or unknowingly contributed to this book's development. Thank you all for being a part of my life.